Faithful Translators

Rethinking the Early Modern

Series Editors
Marcus Keller, University of Illinois, Urbana-Champaign
Ellen McClure, University of Illinois, Chicago

FAITHFUL TRANSLATORS

Authorship, Gender, and Religion in Early Modern England

JAIME GOODRICH

NORTHWESTERN UNIVERSITY PRESS
EVANSTON, ILLINOIS

Northwestern University Press
www.nupress.northwestern.edu

Printed in the United States of America

10 9 8 7 6 5 4 3 2 1

Library of Congress Cataloging-in-Publication Data

Goodrich, Jaime, 1978– author.
Faithful translators : authorship, gender, and religion in Early Modern England / Jaime Goodrich.
pages cm. — (Rethinking the Early Modern)
Based on the author's thesis (PhD)—Boston College, 2008.
ISBN 978-0-8101-2969-6 (cloth) — ISBN 978-0-8101-2938-2 (pbk.)
1. Christian literature—Translations into English—History and criticism. 2. English literature—Early modern, 1500–1700—History and criticism. 3. Women translators—Great Britain—History—16th century. 4. Women translators—Great Britain—History—17th century. 5. Authorship—Great Britain—History. 6. Women and literature—Great Britain—History. 7. Translating and interpreting—England—History—16th century. 8. Translating and interpreting—England—History—17th century. I. Title. II. Series: Rethinking the Early Modern.
PR428.C48G66 2014
820.938209031—dc23
2013025609

♾ The paper used in this publication meets the minimum requirements of the American National Standard for Information Sciences—Permanence of Paper for Printed Library Materials, ANSI Z39.48-1992.

CONTENTS

FIGURES

ACKNOWLEDGMENTS

This book was made possible by generous research support from Wayne State University (a sabbatical leave, a University Research Grant), the Wayne State Humanities Center (a Faculty Fellowship), and the Wayne State English Department (a Josephine Nevins Keal Fellowship). This project grew out of my dissertation, which was supported by the American Association of University Women, the Renaissance Society of America, and the Catholic Record Society.

Librarians and archivists at the Archdiocesan Archives of Mechelen-Brussels, the Archives Départementales du Nord, the Beinecke Library, the Bodleian Library, the British Library, Downside Abbey, the National Archives in Kew, and the Newberry Library kindly helped me locate archival material. Special thanks are due to Abbot Aidan Bellenger and the archivists of Downside Abbey—Dom David Foster and Simon Johnson—for their patient assistance during my many visits. Andrea Clarke of the British Library kindly showed me Elizabeth's fragile embroidered binding for Royal MS 7 D X. I am most grateful to the present Viscount De L'Isle, MBE, DL, for generously allowing me to view and cite MS A of the Sidney Psalter, part of his private collection of family papers. Likewise, David Vaisey, literary executor for Bent Juel-Jensen, kindly allowed me to examine MS J of the Sidney Psalter.

An earlier version of part of chapter 1, "Thomas More and Margaret More Roper: A Case for Rethinking Women's Participation in the Early Modern Public Sphere," appeared in *Sixteenth Century Journal* 39, no. 4 (2008): 1021–40. I would like to thank the editors for allowing me to reprint this material. I am also grateful to the following institutions for permission to reproduce the images within this book: the British Library (the title page and signature A1v of Margaret Roper's *Devout Treatise upon the Pater Noster;* the title page of John Bale's *Illustrium majoris Britanniae scriptorum*), the Folger Shakespeare Library (the title page of Potentiana Deacon's *Delicious Entertainments of the Soule*), the National Archives, Kew (folio 39r of State Papers 12/289), and the Huntington Library (page 1399 of *The Workes of Sir Thomas More;* the title page of *The First Tome or Volume of the Paraphrase of Erasmus upon the Newe Testament;* the title page of Elizabeth Tudor's *Godly Medytacyon of the Christen Sowle*).

While tracing the intellectual coteries of faithful translators, I was lucky enough to benefit greatly from the vibrant academic community at Wayne State University. Arthur Marotti has been an invaluable mentor and guide, patiently commenting on draft after draft of the entire book. Simone Chess read early drafts and was a crucial source of friendly encouragement, while Ken Jackson shared his wisdom on grant writing and publishing. I am grateful for the insights I gained after workshopping these ideas in a doctoral seminar on "Gender and Translation in Early Modern England" as well as at meetings of the Group for Early Modern Studies, an interdisciplinary working group sponsored by the Wayne State Humanities Center. Ginny Owens and Kimberly Majeske provided much-needed assistance in cataloging archival material. A succession of chairs offered logistical aid (Richard Grusin, Arthur Marotti, and Martha Ratliff), but Ellen Barton deserves special thanks for her ever enthusiastic support of my work. I also have a deep appreciation for the camaraderie of a number of colleagues: Caroline Maun, Lisa Maruca, renée hoogland, Lissy Sklar, Sarika Chandra, Gwendolen Gorzelsky, Anne Duggan, Lisa Ze Winters, José Antonio Rico-Ferrer, Michael Scrivener, Robert Aguirre, and Julie Klein.

This book has also greatly benefited from the advice and encouragement of the larger scholarly community. I presented early versions of several chapters at conferences held by the Renaissance Society of America, the Sixteenth Century Society and Conference, the Centre for Early Modern Exchanges at University College, London, and the Wayne State Humanities Center. In addition, I shared part of chapter 3 at an invited talk sponsored by the Classics Department at Smith College. Indeed, without the formative influence of Classics and English faculty at Smith—including Scott Bradbury, Justina Gregory, Bill Oram, Thalia Pandiri, Maureen Ryan, and Nancy Shumate—this project would not have been possible. Justina Gregory deserves special thanks for her kind encouragement of my scholarly potential. I would also like to thank my dissertation committee—Caroline Bicks and Amy Boesky—for their comments, and I am especially grateful to Mary Thomas Crane, my dissertation advisor, for her generous, ongoing mentorship of this "hard wit." Many thanks to Dayton Haskin and Maxim Shrayer for respectively fostering my interest in early modern literature and translation. While I was initially dismayed to learn that Brenda Hosington was also writing a book on female translators, she became less a rival than a treasured collaborator; I deeply appreciate our many inspiring conversations and productive panels at conferences over the years. In addition, many thanks are due to other scholars for their advice and support: Margaret

Hannay, Micheline White, Patricia Phillippy, Susannah Monta, Katherine Kellett, Chris Laoutaris, Elaine Beilin, Caroline Bowden, Nicky Hallett, Claire Walker, Alison Shell, Elizabeth McCutcheon, Jenna Lay, and Victoria Van Hyning.

It has been a pleasure to work with Northwestern University Press, and I am especially grateful to Henry Carrigan, senior editor and assistant director, Nathan MacBrien, special projects editor, and Lori Meek Schuldt, my copyeditor, for shepherding the book through the editorial process with such care.

My parents, Lee and Christine Goodrich, and my brother, Jared, have been a source of unending encouragement throughout this process, supporting this project in tangible and intangible ways. Without their early encouragement of my academic interests, this book would never have been written. Last, but by no means least, Katherine Gurdziel has been an essential source of inspiration and insight, willing to accompany me through every stage of this project—whether driving through the back roads of England in search of remote archives, taking innumerable photographs of manuscripts, or discussing early modern women's translations from morning to night. I am truly indebted to her boundless support.

Faithful Translators

Introduction

Religious Translation in Early Modern England

In dedicating his 1603 translation of Montaigne's *Essayes* to Lucy Russell, Countess of Bedford, and her mother, Lady Anne Harington, John Florio strikingly compared this latest publication to his earlier Italian and English dictionary *Worlde of Wordes* (1598):

> To my last Birth, which I held masculine, (as are all mens conceipts that are their owne, though but by their collecting; and this was to Montaigne like Bacchus, closed in, or loosed from his great Jupiters thigh) I the indulgent father invited two right Honorable Godfathers, with the One of your Noble Lady-shippes to witnesse. So to this defective edition (since all translations are reputed femalls, delivered at second hand; and I in this serve but as Vulcan, to hatchet this Minerva from that Jupiters bigge braine) I yet at least a fondling foster-father, having transported it from France to England; put it in English clothes; taught it to talke our tongue (though many times with a jerke of the French Jargon) would set it forth to the best service I might.[1]

Florio's evocative metaphors of class and gender have become a touchstone for critical discussions of early modern English translations. In 1931, F. O. Matthiessen included Florio in a study that enthusiastically presented translation as a nationalistic exercise parallel to the contemporary colonization of the New World: "The translator's work was an act of patriotism. . . . He believed that foreign books were just as important for England's destiny as the discoveries of her seamen, and he brought them into his native speech with all the enthusiasm of a conquest."[2] Matthiessen saw Florio and other translators of creative works as crucial agents in the development of the English literary canon. While acknowledging the militaristic language used by some translators, Neil Rhodes has more recently claimed that Florio, like other translators, felt an acute anxiety because "Translations are always inadequate."[3] Florio's vaunting therefore disguises his concerns over the status of his work. Despite their different views of Florio, both Matthiessen and Rhodes agree that his translation occupies an inferior position as either a subjugated foreigner or an unsuccessful copy—a perspective that reflects the postromantic tendency to privilege original authorship over so-called secondary activities such as translation.[4] Indeed, Florio has become central to scholarship on early modern translation precisely because he seems to anticipate this modern attitude. Florio clearly depicts his translation as a "defective" version of Montaigne's original, drawing upon the connotations of "femall," a term that could also signify "inferiority," to portray the translation's hierarchical relationship to its source text in gendered terms.[5] This presentation of the translation as "defective" is only underscored by the low social position that it occupies as a metaphoric servant to Bedford and Harington.

Yet we should be wary of obscuring the differences between Florio's views of translation and modern opinions of this activity. In the preface to the reader that accompanies the 1603 edition of his Montaigne, Florio also insists upon the importance of translation as a means of transmitting knowledge and cultural power: "Shall I apologize translation? Why but some holde (as for their free-hold) that such conversion is the subversion of Universities. . . . It were an ill turne, the turning of Bookes should be the overturning of Libraries. Yea but my olde fellow Nolano [Giordano Bruni] tolde me, and taught publikely, that from translation all Science had it's of-spring" ("DP," *Essayes,* A5r). Responding to potential criticisms of translation, Florio then presents another gendered metaphor defending this dissemination of learning: "Learning cannot bee too common, and the commoner the better. Why but who is not jealous, his Mistresse should be so prostitute? Yea but this Mistresse is lyke ayre, fire, water, the more breathed the clearer; the more extended the warmer; the more drawne the sweeter" ("DP," *Essayes,* A5r). Florio's depiction of knowledge as female evokes the previously mentioned birth scenario from his dedicatory preface to Bedford and Harington, which Jonathan Goldberg has characterized as "an allegory about the origin of ideas."[6] In that earlier moment, Florio presents himself as Montaigne's collaborator, assisting with the birth of Minerva, the goddess of learning. Florio's metaphors of class and gender thus negotiate the plural authorship entailed by translation. By portraying the text as a female servant and himself as a midwife, foster father, and instructor who supplants Montaigne, Florio suggests that he, as the translator, bears some authorial responsibility for the work itself. If Florio, like other early modern translators, was clearly aware that translation offered a unique set of authorial ramifications, too often literary scholars have focused on the translator's creative autonomy or lack thereof. This book attempts to reorient critical discussions of early modern translation by considering faithful translators: those who translated biblical or nonbiblical religious works that often required conservative translation strategies. These faithful translators took advantage of the authorial multiplicity inherent in translation to pursue a number of agendas that made their work central to the cultural landscape of early modern England.

This book will primarily focus on female translators, whose works offer an ideal corpus for rethinking the authorial nature and cultural role of religious translation. Scholars have frequently cited these women's translations as evidence that early modern thinkers viewed translation as an inferior and secondary activity. Mary Ellen Lamb turned to Florio's gendered metaphors of translation to explain why women of this period translated so often: "Translations were 'defective' and therefore appropriate to women; this low opinion of translating perhaps accounts for why women were allowed to translate at all. A man who labors in this degraded activity must justify himself, 'since all translations are reputed femalls.'"[7] Much as Matthiessen and Rhodes do, Lamb responds to Florio's apparent anticipation of postromantic views of original authorship and translation, moving swiftly from his assertion that translations, like women, were "defective" to the claim that translation was "therefore appropriate to women," a view never expressed by Florio. If Matthiessen had celebrated the creative independence of male translators, Lamb points to women's religious translations as evidence of their oppression: "The translations by Renaissance women are different from the translations of Renaissance men in being exceedingly literal. Absent are the magnificent and occasionally quirky expansions of Harington's *Orlando Furioso* and Chapman's *Homer;* instead we find line-by-line transliteration. The explanation of the difference lies to some extent in the nature of the task itself. . . . Many religious texts had by their very nature to be translated literally."[8] Despite Lamb's caveats about the conventions associated with religious translation, a critical dichotomy has since developed: while men showed creative liberty by translating freely, women complied with patriarchal expectations by translating faithfully. Massimiliano Morini, for example, recently stated that "translation . . . asked of translators a personal contribution, an infusion, as it were, of their personality in the final result: at least, it did so for men, for with women things stood differently. . . . Translation, particularly if exercised within a devout sphere, could be the only activity permitted to women, for in their case it could be seen as a mechanical exercise, one that would occupy the mind and body much as embroidery did."[9] According to this dichotomy, at worst the female translator submissively acknowledged the (generally) male authority of her source text. At best, translation seemed to provide female translators with a protected agency that met contemporary expectations of feminine modesty.[10] The power of this paradigm may be gauged by its effect on feminist translation theorists, who have relied on Florio and Lamb in their efforts to demonstrate that translation was first regarded as inferior to original composition during the early modern period.[11]

Developments in the fields of Translation Studies and early modern literature have necessitated a reassessment of this assumption that faithful translators were necessarily passive conduits for the original author's text. The work of Roland Barthes and Michel Foucault has opened up new ways of thinking about authorship beyond the single-author model that long governed literary criticism. As Foucault observed, "The author is the principle of thrift in the proliferation of meaning. . . . He is a certain functional principle by which, in our culture, one limits, excludes, and chooses; in short, by which one impedes the free circulation, the free manipulation, the free composition, decomposition, and recomposition of fiction."[12] This poststructuralist decentering of the author implicitly permits recognition of the translator's authorial role. If an emphasis on the author limits the meaning of original writing, then privileging a translation's original author circumscribes the meaning of the translation itself, a literal "recomposition" in which the translator assists with the "proliferation of meaning." Translation theorists reacted to these insights in two major ways: first, by emphasizing the translation's role within its cultural and historical moment, and second, by reconceptualizing translation as a form of writing.[13] Within early modern literary studies, advances in bibliographic scholarship only heightened the importance of poststructuralist views of authorship, and critics began to argue that early modern texts were social productions influenced by any number of collaborative agents.[14] Scholars have now shown that readers and scribes revised and rewrote works that circulated in manuscript.[15] Print also offered a wide range of possibilities for social and collaborative authorship, as a host of agents beyond the original author—including editors and compositors—helped determine a text's form.[16] We now recognize that paratextual devices such as prefaces and marginalia informed reader reception.[17] Dramatic authorship has proved particularly fertile territory since playwrights collaborated with scribes, actors, and many other agents on texts that had to take account of economic, performative, and political exigencies.[18] More recently, scholars have begun to consider how printed books prompted readers to compose annotations and errata lists.[19]

If editors, compositors, and creators of marginalia functioned as authors, then the translator certainly has a claim to authorial agency, as recent scholarship—largely on women's translations—has demonstrated. During the 1990s, critics began to argue that women's translations should be recognized as a form of writing, leading to a fresh awareness of the literary and political agency of the female translator.[20] Danielle Clarke, for example, utterly rejected the earlier critical model in which the female translator submissively acknowledged the authority of her source text: "The practice of translation can only be thought of as 'safe' for women if its functions are reduced to a slavish relationship of translator/reader to the text, where he/she merely passively subordinates him/herself to the original author and his messages."[21] More recently, Peter Burke has noted that early models of translation allowed the translator to exercise authorial freedom: "Early modern translators of medieval or modern works seem to have viewed themselves as co-authors with the right to modify the original text. In the early modern period it was only very gradually that the idea of a text as both the work and the property of a single individual imposed itself."[22] Most important, a series of case studies has now revealed the ways that women used translation to participate in contemporary politics.[23] Micheline White has called for a new way of approaching early modern women's translations by situating Anne Lock's translation of Calvin within its historical context: "Lock's translation was far from 'silent' or passive: undertaken at a specific moment, it responds to the needs of a specific religious community, and it participates in the rhetorical struggle to garner support for their cause."[24] This recognition that female translators could have authorial agency in their own right has opened up a fresh set of questions that are central to any understanding of the role that translation played in early modern England. What were the potential authorial positions available to translators, both male and female? To what extent did contemporaries distinguish between the authority of the translator and that of the original author? What sorts of agency did translators receive from these authorial positions? What cultural work did translation perform?

To answer these questions, this book will explore the authorial strategies and cultural functions of religious translations, both biblical and nonbiblical. With the recent turn to religion in early modern literary studies, the time is ripe for a full-scale discussion of religious translation, particularly of nonbiblical works that offer a useful complement to longstanding scholarly interest in biblical and literary translation.[25] Despite the sizable number of religious works translated during the early modern period, only a few preliminary studies of this corpus have appeared.[26] On the basis of her online bibliography of early modern translations from 1473 to 1641, Brenda M. Hosington recently calculated in a keynote address that 49 percent of the printed translations produced by English men and women during this period were religious in nature, and furthermore that 45 percent of these translations were biblical.[27] Thus almost a quarter of English translations published during this period were nonbiblical and religious in nature. The corpus of nonbiblical religious translations, as important as it is neglected, comprises the second largest body of English translations after the Bible. While with the exception of the book of Psalms women did not translate the Bible, religious translations also dominate their productions, accounting for 60 percent of women's print and manuscript translations during this period, according to Hosington.[28] If women translated religious works more frequently than literary texts, then, they were not out of step with their male counterparts. Without an acknowledgment of this larger cultural impetus to translate religious texts, there can be no fuller understanding of female translators, their relationship to the work of male translators, and their cultural significance in early modern England.

Before examining the cultural functions of early modern religious translation, it is necessary to move beyond generalized statements that translators were authors by establishing just what kind of authorship translation involves. Deborah Uman's work offers a useful starting place for theorizing the authorial role of early modern translators. She and Bistué Belén have described translation as a form of collaborative authorship involving both the translator and the original author.[29] Yet the term "collaborative," which may suggest a dialogue between two or more parties, does not adequately describe the process of translation. It is difficult, for example, to imagine an early modern translator "collaborating" with a classical author, even if the translator is sympathetic to his or her position. André Lefevere illuminates this situation while answering an imagined query about the original author's view of the rewriting involved in translation: "Do writers have to submit to these indignities? First of all, they don't really submit. In many cases they have long been dead, in most they have precious little say in the matter. Writers are powerless to control the rewriting of their work."[30] More recently, Uman has supplied another model of the translator's authorship, claiming that translation "gave women the chance to assume an authorial role—a role that . . . gave them ownership of their words and the chance to achieve profit, fame, status, and influence."[31] Yet because of the authorial multiplicity inherent in this act, translators—whether female or male—never achieve total "ownership of their words." Harold Love's category of executive authorship supplies a fitter paradigm for the authorial positions created by translation. According to Love, in these cases "the maker or *artifex*" serves as "the deviser, the orderer, the wordsmith, or . . . the reformulator" of another author's thoughts.[32] The plurality of executive authorship makes visible the separate authority that a translator and the original author hold. The *artifex* determines the way that a text's content will be expressed, in the process exerting influence on the shape of that content. Similarly, the translator rewrites her source text, basing her work on the original author's language even while assuming the authorial agency to subvert, subsume, and redirect the source text in ways not intended or foreseen by the original author.

A host of cultural factors shaped the ways that the translator's executive authorship operated during the early modern period, and the sociological turn in the field of Translation Studies provides a useful methodology for exploring these factors and their effects.[33] Since the late 1990s, translation theorists have become increasingly interested in the translator's role as a social agent within a larger cultural context, and Pierre Bourdieu's theories of practice have proved especially influential.[34] While this development has not yet affected scholarship on translation in early modern England, the sociological turn offers a new paradigm for understanding the cultural functions of translation during this time. Instead of viewing everyday practices as spontaneous occurrences, Bourdieu proposes that human behavior is actually governed by habitus, or "systems of durable, transposable dispositions, structured structures predisposed to function as structuring structures, that is, as principles which generate and organize practices and representations that can be objectively adapted to their outcomes without presupposing a conscious aiming at ends or an express mastery of the operations necessary in order to attain them." These "dispositions," which are often acquired during an individual's formative years, both "generate" and "structure" the way that an individual behaves even though he or she is not consciously aware of them. The habitus does not predetermine an individual's actions but rather offers a range of possibilities for behavior: "the habitus is an infinite capacity for generating products—thoughts, perceptions, expressions and actions—whose limits are set by the historically and socially situated conditions of its production."[35] Thus the habitus makes possible a vast range of attitudes and behaviors that are constituted within a specific cultural context. In doing so, the habitus enables individuals to participate in particularized fields, each of which is controlled by a distinct set of rules. Bourdieu has defined the field of literature, for example, as "an independent social universe with its own laws of functioning, its specific relations of force, its dominants and its dominated, and so forth."[36] Without knowledge of the proper habitus, or conventions, that govern a given field, individuals lack the ability to participate successfully in that field.

A translator's habitus can be usefully split into functional and practical aspects: that is, *why* and *how* translations were produced. Both of these aspects, which may at times be interrelated, depend on the particular social and cultural situation of the translator. If literature qualifies as a Bourdieusian field constituted by authors, critics, publishers, and other agents, then translation—as a form of writing—could be considered a field as well, populated by translators, publishers, and others.[37] Yet viewing translation as a field in and of itself poses problems due to the incoherence of translation as a sphere. For example, the translator of technical manuals will necessarily differ in attitude and purpose from the translator of novels. Michaela Wolf has offered a way past this problem by proposing the term "translation space" in recognition of the fact that "the translation field or space is always situated *between* various fields, such as the literary field, academic field, political field, and others."[38] Wolf's description of the interaction between translation and these fields is very helpful for understanding early modern religious translation since economic, religious, and political factors shaped this sphere and the functional habitus that existed within it. These factors also influenced a translator's practical habitus, which ran the gamut from faithful to free translation strategies depending upon the translator's attitude toward the source text. As the following overview of early modern religious translation will show, the functional and practical aspects of habitus generated a variety of authorial possibilities that allowed translators to pursue cultural agendas in ways that would have been denied to them as single authors.

Financial, theological, and political imperatives helped determine the functional habitus associated with religious translations, whether of the Bible, polemical treatises, or devotional works. The early modern print shop and bookstall were first and foremost business ventures, and printers and publishers consequently selected religious translations that might be popular enough to turn a profit.[39] William Caxton, for example, printed his own translations, including hagiographic material in step with late medieval interest in saints: Jacobus de Voragine's *Legenda aurea*

(1483) and Robert of Shrewsbury's *Lyf of the Holy Blessid Vyrgyn Saynt Wenefryde* (1485). Caxton's rendering of the *Legenda aurea* proved so profitable that Wynken de Worde reprinted it five times between 1493 and 1527. As the sixteenth century progressed, publishers often turned to translations to meet the increased appetite for devotional material caused by rising literacy rates and a new emphasis on pious reading. During Edward's reign, Walter Lynne printed his own translations of texts by Heinrich Bullinger (*A Treatise . . . Concernynge Magistrates,* 1549) and Martin Luther (*A Frutefull and Godly Exposition . . . of the Kyngdom of Christ,* 1548). Printers and publishers also sought out translators for works that they viewed as potential sources of profit. Arthur Golding may be best known today for his translation of Ovid's *Metamorphoses,* but he translated a number of Protestant works. In the preface to one of these translations, Golding explains that two publishing partners asked him to translate this text: "Lucas Harison and George Bishop Stacioners, men well mynded towards godlynesse and true Religion, taking uppon them too Imprint this woork at their proper charges, requested mee too put the same intoo English, I willingly agreed too their godly desire."[40] This collaboration was clearly successful, as Golding provided five more translations for Harrison and Bishop, either acting together or independently.[41] Some enormously popular translations saw multiple editions that offered a reliable source of profit for printers, as in the case of Calvin's *Catechisme or Maner to Teach Children the Christian Religion.* Yet sales alone did not account for all of the profit that a publisher or translator might receive from these works. As Caxton notes in the preface to the *Legenda aurea,* William Fitzalan, Earl of Arundel, offered him "a yerely fee / that is to wete a bucke in sommer / & a doo in winter" to complete the work.[42] Aristocratic or royal patronage could thus, in effect, decide which works were translated and published. Translators also presented manuscript copies of their works to patrons to gain economic or social profit. In a bid for patronage, Josuah Sylvester gave James I a presentation copy of his version of Guillaume Du Bartas's *Devine Weekes* and later dedicated a print edition of the complete poem to James.[43]

Religious translations—whether in print or manuscript—could reliably generate profit through their ability to bring new doctrinal models to England from the Continent. The five religious translations published in 1526 illustrate the way that translation affected English religious beliefs and devotion. Two of these translations offered material in keeping with late medieval taste and practices: Richard Whitford's version of the *Martiloge* used at Syon Abbey and a reprint of Margaret Beaufort's translation of the treatise *Mirroure of Golde for the Synfull Soule* (first published in 1506). The other publications reflect the pressure that was being placed on this traditional model by reformist agendas originating from the Continent. A pair of Erasmian translations carried a message of reconciliation based on commonalities among Christians, such as the Lord's Prayer: Margaret Roper's *Devout Treatise upon the Pater Noster* and Gentian Hervet's *Sermon of the Excedynge Great Mercy of God.* These publications initiated a trend of Erasmian translation that would persist for decades, yet they also responded to Martin Luther's call for religious reform. The final translation of 1526 shows that Lutheran ideas had already begun to influence English thinkers: William Tyndale's successful printing of his complete English translation of the New Testament at Worms. Tyndale pursued the Lutheran goal of providing literate readers with access to the Bible in the vernacular, creating a text that formed the basis for all subsequent English Bibles.

Because translators of religious texts often reacted to ongoing theological developments, a study of religious translations yields a fairly accurate history of the English Reformation. During the 1520s and 1530s, reformers were strongly influenced by Luther, and translators consequently turned to Luther's polemical tracts urging reform, such as *A Boke Made by a Certayne Great Clerke, against the Newe Idole, and Olde Devyll* (1534). Under Edward, looser restrictions on print caused a spike in the publication of midcentury theologians such as Martin Bucer, Heinrich Bullinger, Philipp Melanchthon, Peter Martyr Vermigli, and Ulrich Zwingli. By the 1570s, however, the increasingly Calvinist atmosphere within England resulted in a marked preference for the works of John Calvin and Théodore de Bèze. Even as the theologians popular under Edward ceased to be translated during the 1580s, twenty of Calvin's works were printed between 1580 and 1589.[44] While Calvin's exegetical treatises and sermons formed the bulk of these translations, his *Institutes* were especially popular and saw at least six editions. Meanwhile, Elizabethan translators largely ignored Luther's controversial literature in favor of his biblical exegesis and pastoral sermons (*A Commentarie of M. Doctor Martin Luther upon the Epistle of S. Paul to the Galathians,* 1575; *Special and Chosen Sermons of D. Martin Luther,* 1578). A similar pattern may be discerned in the translation of Roman Catholic works, which introduced English readers to the theology of Counter-Reformation figures such as Roberto Bellarmino, SJ; Gaspar Loarte, SJ; and Luis de Granada, OP.[45]

Translators' interest in Continental theology—whether Catholic or Protestant—was often a direct product of the political situation within England, as successive regimes found translation useful in defending and disseminating the shifting doctrine of the English church. Henry VIII and his advisers adeptly exploited translation for political purposes, issuing a 1531 translation of a Latin tract defending Henry's intended divorce from Catherine of Aragon and repudiating papal power: *The Determinations of the Moste Famous and Mooste Excellent Universities of Italy and Fraunce That It Is So Unlefull for a Man to Marie His Brothers Wyfe, That the Pope Hath No Power to Dispence Therewith.* Similarly, Elizabeth's regime sponsored Anne Cooke Bacon's translation of John Jewel's *Apologie . . . of the Churche of Englande,* a Latin tract that originally addressed an international audience to defend the Elizabethan settlement. The necessity of providing an English version to combat the criticism of "hotter" Protestants and English Catholics can be seen in the decision to replace an unofficial translation published in 1562 just two years later with Bacon's authorized version. Officially sponsored biblical translations also reflected ecclesiastical policy. The oft-noted lack of polemical marginalia in the King James Bible represented James's irenic stance. The printers, publishers, and translators who produced these books stood to gain substantial profit, but they also collaborated with the government in a less official manner. The anonymous translator of Luther's *A Propre Treatyse of Good Workes* (1535) aimed to bolster the reform initiatives of Thomas Cromwell by spreading Lutheran ideas of justification and by defending "the true & syncere teachers of the infallyble truthe of our savyour Jesu Chryst, . . . falsely defamed unto the unlearned people."[46] The edition gestured at official support for these views with a woodcut featuring the Beaufort portcullis, the Tudor rose, and the royal motto DIEU ET MON DROIT. Other translators took it upon themselves to produce works that supported governmental positions. In the wake of anti-Catholic sentiment caused by the Gunpowder Plot and oath of allegiance controversy, a translator of Pierre du Moulin's defense of Protestantism stated, "such Treatises as this, which afford direction to the Church & Spouse of God, travailing to heavenly Jerusalem, through the Wildernesse of this world, [are] nothing more necessary; being fit to resolve her of doubts in matters of Controversie."[47]

Official religious policies also generated translations opposed to the doctrine of the English church, as translators sought to strengthen support for dissident religious beliefs. Their translations could have dire consequences: Tyndale, for example, was executed for the religious unorthodoxy perceived to be in his biblical translations. Many of these translators therefore worked in exile or published through secret presses. During Mary's reign, a writer using the pseudonym of the church historian Eusebius Pamphilus presented his translation of Luther as a means of warding off divine retribution for the country's return to Catholicism: "Iff such warnings as have proceded of the like spirite as this present advertisement was writton/had bene regarded in time/paraventure god wold have spared us our late Josias/Noble king Edward of famos memory/a little longar. O Ingland/Ingland/that thy sinnes/unthankfulnes and securite were such that thei provoked god . . . to send the[e] such [governors] now as goo abowt to bring the[e] in thraldom and subjeccion unto alienes and to conquer the[e] with tyranny and seduce the[e] with fals relygyon."[48] Likewise, under Elizabeth, the Catholic exile Richard Hopkins noted that Thomas Harding had encouraged him to translate devotional works of the Spanish Counter-Reformation out of a belief "that more spirituall profite wolde undoutedlie ensewe thereby to the gayninge of Christian sowles in our countrie from Schisme, and Heresie, and from all sinne, and iniquitie, than by bookes that treate of controversies in Religion."[49] Eusebius Pamphilus and Harding were not alone in thinking that translation might convert readers to their religious beliefs. Beginning in the reign of Henry VIII, governmental authorities tried to control the dissemination of printed translations that undermined the official church. William Tyndale's translation of the Bible was burned in bonfires during the 1520s, and Thomas Cromwell's attainder for treason included the complaint that he had authorized the translation "into our maternal and English tongue" of heretical books containing material "against the . . . most blessed and holy sacrament."[50] Under Protestant regimes, government officials similarly attempted to limit the importation of Catholic books, causing Jane, Lady Lovell to complain in 1605 to Robert Cecil that pursuivants had taken away her copy of the Rheims New Testament.[51]

The practical habitus of the religious translator generally operated between the poles of faithfulness and freedom, depending on the translator's views of the source text's orthodoxy. Both biblical and nonbiblical translations frequently emphasized faithfulness to the source text, as Flora Ross Amos noted long ago: "Though the translation of the Bible was an isolated task which had few relations with other forms of translation, what few affiliations it developed were almost entirely with theological works like those of Erasmus, Melanchthon, Calvin, and to the translation of such writings Biblical standards of accuracy were transferred."[52] Some spheres of religious translation, particularly the psalms, relied more extensively on freedom than others. A translator might also choose to exercise a localized freedom by emending or emphasizing the source text at certain moments while otherwise remaining relatively faithful.

Both faithfulness and freedom had roots in the early modern schoolroom since translation was central to instruction in foreign languages during the period.[53] Late medieval schoolmasters frequently used "vulgaria," or exercises in translating sentences into and out of English, to teach students French and Latin vocabulary and grammar.[54] Translation was arguably even more important within the humanist curriculum as a means of imparting proper Latin style. Thomas More, John Cheke, and Roger Ascham all used the technique of double translation, although Ascham, Cheke's pupil, is today best known for this method, which he employed to inculcate a Ciceronian style in beginning students. After a young pupil has been introduced to one of Cicero's letters, "the childe must take a paper booke, and sitting in some place, where no man shall prompte him, by him self, let him translate into Englishe his former lesson. Then shewing it to his master, let the master take from him his latin booke, and pausing an houre, at the least, than let the childe translate his owne Englishe into latin againe, in an other paper booke. When the childe bringeth it, turned into latin, the master must compare it with Tullies booke, and laie them both togither: and where the childe doth well, either in chosing, or true placing of Tullies wordes, let the master praise him."[55] In this scenario, the translator practices an extreme form of faithfulness to Cicero's language so that he can easily retranslate his English into Cicero's Latin. Such thorough internalization of Cicero's style would allow the student to use Ciceronian language and phrasing automatically in the future. Double translation is therefore an implicitly hierarchical activity in which the student, at best, replicates an authoritative original word for word. Tutors of vernacular languages also employed this technique, meaning that even students without humanist training might have encountered the precepts of faithful translation.[56]

Yet some humanists had a selective attitude toward the classics, advising that teachers should exercise caution in introducing students to potentially licentious writers such as Ovid.[57] Juan Luis Vives, for example, recommended the expurgation of classical literature that might encourage vice: "It certainly would be very fitting, if, on the account of the weakness and darkness of our mind, hurtful passages could be cleansed, so that there should be no pitfall of harm left, and we should only then wander about in those fields in which grow wholesome or pleasant herbs." Vives proposes that this editing be entrusted to the judgment of a learned Christian who can act as a gatekeeper: "Let some man show us the way, a man not only well furnished with learning, but also a man of honour and of practical wisdom, whom we trust as a leader; who will remove us from danger either quietly without explaining the danger, lest he rouse the desire of curiosity; or, will openly show to those for whom it is fitting, what danger lies hidden. . . . In this manner the heathen woman will be received into marriage, with nails and hair duly cut, according to the rite of the children of Israel, even as S[aint] Jerome expounds."[58] Here Vives alludes to Jerome's suggestion that the captive pagan woman of Deuteronomy 21:11–13, whose hair and nails are cut by the conquering Israelites, could serve as a model for dealing with pagan material in classical texts. Some translators of classical works adopted Jerome's model, viewing their Christianity as justification for assuming a hierarchical superiority over pagan source texts. Thomas Drant, for example, advertised his use of this practice on the title page to his translation of Horace's *Satires: A Medicinable Morall, That Is, the Two Bookes of Horace His Satyres, Englyshed Accordyng to the Prescription of Saint Hierome* (1566). As Drant explains in the preface, he has removed Horace's references to pagan religion as well as material that he deems inappropriate or irrelevant: "I have done as the people of god wer commanded to do with their captive women that were hansome and beautifull: I have shaved of[f] his heare, & pared of[f] his nayles (that is) I have wiped awaye all his vanitie and superfluitie of matter."[59] Instead of submissively acknowledging Horace's authority, Drant highlights his bowdlerization of Horace to assure contemporary readers that the text is now fit for consumption.

These functional and practical aspects of the translator's habitus generated a variety of authorial possibilities ranging from submission to gatekeeping. When translators worked with source texts with an unimpeachable authority, they frequently displayed an authorial deference to the original author. The biblical translator was always the hierarchical inferior of the original author, God, and these translators often cultivated an authorial invisibility reflecting that relationship. In the preface to the King James Bible, Myles Smith articulates this paradigm of executive authorship in which God is viewed as the true author of the translation: "Wee affirme and avow, that the very meanest translation of the Bible in English, set foorth by men of our profession . . . containeth the word of God, nay, is the word of God. As the Kings Speech which hee uttered in Parliament, being translated into French, Dutch, Italian and Latine, is still the Kings Speech."[60] Significantly, the fifty-odd translators involved in the production of this Bible go unnamed. This emphasis on God's authority was further established by biblical translators' claims of faithfulness to the source text.[61] The preface to the Rheims New Testament echoed Jerome's dictum that the Bible must be translated word for word rather than sense for sense:

> We have done our endevour with praier, much feare and trembling, lest we should dangerously erre in so sacred, high, and divine a worke . . . that we have used . . . no more licence then is sufferable in translating of holy Scriptures: continually keeping our selves as neere as possible, to our text & to the very wordes and phrases which by long use are made venerable, though to some prophane or delicate eares they may seeme more hard or barbarous . . . acknowledging with S[aint] Hierom, that in other writings it is ynough to give in translation, sense for sense, but that in Scriptures, lest we misse the sense, we must keepe the very wordes.[62]

The Rheims translators present their work as a sacred endeavor, undertaken "with praier, much feare and trembling" for fear of doctrinal error. Their caveat about "hard or barbarous" language reflects the translators' deference to both their source text and the Catholic ecclesiastical hierarchy, as the Vulgate was their primary source text. By attempting to convey the language of the Vulgate as accurately as possible, the translators created a Latinate English that is notorious for awkward neologisms such as their substitution of "supersubstantial bread" for "daily bread" in the Lord's Prayer.[63] While the Geneva Bible translators attempted to render their Greek and Hebrew source texts by sense rather than by word, they nonetheless incorporated some Hebrew terms unfamiliar to readers: "We have in many places reserved the Ebrewe phrases, notwithstanding that thei may seme somewhat hard in their eares that are not wel practised and also delite in the swete sounding phrases of the holy Scriptures."[64] The Geneva translators also aimed at fidelity by differentiating their interpolations to the text through italics; the King James Bible would later follow suit by using a different typeface for its additions.

Biblical translations provide a useful example of the way that political initiatives might also cause the invisibility of the translator. The anonymous translators of the King James Bible appear to relegate authorship to James himself: "We hold it our duety to offer it to your Majestie, not onely as to our King and Soveraigne, but as to the principall moover and Author of the Worke." The translators are referring to James's role in commissioning this work, as Myles Smith later explains: "What can the King command to bee done, that will bring him more true honour then this? and wherein could they that have beene set a worke, approve their duetie to the King, yea their obedience to God, and love to his Saints more, then by yeelding their service, and all that is within them, for the furnishing of the worke?"[65] Since the translators' work is inscribed within the social hierarchy, this rejection of public credit for their work acknowledges James's royal authority. Other biblical translations with official mandates similarly emphasized the monarch's patronage by minimizing the translator's role. When Coverdale's Bible appeared in 1535, its title page featured a woodcut depicting Henry VIII distributing the Bible to his subjects, reflecting Henry's tacit approval of the work. In the preface, Coverdale invited Henry to take an authorial role as the final editor of his text: "I thought it my dutye and to belonge unto my allegiaunce, whan I had translated this Bible, not onely to dedicate this translacyon unto youre hyghnesse, but wholy to commytte it unto the same: to the intent that yf any thynge therin be translated amysse . . . it may stonde in youre graces handes, to correcte it, to amende it, to improve it, yee & cleane to rejecte it."[66] Later Bibles also relied on visual illustrations of royal approval. The title page to the Great Bible (1540) offered an elaborate woodcut in which Henry passes the Bible to Thomas Cranmer and Thomas Cromwell, who then distribute the work down the ecclesiastical and social hierarchies. At the bottom of the woodcut, joyful commoners shout, "Vivat rex" (long live the king). The translators of the Great Bible are not named, possibly for political reasons as Tyndale was primarily responsible for the translation. The title page of the Bishops' Bible portrayed Elizabeth wearing a crown and holding a scepter, but just a few of the translators were identified, and only by their initials. Thus from the 1530s onward, government-sponsored Bibles suppressed the identity of the translator in order to emphasize royal approval of the translation, which underscored the official nature of these works.

When translators selected theological treatises that reflected their own religious views, they likewise occupied an invisible or inferior role in relation to the original author. As in the case of the Bible, the source text generally held more religious clout than the translator did. In recognition of the source text's doctrinal authority, translators of theological works attempted to render their translations as faithfully as possible. In the second edition of his translation of Calvin's *Institution of Christian Religion* (1562), Thomas Norton explained the difficulties he faced in deciding whether to translate word for word or sense for sense:

> If should folow the wordes, I saw that of necessitie the hardnesse in the translation must nedes be greater than was in the tong wherein it was originally written. If I should leave the course of words, and graunt my self liberty after the natural maner of myne own tong, to say that in English which I conceived to be hys meaning in Latine, I plainly perceived how hardly I might escape error: and on the other side in thys matter of fayth and religion, how perilous it was

> to erre. For I durste not presume to warraunt my selfe to have hys meaning without hys words. For they that wote [know] what it is to translate wel and faythfully, specially in matters of religion, do know that not the onely grammaticall construction of wordes sufficeth, but the very bylding and order to observe all advauntages of vehemence or grace, by placing or accent of words, maketh much to the true setting fourth of a wryters mynde. In the ende, I rested upon thys determination, to folow the wordes so nere as the phrase of the English tong would suffer me.[67]

Like the Rheims translators, Norton fears that a free translation might create room for unorthodox opinions, recognizing that "in thys matter of fayth and religion, how perilous it was to erre." Believing that the "bylding and order" of words creates the sense, Norton equates translating "wel" with translating "faythfully." He was not alone in perceiving a need for an accurate translation of Calvin's text. The first edition of his translation contains a prefatory note from the printers Reynald Wolf and Richard Harrison, who apologize for the delay in printing an English version of this work: "Maister John Dawes had translated it and delivered it into our handes more than a twelvemoneth past . . . [but] we could not wel emprinte it soner. For we have ben by diverse necessarie causes constrayned with our earnest entreatance to procure an other frende of ours to translate it whole agayn. This translation, we trust, you shal well allow. For it hath not only ben faythfully done by the translater himself, but also hath ben wholly perused by such men, whoes jugement and credit al the godly learned in Englande well knowe & esteme."[68] While Wolf and Harrison do not explain their rationale for commissioning a new translation, their claim that Norton's version has been approved by sundry learned men suggests that Dawes's rendering would not pass muster. The printers clearly believed that such an important work needed to be translated "faythfully." Both the first and second editions of Norton's translation further emphasize his submissive relationship to the original text by identifying Norton only by his initials.

Yet the perceived superiority of the original author could also enable the translator to claim literary authority or cultural agency for himself. Lawrence Venuti has characterized translation as "a form of scholarship" because this activity implicitly displays the translator's learning.[69] It is this very ability to disseminate knowledge that made translation a vital activity during the English Reformation, and translators leveraged their learning into a source of self-authorization and self-advancement. For example, when William Tyndale sought Cuthbert Tunstall as a patron for his translation of the Bible, he brought a translation of Isocrates as evidence of his Greek skills.[70] Translators also used their work as a platform for legitimating their own compositions, moving from executive authorship into original authorship. When Nicholas Lesse published a translation of Philipp Melanchthon in 1548, he appended a tract of his own composition: *The Justification of Man by Faith Only: Made and Written by Phylyp Melanchton and Translated out of the Latyn in to This Oure Mother Tonge by Nicholas Lesse of London. An Apologie or Defence of the Worde of God, Declaringe What a Necessary Thynge It Is, To Be in All Mennes Handes, the Want wher of is the Only Cause of Al Ungodlienes Committed thorowe the Whole Earth, Made by the Sayde Nicholas Lesse* (STC 17792). By pairing his treatise with Melanchthon's text, Lesse both indicated the reformist orientation of his tract and capitalized on recent interest in German reformers. In fact, three other translations of Melanchthon saw print between 1547 and 1548.[71] Finally, translators co-opted the authority of their source texts in ways that conflicted with the original author's religious views. In 1534, Leonard Cox paired a translation of the Epistle of Paul to Titus with an English version of Erasmus's *Paraphrase* on this epistle. Cox's preface to this publication defended Henry's repudiation of papal authority by identifying the pope with the inattentive shepherds of Ezekiel 34:1–16, whose neglected sheep become the prey of beasts: "Se here most gentle reader the angre of god evydently fallen upon the bysshop of Romes tyrannye/and his adherentes whose proude power daylye decreaseth . . . for theyr devourynge of Chrystes flocke. And se also on the other syde the greate goodnes of god towarde our Englysshe nacyon/whiche hathe delyvered us oute of his ravenyng mouth/and gyven us our hed & herdes man our moste redoubted soverayne."[72] Despite his criticisms of ecclesiastical abuses, Erasmus would have never advocated outright rejection of the pope, but Cox's translation positions Erasmus as a supporter of English schism.

Protestant translators working with Catholic texts claimed authorial agency even more openly by taking advantage of the gatekeeping aspect of translation. These translators unapologetically exercised freedom in removing potentially offensive or doctrinally unacceptable material, presenting themselves as endorsers of their translations' orthodoxy. Some of these translators appropriated contemporary Catholic devotional works for Protestant audiences. Francis Meres's preface to his 1598 translation of Luis de Granada explained that he had "remov[ed] corruptions, that as Rocks would have endangered many."[73] The church fathers posed special problems, as both Catholics and Protestants cited patristic texts as evidence for their doctrinal positions. The Protestant translator Thomas Rogers, for example, sought to reclaim works attributed to Augustine by zealously adding biblical marginalia and removing references to Roman Catholic doctrine.[74] Rogers's revision of Thomas à Kempis's *Imitatio Christi* is especially illustrative of his views about the translator's responsibility for the orthodoxy of a translation. Earlier Protestant recensions of the *Imitatio* had removed Kempis's fourth book on the Eucharist, but Rogers criticizes these versions for retaining other Catholic material: "I grant they have done the dutie of translators: yet sure I am they have neglected a greater dutie than of translatorship. For my part I had rather come into the displeasure of man, than displease God; and rather move the obstinat heretike, than offend the weake & simple Christian."[75] Rogers prioritizes reformed orthodoxy over fidelity to the source text, placing Kempis in an inferior position to himself as a Protestant who rejects Catholic innovations. He felt no scruples in tampering with Kempis's text, offering an English translation of Kempis's *Soliliquium animae* in 1592 as a substitute for the missing fourth book. In the preface to this translation, Rogers transforms Kempis into a would-be Protestant: "I have as little as might bee varied from the auctors words and phrazes, and no where from the sense, but where he himselfe hath varied from the truth of God, and, I doubt not, would have redressed, had hee lived in these daies of light, as he did in the time of most palpable blindnes."[76] By presenting the translation as compatible with the "truth of God," Rogers endorses its doctrinal purity, authorizing Kempis as suitable reading for Protestants.

In many ways the functional and practical habitus of female translators resembled the attitudes toward translation displayed by their male counterparts. Nevertheless, female translators faced an additional burden of conforming to contemporary expectations of feminine virtues, such as chastity, silence, and obedience. Perhaps the most noticeable difference between the male and female translator, then, is the overwhelming tendency for women's translations to be characterized as private works based in the domestic sphere. In Nicholas Breton's *Olde Mans Lesson* (1605), the titular character Chremes advises a younger man that learned wives should occupy their time with translation: "If she be learned and studious, perswade her to translation, it will keepe her from Idlenes, & it is a cunning kinde taske: if she bee unlearned, commend her huswifery, and make much of her carefulnesse."[77] This view of translation as an appropriate domestic activity for women originated in the circle of Thomas More, which contended that humanist education—usually framed as a means of training young men for government careers—could be adapted to prepare women for their roles as wives and mothers.[78] Such arguments attempted to forestall objections that learning might encourage women to indulge in supposedly feminine vices such as lust. Breton's use of the term "cunning" to describe translation inadvertently gestures at this possibility as this word could mean both "learned" and "sly."[79] If Florio felt compelled to defend the way that translation could disseminate knowledge, then female translators had to be particularly careful in circulating their work, which might be perceived as trespassing on the masculine sphere of learning. Two seventeenth-century assessments of Elizabeth I's translation of Boethius suggest the potential range of reactions to women's translations. William Camden admiringly claimed that Elizabeth translated Boethius after Henry IV's conversion to Catholicism, implying that such a learned activity was fit for a queen: "At this time, she daily turned over Boetius his books, *De Consolatione,* and translated them handsomely into the English tongue."[80] The French Jesuit Nicolas Caussin, however, criticized Elizabeth for this translation while praising Mary, Queen of Scots for avoiding such learned displays: "[Mary] was experienced in the knowledge of tongues and sciences, as much as was necessary for an honest Lady, who ought not to appear too learned. [Elizabeth] gave her self to such a vanity of study, that oftentimes she committed some extravagances; as when she undertook to translate the five books of the Consolation of Boëtius, to comfort her self on the Conversion of Henrie the Fourth."[81] If an "honest Lady" should refrain from seeming "too learned," then Elizabeth's demonstration of her facility with Latin merely shows her "vanity" and "extravagances." Of course, these different assessments of Elizabeth's translation reflect Camden's and Caussin's divergent religious beliefs. Nevertheless, Caussin's reaction is a useful reminder that the activity of translation itself did not spare female translators from attack. Female translators and their allies therefore countered any potential criticism of the translator's virtue by framing this activity as a suitably domestic exercise, subsuming potentially unacceptable displays of learning within a patriarchal structure.

Despite these domestic frameworks, the cultural agendas of women's and men's translations bear striking similarities. Just as printers and male translators used translation to generate economic profit and to seek patronage, so women offered translations to potential or actual patrons. Mildred Cooke Cecil straightforwardly presents her translation of Basil the Great to Anne Somerset, the Duchess of Somerset, as payment for previous favors: "I . . . thought mete with these fewe leaves thus by me translatyed to move your goodnes ether to take them as some small parte of my service I owe, or in sted of some meane frende to intreat for my dett."[82] Male translators were not alone in using their work to import theology and devotional practices from the Continent. Francis Bell, OFM, for example, explained that he hoped to provide a model of Franciscan piety for readers by publishing a life of Saint Elizabeth of Portugal translated by Abbess Catherine Greenbury of the Third Order Franciscans in Brussels: "I had scruple to hide what was so behovefull for the commun good. . . . For nothing moveth more to perfection then the examples of those saintes that were in all respectes of the same profession that our selves are."[83] Greenbury's translation offered English readers an example of Continental hagiography even as it publicized the newly resurgent English Franciscan order. Finally, women used translation to support or oppose the official church much as their male contemporaries did. A notable example is Anne Bacon's translation of Jewel's *Apologie,* which Matthew Parker, Archbishop of Canterbury, presented as a substantial contribution to current ecclesiastical policy: "By which your travail (Madame) you have expressed an acceptable dutye to the glorye of God, [and] deserved well of this Churche of Christe . . . and besides the honour ye have done to the kinde of women and to the degree of Ladies, ye have done pleasure to the Author of the Latine boke, in deliveringe him by your cleare translation from the perrils of ambiguous and doubtful constructions: and in makinge his good woorke more publikely beneficiall: wherby ye have raysed up great comforte to your friendes."[84] Parker's oblique allusion to the defects of the previous English translation ("perrils of ambiguous and doubtful constructions") only reinforces the public necessity of Bacon's translation. Meanwhile, Elizabeth Cary framed her translation of Jacques Davy Du Perron's defense of Catholicism as an intervention in the largely Protestant culture of English universities: "I was mooved to it by my beleefe, that it might make those English that understand not French, whereof there are ma[nie], even in our universities, reade Perron."[85] These parallels between the functions of religious translations by men and women suggest that women were well aware of the cultural and political uses of translation.

The practical habitus of the female translator typically hewed closer to faithfulness than freedom. If Meres and Rogers sought to reclaim authors such as Augustine and Granada for Protestant readers, female translators were less likely to work with texts outside of their confessional identities. This difference may reflect contemporary views that women should not be exposed to doctrinally suspect works. Anne Gawdy Jenkinson, a Protestant woman who translated a Catholic work by Guillaume du Vair, Bishop of Lisieux, offers an important counterexample to this trend.

Jenkinson's rendering of du Vair's *Meditations upon the Lamentations of Jeremy* (1609) carefully aligns the work with Protestant beliefs, but she does not mention these alterations in her preface.[86] Rather, Jenkinson notes that her father both presented the text to her and asked her to translate it, thus giving her translation a paternal seal of approval. Women who translated conservatively had the same incentives as faithful male translators. Some had encountered double translation as part of their education and subsequently applied its principles to their work. The stylistic awkwardness of Elizabeth I's surviving translations from Latin may be explained in part by her familiarity with double translation, as she replicated her source texts as exactly as possible.[87] Yet women's faithfulness in translating religious works also resulted from their perception that authoritative source texts needed to be rendered precisely so as to preserve proper doctrine. Like Thomas Norton, Anne Lock intended her translation of Calvin to be as faithful as possible to the original: "I have rendred it so nere as I possibly might, to the very wordes of his text, and that in so plaine Englishe as I could expresse."[88] Women, like men, often exercised a localized freedom in their translations, but women were much more likely to translate approved religious authorities whose texts required close translation, with the exception of the psalms.

In keeping with these functional and practical aspects of habitus, the female translator generally took a submissive authorial position that emphasized the original author but that could also authorize the translator—a practice that once again parallels the authorial poses of male translators. Some female translators were completely invisible to the wider public, even if selected readers might have known their identity, as with Katherine Parr's anonymous translation of John Fisher (*Psalmes or Prayers Taken out of Holye Scripture,* 1544). As in the case of the English Bible, the translator's invisibility allowed her work to become part of a larger governmental agenda to popularize vernacular piety. Other translators invoked the prestige of their source texts in ways that developed their own literary and scholarly credibility. Mary Basset claimed that she hesitated to present Mary Tudor with her manuscript translation of Eusebius's *Ecclesiastical History* because such an important work "requyred . . . the dylygent labour of a wyse, eloquent, expert, and in all kyndes of good lyterature, a very well exercysed man."[89] Nevertheless, her dedicatory preface demonstrated an outstanding grasp of Greek and Latin by identifying errors in both the printed Greek edition of Eusebius as well as in Rufinus's Latin version, knowledge befitting her role as Thomas More's granddaughter. Meanwhile, Lock compared the production of her translation of Calvin to the preparation of medicine: "This receipte God the heavenly Physitian hath taught, his most excellent Apothecarie master John Calvine hath compounded, & I . . . have put into an Englishe box."[90] By presenting herself as a mere packager of Calvin's divinely inspired wisdom, Lock minimizes her role in the creation of the translation. At the same time, Lock—like Nicholas Lesse—uses her association with an authoritative theologian to legitimate the publication of her own work. Lock appends a sonnet sequence on Psalm 51 to her translation, characterizing it as the work of a friend. The likelihood that Lock herself composed this work is heightened by the fact that her later translation of Jean Taffin was also accompanied by a poem inspired by her source text.[91] Finally, just as Cox had appropriated Erasmus for his own ends, some female translators reframed or rewrote their source texts to serve new purposes. Catherine Magdalen (Elizabeth) Evelinge, a Poor Clare, asserts that her translation of the life of Saint Clare came "totally out of the R[everend] F[ather] Francis Hendriques," even though she, or her collaborators, added a lengthy new section compiled from fifteen or more different sources: "Of many and admirable acts wrought by the holy Order of S[aint] Francis in the Church of God. But more especially in these latter ages, in the Indies."[92] This interpolation transformed the text from a simple hagiography of Saint Clare into a history of the Franciscan order, offering English readers evidence of the Franciscans' vitality as agents of conversion. As these examples suggest, female translators—like their male counterparts—found the authorial multiplicity of translation a productive means of assuming authorial poses that established their personal credibility and advanced larger political and religious agendas.

The following chapters explore the major cultural functions and authorial roles associated with early modern Englishwomen's religious translations. Since women generally did not translate the Bible, I largely concentrate on women's translations of nonbiblical religious texts. The lone exception to this rule is Mary Sidney Herbert's *Psalmes*, a work that represents the importance attached to psalm translations and paraphrases during this period. Rather than focusing on female translators in isolation, I situate these women within their social networks as well as their broader cultural contexts. In each chapter, I examine one cultural function performed by translation by surveying its appearance in a range of early modern translations. I then trace the way that religious, pedagogical, and political factors affected the manifestation of this phenomenon by focusing on two interrelated case studies of translations by women from the same family or milieu. Placing the female translator in the context of other translators from her immediate circle (whether family members, tutors, or members of her religious community), I reveal that these women's translations were not anomalous but rather emblematic of specific cultural agendas linked to translations emerging from these social groups. After establishing the functional habitus of translation particular to these women's coteries, I analyze the historical and literary contexts of their translations. Through material characteristics (such as title pages, woodcuts, and scribal hands), female translators and/or their editors created distinct authorial personae that positioned these works as contributions to ongoing debates. I then consider the translators' practical habitus, identifying translation choices that react to the translators' historical contexts and authorial roles. This interplay of methodologies drawn from historicism, textual studies, and Translation Studies allows for a detailed understanding of the similarities and differences between male and female translators of the period. More important, this book outlines how early modern translators—whether male or female—manipulated the authorial connotations of translation to legitimate their participation in ongoing religious and political controversies.

Chapters 1 and 2 focus on the ways that women's translations exercised political agency and thus circumvented restrictions on women's participation in the public sphere. Chapter 1 examines translation's role as a leisure activity, which translators emphasized to present their publications as evidence of their private lives. Printed translations by Margaret Roper and Mary Basset, the daughter and granddaughter of Thomas More, took advantage of this connection between translation and domesticity to shape public ideas about More himself. Chapter 2 discusses the use of translation as propaganda, particularly in cases where translations gained cultural significance thanks to the fame of the translator. Male editors of translations by Mary and Elizabeth Tudor appropriated the princesses' works as propaganda for the Edwardian Reformation, using the translators' rank as a means of authorizing religious change. Chapters 3 and 4 turn to female translators who restricted public awareness of their roles as translators, in the process enhancing their own legitimacy as spiritual and political authorities. As chapter 3 shows, learned courtiers offered counsel to their patrons through manuscript presentation copies of translations with lavish physical characteristics. Both Mary Sidney Herbert and Elizabeth I prepared unique manuscript translations in response to contemporary debates over England's support for foreign Protestants, transforming their educations into justification for their political views. Chapter 4 addresses the tendency among members of dissident religious groups to issue anonymous translations that spoke on behalf of their factions. Mary Percy and Potentiana Deacon, Benedictine nuns living on the Continent, each published translations endorsing Jesuit practices that were controversial within their convents. Neither Percy nor Deacon could claim to represent their convents' spiritual practices, but anonymity allowed them the appearance of doing just that.

These case studies demonstrate the cultural importance of faithful translation as an agent of religious change and as a source of political controversy. Like their male contemporaries, female translators participated in a vital activity whose authorial connotations offer new models of early modern authorship. Translators, editors, and others working within the space of religious translation cultivated a rich variety of possible authorial poses, ranging from the private citizen to the famous aristocrat to the learned counselor to the anonymous member of a religious group. Instead of simply foregrounding a text's original author, these authorial strategies often helped advance the cultural and religious agendas of the translators or their editors. Gender expectations may have played an important role in determining the way that women made use of translation and its authorial possibilities, leading them to ward off criticism of their displays of learning through devices such as the modesty topos. Nevertheless, religious translation offered women as well as men a significant, if often overlooked, means of contributing to larger cultural conversations sparked by the English Reformation.

CHAPTER ONE

Private Spheres

Margaret Roper, Mary Basset, and Catholic Identity

When Richard Hyrde introduced Margaret More Roper's translation of Erasmus's *Devout Treatise upon the Pater Noster* (1526) to English readers, he helped forge an enduring link between translation, humanist study, and leisure time. As John Archer Gee noted decades ago, Roper's work was one of the first published translations to follow humanist standards, and Hyrde's preface is likewise an early presentation of humanist translation as a private activity.[1] Hyrde defended women's training in classical languages by noting the ability of humanist learning to stave off dangerous fantasizing:

> Redyng and studyeng of bokes so occupieth the mynde/that it can have no leyser to muse or delyte in other fantasies/whan in all handy werkes/that men saye be more mete for a woman/the body may be busy in one place/and the mynde walkyng in another: & while they syt sowing & spinnyng with their fyngers/maye caste and compasse many pevysshe fantasyes in their myndes/whiche must nedes be occupyed/outher with good or badde/so long as they be wakynge.[2]

While those opposed to women's learning had suggested that women need only be occupied with physical labor such as "sowing & spinnyng," Hyrde notes that these activities allow women to "caste and compasse . . . pevysshe fantasyes in their myndes." An education, however, leaves no room for this problematic mental "leyser." This need to avoid idleness was not gender-specific, for John Wilkinson prefaced his 1547 translation of Aristotle with a similar concern about wandering minds: "Although the feble and werie bodye . . . be satisfied with a restinge place: yet the mind cannot be so quieted or reposed, but that of necessitie it is evermore busi. Therfore it shal be good for every man to provide for some vertuouse occupiyng [*sic*], against the multitude of phantasies, wherin may be fixed the labour of the mind, so that it stray not to[o] ferre in vaine."[3] These concerns about leisure reflect two humanist contentions: that idleness was unprofitable and even detrimental to the state and that classical study provided an appropriate activity for spare time. Translators could in turn frame their work as tangible evidence of their private occupation and its profit to the nation.

Hyrde was only the first of several male editors who presented women's translations within a domestic framework. Since women generally could not hold public roles in early modern England, scholars have often taken these claims of female translators' privacy at face value, inadvertently minimizing the public aims of their works. For example, the *Oxford History of Literary Translation in English* relegates its only sustained discussion of early modern female translators to a chapter by Gillian Wright entitled "Translating at Leisure: Gentlemen and Gentlewomen." If this title suggests that women's translations had few public applications, Wright emphasizes the private nature of translation during this period: "As the holdings of major manuscript repositories show, translation was commonly performed throughout the early modern period for private purposes (such as education and spiritual devotion) by both women and men of the leisured classes."[4] Yet Wright primarily discusses printed translations by women such as Anne Cooke Bacon, Anne Lock, and Elizabeth Cary, whose works may have had private origins yet nevertheless clearly participated in public religious debates. A similar tension appears in Peter Burke's recent distinction between amateur and professional translators: "a relatively small number of translators were professional, at least in the general sense of devoting a considerable amount of their life to this task, often for money." Burke categorizes female translators as amateurs, mentioning women such as "Margaret Beaufort, Aphra Behn, Elizabeth Cary, Ann Cook, Ann Lok, Jane Lumley, Margaret Roper, Mary Sidney and Margaret Tyler."[5] Most of these women translated at least two works, and some of them—such as Lumley and Sidney—translated regularly over a span of years. The inclusion of Behn on this list further reveals the problems caused by identifying female translators as amateurs. A woman often seen as the first professional female author, Behn relied in part on translation to make a living by her pen. This impulse to view women's translations as private or amateur responds to the frequency with which female translators and their editors positioned women's translations outside of the public sphere.[6] Such characterizations may have helped preserve the female translator's virtuous reputation, but her apparently private work could also publicly symbolize her family's piety.

This chapter will examine the way that printed translations by Margaret More Roper and her daughter Mary Roper Basset helped establish this tradition of the female translator's domesticity. Both women's published translations were strongly associated with the private life of Thomas More. Margaret Roper's translation of Erasmus suggested the connection between the female translator and her family's religious and political agendas, and scholars have been particularly interested in considering the extent to which Roper's work can be separated from the life and legend of her father.[7] Mary Basset followed the example set by her mother, using translation to advance the cause of English Catholicism and to emphasize More's legacy as a martyr. Indeed, Roper and Basset subtly rework their source texts in ways that intersect with their translations' political contexts and paratextual agendas, suggesting that neither woman was a submissive tool of patriarchal agendas. Rather, both Roper and Basset actively participated in the familial and political causes evoked by their editors. The ways that their translations attempted to shape public conceptions of Thomas More reveal that the female translator could possess an oblique political power despite her apparent confinement within the domestic sphere. The translations of the More women consequently offer new ways of viewing women's use of the modesty topos and their involvement in the early modern public sphere.

Leisure Pursuits: Translation and Humanist Study

As humanist education gained traction in early modern England, translation became associated with the private sphere. Proponents of the new learning had presented reading as a worthwhile alternative to other leisure pursuits, and male translators built on this development to cast their work as the product of a leisure time that complemented their public careers and aspirations.[8] Thomas Elyot's *The Boke Named the Governour* (1531) characterizes idleness as a lack of profitable labor: "It is nat onely called idlenes/wherin the body or minde cesseth from labour/but specially idlenes is an omission of al honest exercise: the other may be better called a vacacion from seriouse businesse: whiche was some tyme embraced of wise men and vertuous."[9] This redefinition of spare time as "a vacacion from serious businesse" echoes the preface to Elyot's translation of Plutarch (*The Education or Bringinge Up of Children*, 1530): "I therfore in tymes vacant from busynes & other more serious study, as it were for my solace & recreation, have translated . . . this lytell treatise."[10] Elyot, then senior clerk of the king's council, presents his translation as the fruit of private "study," suggesting that it provides concrete evidence of how he profitably disposes of the time not devoted to "busynes." Similarly, Thomas Phaer, solicitor to the council in the Welsh marches, dedicated his translation of Virgil to Mary I, portraying it as the natural counterpart to his "diligence [while] employed in [her] service in the Marchies": "So your highnes hereby maie receive the accomptes of my pastyme, in all my vacations, in whiche vacations I made the saied worke, since I have been preferred to your service."[11]

Jürgen Habermas's concept of representative publicity provides a useful way of understanding how Elyot and Phaer manipulated their public and private personae through translation. Before the emergence of the modern public sphere, noblemen held public roles by virtue of their ability to govern: "In medieval documents 'lordly' and 'publicus' were used synonymously; publicare meant to claim for the lord."[12] As a result, an aristocrat or officeholder had a public role insofar as he represented the king or his office: "This *publicness* (or *publicity*) *of representation* was not constituted as a social realm, that is, as a public sphere; rather, it was something like a status attribute, if this term may be permitted. In itself the status of manorial lord, on whatever level, was neutral in relation to the criteria of 'public' and 'private'; but its incumbent represented it publicly. He displayed himself, presented himself as an embodiment of some sort of 'higher' power."[13] By the early sixteenth century, both aristocrats and bureaucrats connected with the state held representative publicity as signifiers of Henry VIII's power, and male translators associated with the state took advantage of this phenomenon to craft an appearance of privacy that served more public ends. By mentioning their leisure time so pointedly, Elyot, Phaer, and other translators of literary works both advertised their private devotion to learning and publicized their own capacity for government service. Nevertheless, references to leisure time are far less common in prefaces to men's translations of religious works, even though these translations could be taken as evidence of the translator's personal virtue. For example, William Caxton notes that he translated the *Legenda aurea* (1483) to avoid the vice of idleness condemned by Saint Jerome and Saint Bernard: "I have concluded & fermelye purposed in my self nomore to be ydle but wyl applye my self to laboure and suche ocupacion as I have be acustomed to do."[14] After the Reformation, men translated devotional and doctrinal works related to public debates over religion, presenting these translations as urgent interventions in ongoing controversies. While Thomas Hoby characterized his translation of Castiglione's *Courtyer* as a product of his "time and leyser," he had framed his earlier translation of Martin Bucer as a timely contribution to the Edwardian Reformation, stating that he would be remiss to "let slippe suche a mete, apt, and necessarye epistle . . . written and indited to the whole churche, or congregation of Englande."[15]

If male translators of religious works could openly participate in religious controversies, women rarely had any such expectations of taking on a public role. As a result, women's translations—whether secular or religious in nature—were frequently presented as part of their leisure time, both by female translators themselves and by their editors. Nicholas Udall described the Edwardian court as a locus of women's pious reading in his preface to Mary Tudor's translation of part of Erasmus's *Paraphrases* (1547): "It is nowe no newes at all to see Quenes and Ladies of moste highe estate and progenie, in stede of Courtly daliaunce, to enbrace vertuous exercises of readyng and wrytyng."[16] Much as Hyrde had done with Margaret Roper, Udall sets up Mary as an exemplar of studious piety by revealing that she is one of the aristocratic women who have replaced "Courtly daliaunce" with "readyng and wrytyng." Likewise, G. B.'s preface to Anne Cooke's translation of Bernardino Ochino anticipates potential criticism by reminding readers of the aristocratic indolence typically associated with her rank: "remember it is a womans yea, a Jentylwomans, who commenly are wonted to lyve Idelly."[17] Through prefaces that emphasized the female translator's abhorrence of idleness, male editors situated these texts within the larger humanist tradition of profitable leisure time. While these women did not have public occupations, both were related to well-known men, and their translations could in turn symbolize their families. Such assertions of the female translator's domesticity indicate that the privacy associated with translation was not enough to protect the female translator from scorn. Prefaces composed by male editors therefore placed the female translator at a double remove from the public sphere, as if to guarantee the translator's feminine virtue.

When circulating their work in manuscript, women may have felt more freedom to address readers, but they nonetheless expressed similar sentiments about the privacy of their compositions. William Rastell's preface to Mary Basset's printed translation of Thomas More (*Of the Sorowe of Christ,* 1557) indicates Basset's reluctance to enter the public sphere associated with print, reporting that Basset had translated the work "for her owne pastyme and exercyse."[18] Rastell's language echoes Basset's own dedicatory preface to her manuscript translation of Eusebius

(c. 1547–53), in which she informs Mary Tudor that the work was done "for myne owne onely exercyse."[19] In both cases, Basset's work is associated with leisure activity ("pastyme," "exercyse"), yet her refusal to speak on her own behalf in print indicates her awareness of contemporary restrictions on women's public speech. Likewise, John Bale presents Elizabeth Tudor's translation of Marguerite de Navarre as a personal enterprise meant to increase her knowledge and devotion: "Chefely have she done it for her owne exercyse in the frenche tunge, besydes the spirytuall exercyse of her innar sowle with God."[20] By characterizing the translation as simply intended for individual use ("her owne exercyse," "her innar sowle"), Bale heightens the privacy associated with this translation, which was originally a New Year's gift for Katherine Parr. Bale also removes Elizabeth's preface to this manuscript version of the translation, which asks that "no other, (but your highnes onely) shal rede it, or se[e] it, lesse my fauttes be knowen of many."[21] Both Basset and Elizabeth found limited manuscript circulation an appropriate arena for a female voice, yet each one shows concern about circulating their translations within a more public realm. Whether early modern readers encountered women's translations in manuscript or print, the translator's apparent privacy would have met expectations about the domesticity associated with both women and translation.

The Doctor and the Gentlewoman: Margaret Roper, Erasmus, and Anti-Lutheranism

Within the familial and scholarly circle surrounding Thomas More, translation was a practice strongly linked to humanist pedagogy that emphasized training in Latin and Greek. Translation is an ideal activity for language instruction, as the translator must inevitably pay close attention to the nuances of diction, syntax, and style. While the schoolroom and the translations composed there might appear to be ideologically neutral, many of the translations published by members of the More circle promulgate a radical outlook indicative of Morean pedagogy: that humanist tenets could inculcate pious morality, particularly in women. As Lutheranism gained strength within England, the circle's translations began to address the threat of heresy, which was of prime concern to More during the 1520s and 1530s. The only woman from the More circle to publish a translation, Margaret More Roper played a unique role in this program, for her work—itself the product of Morean pedagogy—could help justify women's education.[22] At the same time,

Roper was the first to follow her father's example and publish an English translation, providing a model for later printed translations by her tutor and her brother.

Members of the More circle valued translation as a pedagogical tool that permitted the translator to acquire and display linguistic skills. More himself engaged in competitive translations to hone his Greek, translating epigrams from the *Anthologia Graeca* with William Lily (*Progymnasmata,* c. 1504, published 1518) and Lucian's dialogues with Desiderius Erasmus (1506).[23] More prefaced his translations of Lucian by emphasizing their moral and religious applications: "*Philopseudes* . . . will teach us this lesson: that we should put no trust in magic and that we should eschew superstition, which obtrudes everywhere under the guise of religion."[24] Erasmus's preface to his Latin translation of the Greek tragedy *Hecuba* (1506) also suggested the possible religious applications of secular translation: "Having resolved . . . to translate Greek authorities in order to restore or promote, as far as I could, the science of theology . . . but wishing to avoid risking my potter's skill all at once on a great jar, as the Greek adage has it, or rushing into such a large enterprise with feet as yet unwashed, as the saying goes, I determined first to test whether the labour I had spent on Greek and Latin had been wasted by experimenting on a subject which, though very taxing, was secular in nature."[25] Recognizing the pedagogical value of translation, More ensured that his children's schooling included this activity. As Thomas Stapleton recorded, More's children frequently practiced double translation: "The pupils exercised themselves in the Latin tongue almost every day, translating English into Latin and Latin into English."[26] More himself instructed his children to begin their letters to him in English and then translate their compositions into Latin: "It will do no harm if you first write the whole in English, for then you will have much less trouble and labor in turning it into Latin; not having to look for the matter, your mind will be intent only on the language."[27] Furthermore, two of More's daughters translated his Latin letter to Oxford defending the study of Greek, as Stapleton notes: "I have seen another Latin version of this [letter] made by one of his daughters, and an English version by another."[28] This exercise was not merely a show of filial piety but also representative of the More family's controversial views on education. While a group of Oxford faculty calling themselves "Trojans" had publicly attacked the utility of learning Greek, More endorsed Greek by citing its religious value: "To whom is it *not* obvious that to the Greeks we owe all our precision in the liberal arts generally and in theology particularly."[29] For More and his children, translation was simultaneously a means of exercising the linguistic skills acquired through a humanist education and of pursuing the larger Morean ideal of learned piety.

Five translations linked to the More circle, including Roper's Erasmus, were published during Henry's reign, and these works provided a public record of the household's pedagogical and religious programs. More initiated this practice in 1510 by printing his translation of Gianfrancesco Pico's life of his uncle Giovanni Pico della Mirandola as well as several texts by Pico. Scholars have proposed that More translated the work in 1504 as a means of considering his potential vocation at the Charterhouse.[30] Whether or not the translation was completed earlier, its publication in 1510—the same year that More entered into a public career by becoming undersheriff of London—is suggestive. More's own dedicatory preface of this work as a New Year's gift to Joyce Leigh, a nun and family friend, positions the translation as a vehicle for his moralistic view of humanist learning. More emphasizes the spiritual worth of his translation in contrast with the typical presents exchanged at this time: "I . . . have sent you such a present as may bere witnes of my tendre love and zele to the happy continuannce and gracious encrease of vertue in your soule: and where as the giftis of other folk declare that thei wissh their frendes to be worldeli fortunate myne testifieth that I desire to have you godly prosperous."[31] As critics have noted, More reworks the *Life* so that it has a more devotional nature by removing references to Pico's literary achievements as well as his rejection of a political career.[32] By reshaping the work in this way, More publicly indicated his continued interest in learning despite his nascent public career. In 1529 Richard Hyrde, a tutor at More's "school," translated Juan Luis Vives's *De institutione foeminae christianae,* a treatise that defended women's learning and praised the More women's exemplary education. Hyrde's dedicatory preface to Catherine of Aragon makes it clear that More, who corrected Hyrde's translation, strongly approved of the book: "He had entended/his manyfolde busynes nat withstandyng/to have taken the tymes to have translated this boke hym selfe/in whiche he was (as he said) very glad that he was nowe prevented/nor for eschewyng of his labour/whiche he wolde have ben very glad to bestowe there in/but for bicause that the frute therof may nowe soner come forthe."[33] The work thus became a public expression of More's personal support for women's education.

The More circle also utilized translation to spread religious views that dovetailed with More's efforts to stamp out heresy. After More resigned his office as lord chancellor in 1532, he penned original works that attacked heresy as well as Henry's separation from Rome. In 1533, his son John More published two translations of recent works that actively complemented these treatises: Damião de Góis's *The Legacye or Embassate of the Great Emperour of Inde Prester John* (*Legatio magni Indorum Imperatoris,* 1532) and Frederic Nausea's *A Sermon of the Sacramint of the Aulter* ("Hoc facite in mei commemorationem" from *Tres evangelicae veritatis homiliarum centuriae,* 1530). A Portuguese humanist, Góis had translated several Portuguese documents concerning Prester John into Latin. John More asserted that these works revealed that the legendary Christian kingdom ruled by Prester John had preserved the primitive church established at Jesus's death and thus justified the Roman Catholic Church's rejection of heretical doctrines: "In this treatyse ye also se[e], that the great thynges which have ben byfore this tymes establyshed agaynst heretyques by generall counsayles of olde, agaynst whych old determynacyons these new heretyques make newe besynesse nowe, the selfe same thynges have the chrysten people of that great chrysten empyre from the tyme of theyre fyrste conversyon, whych was forthwyth upon the deth of Chryste, contynually byleved."[34] These "thynges" included transubstantiation, veneration of saints, the seven Catholic sacraments, and the pope's authority, all of which had been challenged by Luther and other reformers.[35] While More's preface to his translation of Frederic Nausea, bishop of Vienna, was not polemical, the sermon itself defended transubstantiation ("what more mervaylous then this sacrament, in whych brede and wyne is veryly converted into the body and blood of Jesu Cryste") and suggested that recent epidemics and riots in Germany had occurred because the sacrament was mishandled.[36] If the More circle had a vested interest in translating and publishing texts related to their educational and religious agendas, Margaret Roper's translation of Erasmus first suggested the political and religious work that could be performed by this activity.

As English authorities grew increasingly concerned about Lutheran heresy, Roper's published translation of Erasmus's *A Devout Treatise upon the Pater Noster* (*Precatio dominica,* 1523) tacitly argued for the doctrinal orthodoxy of Erasmus himself. Before Pope Leo X excommunicated Luther in 1520, Erasmus and Luther had been fairly friendly due to shared concerns about corruption within the church.[37] Luther's condemnation of church abuses followed Erasmus's earlier complaints, and both men agreed that commoners should have access to vernacular versions of the scriptures. Because of such similarities, some contemporaries suspected that Erasmus was secretly a heretic, and even a few of Erasmus's most ardent supporters believed that he was directly responsible for the spread of Lutheranism.[38] Erasmus's reputation was especially fragile in England since evangelists like William Tyndale and Thomas Bilney had been inspired by his writings.[39] By June 1524, Vives was warning Erasmus about the ramifications of an intended visit to England that had fallen through: "Your arrival would have been popular and welcome with the king, the cardinal, and all the nobility. But if you do decide to do so, begin at the same time to write something against the man [Luther]; for otherwise you will raise a frown on some faces when it is particularly important for you that they should be all smiles."[40] When Erasmus finally did attack Luther with the publication of *De libero arbitrio diatribe sive collatio* (*On the Freedom of the Will*) in September 1524, he took special care to inform his English friends of this fact. Henry VIII and Wolsey had long urged Erasmus to refute Luther, and Erasmus sent copies of his new work to both of them. In addition, Erasmus immediately informed several other prominent allies—Cuthbert Tunstall, bishop of London, and John Fisher, bishop of Rochester—of the publication of his work. That November, Vives reported to Erasmus that the king and queen were pleased with his treatise: "Your book on the freedom of the will was handed to the king yesterday, and he read several pages of it between services and showed signs of being very much pleased with it. . . . The queen too is quite devoted to you as a result of this same book."[41] Indeed, in 1525 Catherine of Aragon asked Erasmus to write a treatise on marriage, a commission indicating her continued favor. Yet despite this success, Erasmus's reputation in England remained problematic, and by April 1526 he complained to Wolsey: "I am told that my *Colloquies* have been banned in your country."[42] While this rumor was false, it nevertheless suggests the potential for English mistrust of Erasmus's works. In this same letter, Erasmus expresses concern that Henry Standish—who had once tried to persuade Henry and Catherine to burn his books—had now been appointed to lead a commission that dealt with heretical books. Erasmus laments, "If the outcome is to depend on the judgment of such men, no book of mine will escape the flames."[43] He furthermore reports that some parties in England welcomed the personal attacks and vitriolic criticism directed his way: "Recently a Dominican brought into England on his back some volumes containing a scurrilous attack on me. . . . They found a purchaser, while my *Colloquies* are banned from the bookshops."[44] That December, Robert Aldridge wrote to Erasmus with a fresh account of public reactions to Erasmus's corrections of errors in religious texts: "At noisy public meetings, in the buzz of conversation, at the table, even from the pulpit one hears that Erasmus is ruining good and holy books, because he is replacing old and ingrained errors with something new and apt."[45] These incidents suggest that Erasmus was strongly linked with religious innovation and even heresy in the minds of many English men and women, no matter how much he refuted Luther.

This connection between Erasmus and heterodoxy caused Roper's translation to come under scrutiny in March 1526, when Richard Foxford, vicar-general of the bishop of London, investigated Thomas Berthelet for publishing several works without approval: Roper's *Devout Treatise,* Berthelet's translation of Erasmus's *Dicta sapientum,* Gentian Hervet's translation of Erasmus's *De immensa dei misericordia,* and a sermon by John Fisher, a friend of Erasmus as already noted.[46] A close look at these unlicensed publications suggests that Berthelet was interested in cementing Erasmus's reputation as a scholar and in publishing humanist texts that opposed Luther. *Dicta sapientum* was a widely used grammar school text with sayings from Cato and other classical authorities.[47] Fisher's sermon was directly connected with efforts to root out Lutheran heresy, as the title indicates: *A Sermon Had at Paulis . . . Concernynge Certayne Heretickes, Whiche Than Were Abjured for Holdynge the Heresies of Martyn Luther.* Indeed, Fisher praises "the boke of maister More," or the *Responsio ad Lutherum* (1523), for its successful refutation of Luther.[48] In addition, scholars have characterized both *De immensa* and *Precatio dominica* as subtly anti-Lutheran because of their advocacy of mutual forgiveness.[49] Erasmus composed these texts between 1522 and 1524, while he refused to choose sides in hopes of healing the Reformation, a split which he described as "almost more incurable" than war, his bête noire.[50] During this period, Erasmus attempted to play peacemaker by urging mutual reconciliation between Catholics and Protestants. In 1523, Erasmus laid out a plan for peace to Pope Adrian VI that called for general amnesty: "If God deals with us on that principle every day, forgiving all our offences as often as the sinner shows himself penitent, is there any reason why God's vicegerent should not do the same?"[51] *De immensa* also advocates reciprocal forgiveness through its repeated calls for reconciliation: "Forgyve/& ye shalbe forgyven: And by what measure ye have met[e] to your neyghboure/by the same god shall met[e] to you."[52] As Hilmar Pabel has demonstrated, the *Precatio* linked this idea of reconciliation with the Lord's Prayer, which Erasmus saw as "a communal Christian prayer."[53] Berthelet's publications therefore defend Erasmus by emphasizing his anti-Lutheran position as well as his connection with Fisher, an established Lutheran foe.

Despite the orthodoxy of these particular works, Berthelet's publications were swept up in the campaign to prevent the importation of

Lutheran books into England. In October 1524, Foxford had ordered London booksellers, including Berthelet, to cease purchasing and selling foreign texts and to submit all newly imported books to a council of bishops: "Should they import new books into England or buy books already imported, provided that these were newly composed and made, they were not to sell or part with them unless they first showed them either to the Lord Cardinal [Wolsey], the Archbishop of Canterbury [William Warham], the Bishop of London [Tunstall] or the Bishop of Rochester [Fisher]."[54] Berthelet freely admitted that he had failed to follow this order, and Foxford "enjoined him that he should not hereafter sell any copies of the above works, and that he should not print any works without first exhibiting them before him in Consistory."[55] Despite noting the "curiously Erasmian" nature of these books, James McConica concluded that Berthelet was in trouble for a regulatory slip alone, and therefore there was no "apprehension about Erasmian opinion."[56] The religious authorities whose permission Berthelet had failed to gain were all allies of Erasmus, and the books were subsequently licensed without a problem. Foxford's targeting of Fisher's sermon certainly indicates that he was making an example of Berthelet. The order in question only concerned "imported," or foreign, books, and since Fisher was one of the bishops responsible for authorizing publications, his orthodoxy was clearly undeniable. Yet the preponderance of Erasmian texts here seems too marked to be a coincidence. Erasmus's dubious reputation in England suggests that these translations were suspect precisely because they had a potential connection to Luther. Foxford's concern, then, was probably with Erasmian humanism itself, which remained a possible source of quasi-Lutheran ideas despite Erasmus's own refutation of Luther.

If Foxford's investigation suggested potential English hostility toward Erasmian texts, the second and licensed edition of Roper's translation offered visual evidence that English authorities supported Erasmus. This edition interposed a woodcut of Cardinal Wolsey's coat of arms between the title page and the dedication (see figure 1).[57] Wolsey was one of the clergymen appointed to approve imported texts, and his arms may simply indicate that he had licensed the work. Yet none of Berthelet's other reissued publications features this woodcut, hinting that Roper's translation was particularly important, perhaps due to its association with More. Suggestively, the woodcut obliquely indicates royal support of this publication, as its border contains the Tudor rose associated with Henry VIII and a pomegranate emblematic of Catherine of Aragon, along with a cardinal's hat symbolizing Wolsey himself. This second edition

Figure 1. Signature A1 verso of *A Devout Treatise upon the Pater Noster* (1526), Margaret Roper's translation of Desiderius Erasmus.

of Roper's translation therefore evoked a courtly coterie of prominent humanists who presumably endorsed Erasmus's views. Notably, however, none of their names appears within the text or paratexts, a fact perhaps explained by hardening attitudes toward heresy. Wolsey had already conducted public burnings of Luther's works in 1521 and then again in February 1526, while More himself was busily leading raids to uncover and burn Lutheran books.[58] Since Wolsey and More were taking ever harsher measures against heretics on Henry's behalf, they may have realized that overtly linking their names with Erasmus would have seemed contradictory to an English public that associated the Dutch scholar with unorthodox opinions. Indeed, More was famously later forced to defend his friendship with Erasmus in the face of William Tyndale's attacks: "He asketh me why I have not contended with Erasmus whom he calleth my derlynge. . . . I fynde in Erasmus my derlynge that he detesteth and abhorreth the errours and heresyes that Tyndale playnely techeth and abydeth by/and therfore Erasmus my derlynge shall be my dere derlyng styll."[59] Furthermore, More may have felt that the ramifications of his political career prevented any public defense of Erasmus. During the mid-1520s, More served as Henry's private secretary, an association that heightened More's representative publicity for Henry. As John Guy has noted, those who took up this position "could not act independently."[60] While More did compose the *Responsio* to refute Luther, he probably did so at Henry's command.[61] More did not write against Lutheranism again until he received a commission from Tunstall in 1528 to rebut heresy. This pattern suggests that even if More felt inclined to defend Erasmus's reputation, he could not do so publicly without coming into conflict with his position as a state servant.

Margaret Roper, however, was under no such obligation to refrain from defending Erasmus, and the paratexts to her translation suggest the More family's support of Catholic piety based on humanist ideals. Both the title page and dedicatory preface written by Richard Hyrde, a tutor for the More "school," use the modesty topos to define Roper's voice as strictly private. The full title presents Erasmus as a "moost famous doctour" and Roper as "a yong vertuous and well lerned gentylwoman of .xix. yere of age," contrasting a publicly renowned male humanist with a modest female scholar to create a divide between the public realm of Erasmus and the private sphere of Roper. Furthermore, Roper's anonymity implies her lack of interest in fame or public agendas, and the title page's woodcut continues this impression by presenting a woman apparently reading for her own personal benefit (see figure 2). Quentin Metsys's 1517 portrait of Erasmus had influentially portrayed the Dutch

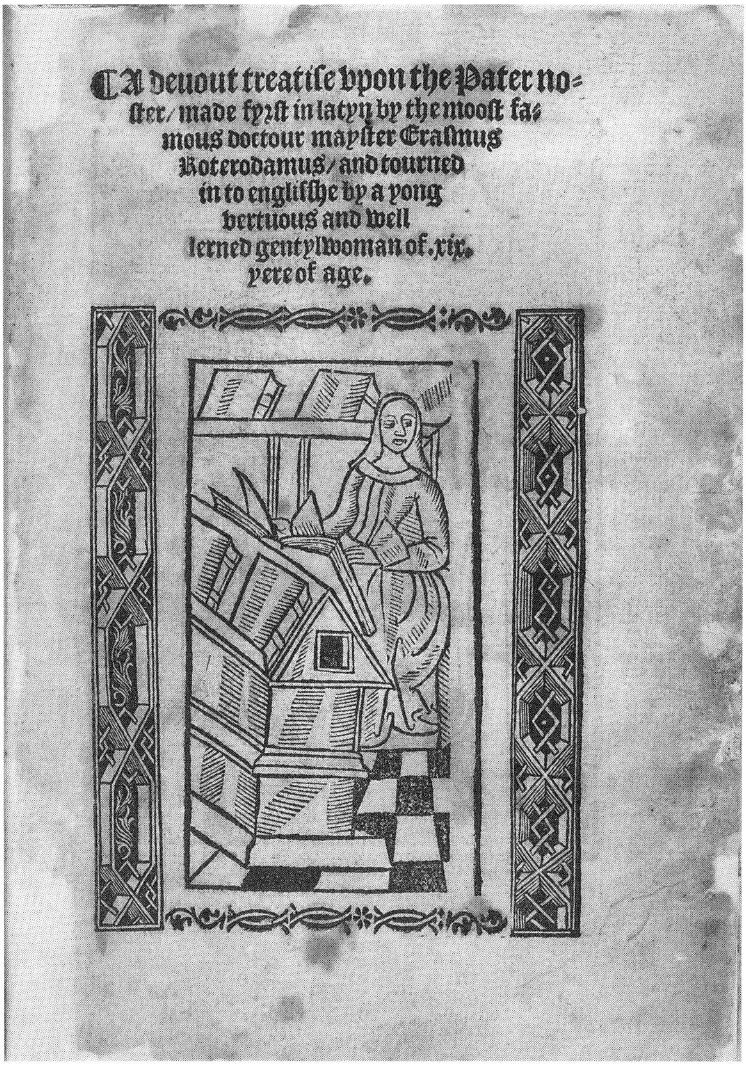

¶A deuout treatise vpon the Pater no=
ster/ made fyrst in latyn by the moost fa=
mous doctour mayster Erasmus
Roterodamus/ and tourned
in to englisshe by a yong
vertuous and well
lerned gentylwoman of .xix.
yere of age.

Figure 2. Title page of *A Devout Treatise upon the Pater Noster* (1526), Margaret Roper's translation of Desiderius Erasmus.

humanist in his study, an apparently private space that nevertheless evoked typical portrayals of Saint Jerome and thus gestured at Erasmus's role as Jerome's biographer and editor.[62] On the title page to Roper's translation of Erasmus, the female reader similarly sits alone in a room with her books, gazing out into space as she turns the pages of the book before her, so that the reader seems to catch Roper in the act of solitary contemplation that defines her personal virtue. Although publication may have been a radical step for a woman, the title page's depiction of Margaret Roper as an exemplar of self-contained study implies that her work is "private" and therefore appropriately feminine.

In keeping with this restriction of Margaret Roper's work to the private sphere, Richard Hyrde's dedication presents her learning within a domestic and familial context. Hyrde frames the translation as an expression of her personal sentiment, praising Margaret Roper as a model of "prudent/humble/and wyfely behavour/charitable & very christen vertue" ("DP," *DT,* A4v). Hyrde's inclusion of "wyfely" within this catalog of praiseworthy traits reinforces his contention that learning enhances traditional feminine roles. Indeed, Hyrde claims that Roper's education has only strengthened her bond with husband William Roper: "With her vertuous/worshipfull/wyse/and well lerned husbande/she hath by the occasyon of her lernynge/and his delyte therin/suche especiall conforte/pleasure/and pastyme/as were nat well possyble for one unlerned couple/eyther to take togyder or to conceyve in their myndes" ("DP," *DT,* B1r). Roper's learning, witnessed by her translation, provides an example of worthwhile leisure activity ("pastyme") that not only is studious but also increases marital "delyte." Hyrde's presentation of Roper as an ideal spouse both justifies the More family's project of female education and situates her translation within the private sphere. As if to drive home the idea that Roper has composed her translation for a domestic audience, Hyrde states that she prefers private esteem over public praise: "She is as lothe to have prayse gyvyn her/as she is worthy to have it/and had leaver her prayse to reste in mennes hertes/than in their tonges/or rather in goddes estimacion and pleasure/than any mannes wordes or thought" ("DP," *DT,* B2v). Hyrde denies that Roper takes any interest in the presumable outcome of her publication—that is, "prayse" expressed through her readers' "wordes or thought." Furthermore, Hyrde suggests that the translation does not contain Roper's voice by assuring the reader that she has accurately rendered Erasmus's original, praising her "dyscrete and substancyall judgement in expressynge lively the latyn" ("DP," *DT,* B2v). These strategies allow Hyrde to separate Roper from the public realm by locating her work within a space devoted to private study.

This emphasis on Roper's domesticity signals Hyrde's participation in a larger effort to establish Margaret Roper as a model of female erudition. One of the few Englishwomen of her time to learn Latin and Greek, Roper was known throughout Europe thanks to the commendations of several learned men associated with her father. Roper's learning was praised by both Juan Luis Vives (*De institutione foeminae Christianae,* 1523) and Erasmus (published letter to Guillaume Budé, 1521; dedicatory preface to his commentary on Prudentius's *Christmas Hymn,* 1523; "The Abbot and the Learned Lady" in his *Colloquies,* 1524). Mary Ellen Lamb has shown that their testimonials, dedications, and letters constituted an elaborate publicity machine intended to spread Margaret Roper's fame to an international audience.[63] Many of these works insisted that Roper's learning helped enhance household piety, fending off potential criticism that education was unfit for women. Such precautions were necessary since humanists had framed the new learning as a means of preparing young men for government service, which meant that women's education might seem unjustified.[64] In contrast, Erasmus's dedicatory preface to his commentary on Prudentius's *Christmas Hymn* imagines that the text will be of use in the nursery as the infant Jesus "will give the offspring of your marriage a happy outcome and be the true Apollo of all your reading, whose praises you will be able to sing to your lyre instead of nursery rhymes to please your little ones."[65] Margaret Roper may have had a relatively high degree of public fame for a gentlewoman, but contemporary praise of her talents portrayed Roper within a domestic sphere associated with Thomas More. The publication of her translation, an activity associated with both the private sphere and her humanist training, thus allowed Roper to take on a public role without flouting limitations on women's participation in the public sphere.

The paratexts to this publication carefully situate Roper's translation within a public arena by hinting at her identity as More's daughter. The title page provides the anonymous translator's social rank, "gentylwoman," and age, ".xix. yere[s]." The dedication gives even more specific clues: Hyrde was a tutor at the More "school," while the dedicatee, "Fraunces S.," could be identified as Frances Staverton, Margaret Roper's cousin. Finally, Hyrde wrote the dedication "At Chelcheth," or Chelsea, a town internationally famous as the site of More's household. Anyone familiar with the More "school," More's children, or the More clan could have unraveled these hints. In addition, the dedication's defense of female education and praise of the translator as a model wife would have revealed her identity to any reader aware of the More circle's campaign to publicize women's learning through Roper. No other young Englishwoman of her generation lived in such a household and was so famous for her learned devotion to husband and family. After all, female education was rare enough that the More daughters' scholarship preceded even the classical training of Mary Tudor, their nearest contemporary. The paratexts therefore frame her voice as private—even as they continually hint at her identity—using the modesty topos to excuse the publication of her work. More important, the paratexts allow her private voice to be identified in concert with More's personal voice. If the More circle used Roper's scholarship to indicate her father's humanism, Margaret Roper's translation in turn signaled More's approbation of Erasmus. Roper's translation carefully positions her as a representative of the More household to underscore the bond between More and Erasmus in a coded, protected manner.

Roper's strategic alterations of Erasmus's original text suggest that she enthusiastically participated in this effort to reclaim Erasmus's English reputation. While Roper's translation is largely conservative in nature, she freely enlarges on the text through doublets. These alterations help associate Erasmus with a scholarly piety that supports Catholicism rather than Lutheranism. Throughout, Roper emphasizes the idea of following divine will, strongly contrasting the antiauthoritarian tendencies perceived in Lutheran tenets. For example, Luther's *Babylonica* had angered Catholics because it threatened to demolish not just the traditions of the church but also papal authority, the basis for many of those traditions, by suggesting that Christians should adhere to only religious practices present in the gospels.[66] Erasmus refutes this antiestablishment view by arguing that true Christians should continually seek to obey heavenly dictates without questioning God's purpose:

> They . . . in this worlde/go about to folowe the *unite and concorde* [concordiam] of the hevenly kyngedome/whiche all the tyme they lyve bodily in erthe/as it becometh naturall and obedient children/*studye with all diligence* [student] to fulfyll those thynges/whiche they knowe shall content thy *mynde & pleasure* [voluntas]/and nat what their owne sensuall appetite gyveth them/ne *jugyng or disputyng* [dijudicantes] why thou woldest this or that to be done/but thynkyng it sufficient/that thus thou woldest it/whom they knowe *surely* [added] to wyll nothing/but that that is best.[67]

Roper highlights Erasmus's emphasis on union with God by translating "concordiam" (concord) as "unite and concorde" and "dijudicantes" (judging) as "jugying and disputying." More important, her translation promotes scholarship as a means of achieving this compliance with God's will. By adding the intensifier "surely" to "knowe," Roper indicates that study can allow Catholics a reliable means of understanding heavenly precepts. Furthermore, she translates "student" (strive) as "studye with all diligence," combining the primary meaning of this verb (to be diligent) with a secondary meaning (to study) that evokes scholarly piety. Similarly, Roper renders "voluntas" (will) with the doublet "mynde & pleasure," adding an intellectual valence that is not present in the original Latin.[68] Erasmus thus seems to argue that by engaging in rigorous "studye" of heavenly dictates, Catholics can "knowe" God's "mynde" and so form an intellectual bond with the divine. Neither "jugyng or disputyng" God's will, as Luther has done, true Christians carefully engage in cerebral activities of "thynkynge," "know[ing]," and "study[ing]." Such thorough consideration of God's "pleasure" allows Catholics a sound basis for asserting that Catholic devotional practices have divine approval, since God "wyll[s] nothing but that is best." This contention that Catholics can come to know God's mind gives humankind a larger agency for salvation within the divine framework than is possible in Protestantism, confuting Protestant emphasis on faith alone. Besides rejecting the idea of abandoning devotional customs unsupported by the gospels, Roper's interventions also indicate that thoughtful practice of such customs is not simply valuable but in fact the hallmark of true religion. Roper's translation therefore distinguishes Erasmus's views from Lutheran theology while refuting the argument that Catholics practice mindless conformity to papal authority.

Roper also defends the classical study promoted by More and Erasmus by justifying its applicability to Christian worship. Erasmus presents Jesus Christ as a teacher who came to earth to instruct humankind in heavenly knowledge. The Lord's Prayer is one example of Christ's teachings, as Christ has "assigned us also a way of prayeng to the[e]" (Roper, *DT,* B4v). By paying close attention to Christ's teachings, a Christian will be able to discern the correct spiritual mode. For example, Erasmus rejects aspersions that learning decreases Christian piety with a reference to the living bread of heaven in John 6:32: "For verily/the *breed* [bread] *and teachynge* [panis] of the proude philosophers and pharises/coude nat suffice and content our mynde: But that breed of thyne/whiche thou sendest us . . . by this breed we are norysshed and fatted" (Roper, *DT,* E3r; Erasmus, *Pd,* 1225B). Roper expands Erasmus's reference to the intellectual component of Christian piety by translating "panis" (bread) with a doublet that underscores Erasmus's point: "breed and teachynge."[69] In Roper's rendering, Christian devotion has an intellectual basis, allowing the humanist student to reject the "teachynge of the proude philosophers" in favor of Christian "breed" that will "norysshe" the "mynde." As a result, Roper causes Erasmus to signal his support of Christian humanism while scoffing at the religious limitations of pagan learning ("philosophers") and Judaism ("pharises"). The translation also validates scholarly study of Christ's teaching as an effective means of defeating the devil: "As we . . . onely worshyp and enbrace the *precious and gostly lernyng of the gospel* [margaritum Evangelicum] . . . So often father thou warrest in us/and overcomest the realme of the devyll" (Roper, *DT,* D2v; Erasmus, *Pd,* 1223A). Here Roper translates "margaritum Evangelicum" (the pearl of the gospel) as "the precious and gostly lernyng of the gospel," in turn endorsing biblical study ("lernyng of the gospell") as a means of serving God even more strongly than her source text does. Roper's version could thus be taken as evidence of the Christian humanist premise that study of classical languages would facilitate pious reading of religious texts. This alteration allows the translation to subtly reject the Lutheran idea that study of the gospels would lead to a purer form of worship since Catholic study instead authorizes existing rites. Indeed, Erasmus condemns those who offer Christ's teachings without a true understanding of their purposes: "He that teacheth the *lernyng* [sermonem] of the gospell/he is he/that gyveth us forthe this breed/whiche yet he gyveth all in vayne/except it be also gyven by the[e]" (Roper, *DT,* E3v–E4r; Erasmus, *Pd,* 1225E). Once again, Erasmus seems to champion pious scholarship since Roper strengthens the pedagogical nuances of his language ("docet"; "teacheth") by rendering "sermonem" (speech) as "lernyng." As a result, Roper's version of Erasmus might appear to allude to the false teachings of Luther, who may cite "the lernyng of the gospell" but whose tenets do not stem from a reasoned understanding of the doctrines provided by God and so are "in vayne." Through her translation, Roper reshapes Erasmus's English reputation both by validating the importance of biblical scholarship as a devotional tool and by hinting at Erasmus's own doctrinal correctness.

Finally, Roper's version of the paraphrase takes on an important role as a means of reuniting a church torn apart by schisms and even extending its reach. The universality of the Lord's Prayer among Christians makes it an ideal tool for unifying them into one body: "We all one thynge praye for and desyre/no man asketh ought for hym selfe *specially or a parte* [peculitariter]/but as membres of one body/quyckened and releved with one soule" (Roper, *DT,*C1r; Erasmus, *Pd,* 1219D–1220A). By reciting the Lord's Prayer, even separately, Christians are unified into "one body" and share "one soule." Roper emphasizes this unity with a doublet for "peculitariter" (specially): "specially or a parte." More important, Roper's translation of Erasmus itself has the potential to unite England and the international Catholic community. By providing the public with an English version of Erasmus's treatise, she allows readers without knowledge of Latin to join the larger group of petitioners evoked by the paraphrase. If Christians follow Erasmus's counsel of obeying God's commands, then they will facilitate the mending of breaches within the church: "All the *membres and partes* [membra] of thy sonne be gathered together/and . . . the hole body of thy sonne/safe and sounde be joyned to his heed [head]/Wherby neyther Christe shall lacke any of his *partes and membres* [membrorum]" (Roper, *DT,* D4v; Erasmus, *Pd,* 1223F–1224A). Roper's chiasmatic doublets for "membra" (limbs) indicate that while Christians are simultaneously identifiable as separate "partes," they are also "membres" of a larger body. This spiritual cohesion is particularly important in accomplishing the greatest task remaining to Christians, which is to unify all humankind within the larger body of Christ: "There is nat yet one herde/and one herde mayster/whiche we hope shalbe/whan the jewes also shall bryng and submyt them selfe to the *spirituall and gostely lernyng of the gospell* [in regnum Evangelicum]" (Roper, *DT,* D3r; Erasmus, *Pd,* 1223B). Roper again emphasizes biblical study by rendering "in regnum Evangelicum" (in the kingdom of the gospel) as "the spirituall and gostely lernyng of the gospell," a translation indicating that the conversion of the Jews depends on their intellectual acceptance of Christ. Once more, Roper's version suggests that the ability to "submit" to God's doctrine extends from a person's knowledge of Christian doctrine, a contention that justifies the importance of Erasmian humanism as a means of ratifying and empowering the church rather than destroying it.

Roper's *Devout Treatise* performs the sort of Catholic intellectual inquiry that Erasmus advocated, suggesting an alternative to Reformation spirituality endorsed by Luther. Furthermore, the paratexts and the text's reception all reveal that Roper's work contributed to the ongoing political controversy linked to Lutheranism during the 1520s. Roper's small but crucial interventions in the source text promote a piety based in humanist scholarship even as they establish Erasmus's orthodoxy. Given Foxford's concerns about the publication of this translation, contemporaries probably viewed Roper's work as part of a confessional struggle with larger public implications rather than as a solely personal exercise. While the paratexts might seem to contradict the public applications of Roper's work, their emphasis on Roper's privacy paradoxically assured the translation's larger importance by associating it with More and other courtly humanists. By evoking Roper's private world, Hyrde presented the translation as evidence of her profitable pastime and consequently guaranteed its authenticity as a reflection of the More family's support for Erasmus. Rather than being silenced by patriarchal agendas, Roper was at the center of this familial effort, actively reworking Erasmus's text so that it promoted the More circle's identification with and endorsement of humanist scholarship and Catholic doctrine.

More's English Tongue: Mary Basset, Thomas More, and the Marian Counter-Reformation

During the mid-Tudor era, the Morean tradition of translation entered a new phase as the circle around Mary Roper Clarke Basset, the daughter of Margaret Roper, used this activity to disseminate staunchly Catholic views. Roper created a home school along Morean lines for her own children, meaning that translation very likely played a role in Basset's education. Yet the translations produced by Basset and her tutors John Christopherson and John Morwen did not have a pedagogical purpose. If Margaret Roper and John More had translated works that participated in religious controversies of the Henrician era, Basset's circle produced translations of Greek works, particularly by the church fathers, to strengthen underground Catholic resistance to the Edwardian Reformation. The core religious debates of this period revolved around the practices associated with the primitive church, and translation of patristic texts—particularly by the Eastern church fathers, whose works often remained unknown even among the educated—offered crucial testimony regarding the early Christian church. Basset herself helped establish her circle's association with Greek patristic texts by translating Eusebius's *Ecclesiastical History* into Latin and English during the Edwardian period. The 1557 publication of Basset's translation of More's final Tower treatise, *De tristitia Christi* (*Of the Sorowe of Christ*), was closer to the model pioneered by her mother but nevertheless maintained the link between translation and Catholic polemic forged by Basset's circle.

If Mary Basset, like her mother, first encountered translation in the schoolroom, her education took place in a more politically charged atmosphere. Basset's interest in the Greek church fathers stemmed from the Morean ideal of pious training in Latin and Greek. More's 1518 letter to Oxford had noted the need for translations of Greek literature, including the church fathers: "However much was translated of old from Greek, and however much more has been recently and better translated, not half of Greek learning has yet been made available to the West."[70] John Clement, one of the tutors at More's "school," later translated Gregory Nazianzen's letters and Nicephorus Callistus's *Synaxarion,* containing saints' lives, from Greek into Latin with the assistance of his wife Margaret Gigs Clement.[71] Roper herself was committed to finding tutors who could provide instruction in Greek, particularly from a Catholic perspective. While she unsuccessfully attempted to hire Roger Ascham, a Protestant well versed in Greek, both Christopherson and Morwen had attended colleges with Greek readers (respectively Trinity College, Cambridge and Corpus Christi College, Oxford), and Morwen became the Greek reader at Corpus Christi. The careers of both men flourished under Mary I. Christopherson, who had entered exile under Edward, would become Mary's chaplain and bishop of Chichester, while Morwen served as secretary and chaplain to Edmund Bonner, bishop of London and a dogged opponent of heretics. Christopherson himself participated actively in the governmental campaign against heresy, along with Henry Cole, another of Basset's tutors who was appointed dean of Saint Paul's in 1556. Basset's education thus fused the humanist training of Roper's own schooling with an emphasis on Catholic orthodoxy.

As the Edwardian Reformation unfolded, Basset's circle turned to translations of Greek religious works to establish the continuity between Catholic tradition and the primitive church. While Greek patristic texts do not appear to have been an established part of the university curriculum, reformers such as John Cheke and Roger Ascham had already translated the Eastern fathers into Latin to demonstrate their Protestant credentials.[72] The translations of Basset's circle held a similar polemical weight. In 1553, Christopherson published a Latin translation of four works by Philo, a first-century Jewish writer, that made clear his personal interest in translation of Greek texts: "Nam nihil nobis magis in optatis est, quam ut omnes Graeci authores in Latinum sermonem quam elegantissime convertantur" (For I hope for nothing more than that all the Greek authors should be translated into the Latin language as elegantly as possible).[73] Perhaps because the work was dedicated to Trinity College, which had funded his exile, Christopherson only mentions the translation's relevance for Christians in general: "nihil certe vel meis studiis aptius, vel utilius reip[ublicae] Christianae putavi" (I certainly thought nothing more apt for my studies or more useful for the Christian commonwealth).[74] That same year, Christopherson intended to print his Latin translation of Eusebius's *Ecclesiastical History* but did not, perhaps as a result of Edward's impending death and Christopherson's return to England.[75] This translation was posthumously published at Louvain in

1569, and Christopherson's preface explicitly asserts Eusebius's value in relation to the Reformation and its effects: "Nam quid est, in quo majore cum fructu quisquam tempus suum, studium & diligentiam ponere possit, his praesertim temporibus, cum tot sectae, tot schismata in variis locis oberrantia, veram Evangelii lucem obscurare, veros Dei cultus adulterare, tranquillam Ecclesiae concordiam disturbare, superstitionis caecitatem defendere, errorum perversitatem propugnare assidue pro viribus moliantur" (For what is there, in which anyone can invest his time, study, and diligence with greater fruit, especially in these times, when so many sects, so many schisms blundering in various places, strive assiduously according to their strength to obscure the true light of the Gospel, to adulterate the true worship of God, to disturb the tranquil concord of the church, to defend the blindness of superstition, to fight for the perversity of errors).[76] Christopherson clearly viewed Eusebius as a useful ally in refuting Protestant tenets and promoting Catholic doctrine.

Morwen, meanwhile, composed several manuscript translations that were even more polemical in nature, possibly because he hoped these displays of learning would secure patronage from prominent Catholics. He sent William Roper four Latin translations of Greek works: Basil the Great's letters "To a Lapsed Monk" (45), "To a Fallen Virgin" (46), and "To Optimius the Bishop" (260); and Cyril of Alexandria's homily on hell (*De exitu animi; Homilia* 14).[77] While "To a Lapsed Monk" had obvious relevance to the dissolution of the monasteries, Morwen's translation of Cyril paid an elaborate compliment to William Roper as Basset, his daughter, had given Morwen his Greek exemplar. Similarly, Morwen dedicated a Latin translation of a fragmentary portion of Symeon Metaphrastes's *Menology,* a work containing saints' lives, to Mary Tudor during Edward's reign. Morwen's dedicatory preface observes that Basset had inspired his work with her translation of Eusebius: "Optimum itaque mihi visum est, si illius vestigia subsequerer; & quod illa in Eusebii interpretatione in patrium sermonum longe purissime, ac exactissime traducta perfecerat, id ego in graeca quodam authore, qui latine loqui non didicerat, pro virili prestarem" (It therefore seemed best to me, if I followed in her footsteps; and what she had accomplished in the translation of Eusebius, rendered most purely and most exactly by far into the language of our fatherland, for my part I would surpass that with some Greek author who had not learned to speak Latin).[78] As Morwen notes, the difficulty of this task was increased by the lack of Latin translations of his source text. Morwen then demonstrates his Catholic credentials with a defense of transubstantiation based on patristic authorities such as Basil, Clement, Cyprian, and Augustine: "Hanc ob causam tam multis sum usus, ut excellens tua prudentia perspiciat, quanta haeretici impudentia, sint praediti, qui nunc corpus, nunc sacrificium, nunc presentiam, nunc humanitatem in sacramento pernegant, & nuda esse symbola, ad propriam ipsorum damnationem contendunt" (I have used so many [examples] for this cause: that your excellent wisdom may see with how much imprudence the heretics are furnished, who deny now that a body, now that a sacrifice, now that a presence, now that humanity are in the sacrament, and they assert it is a bare symbol, to their own personal damnation).[79] Just as Protestants cited the church fathers on behalf of religious reform, so Morwen could invoke Greek authorities to defend Catholic tradition.

Basset was the only member of this circle to translate Greek into English, thus combining the Morean precedent of Englishing works from classical languages with her circle's interest in patristic texts. Sometime during Edward's reign, Basset presented Mary Tudor with a manuscript containing a Latin translation of book 1 of Eusebius's *Ecclesiastical History* and an English translation of books 1 through 5. Basset's partial Latin translation participated in Christopherson's and Morwen's agenda of turning the Greek fathers into Latin, and she cut short her endeavor only after learning of a competing Latin version (possibly by Christopherson). Yet the primary model for Basset's Eusebius is that of Margaret Roper's Erasmus. Basset's dedicatory preface demonstrates a deep modesty that is consistent with her mother's own reputation for humility, framing the text as a product of her leisure time even though she circulated the work among her friends as well as "mo then one or twayne very wyse and well learned men."[80] In disseminating her work and presenting a copy to Mary, Basset promoted a shared sense of Catholic identity that was opposed to Edwardian religious policy.[81] The dedicatory preface only obliquely suggests the work's relevance by praising the "prymytyve churche, in which floryshed so many gloryouse martyrs, so many holy confessors, so excellent, so sincerely learned doctors, so notable worckers of myracles, so noble prelates, and bysshoppes, so dylygently tendring the weale of theyr flocke."[82] Yet the effect of Basset's translation on Morwen suggests just how charged this text could be, and her encouragement of Morwen indicates Basset's personal investment in using translation to support Roman Catholic doctrine. When Basset and her tutors translated, then, they engaged in an activity meant to assert the doctrinal validity of Roman Catholicism.

By contributing an English version of Thomas More's final treatise, *Of the Sorowe of Christ* (*De tristitia Christi,* 1535), to the publication of *The*

Workes of Sir Thomas More Knyght (1557), Mary Basset adapted her circle's interest in translation so that it served a new purpose: establishing the saintly legacy of her grandfather. John Fisher and Thomas More had been executed in 1535 for refusing to accept Henry's separation from Rome, and the two men's deaths were consequently linked in the popular imagination. By the Marian era, however, Fisher had come to overshadow More. As a bishop and, briefly, a cardinal, Fisher may have had more symbolic resonance as an example of Henry's tyranny than More possessed as a layman. Fisher may also have taken precedence because he opposed Henry's divorce vocally, unlike More. Fisher publicly validated Henry's marriage to Catherine of Aragon in *De causa matrimonii . . . Henrici VIII cum Catharina Aragonensi* (1530), and while Fisher's *Brevis apologia* (c. 1532) was never published, this work directly refuted Henry's justification of the divorce (*Gravissimae censurae*).[83] More, meanwhile, indirectly criticized Henry's proceedings by attacking governmental apologist Christopher Saint German in the *Apology* (1533) and the *Debellation of Salem and Bizance* (1533). During the Edwardian period, the publication of an English translation of *Utopia* (1551) drew attention to More's fame as a witty secular author rather than a martyr. Thomas Wilson consequently praised More for his rhetorical abilities in two Edwardian treatises (*The Rule of Reason,* 1551; *Arte of Rhetorique,* 1553), suggesting in the *Arte* that More deserved eternal fame for his jesting: "Sir Thomas More with us here in England, had an excellent gifte not onely in this kinde, but also in all other pleasaunt delites, whose witte even at this houre is a wonder to al the worlde, & shalbe undoubtedly, even unto the worldes ende."[84] The republication of More's works during Mary's reign suggests that this view of More remained potent. Only two works specifically attributed to More were reprinted before 1557: *A Dialoge of Comfort Against Tribulacion Made by Syr Thomas More Knyght* (1553) and *Utopia* (1556). Neither of these works deals directly with Protestantism, and both display More's talent for writing fictional humanist dialogue. Meanwhile, Fisher's fame for devoutness and orthodoxy was reinforced by the republication of his 1526 sermon against Luther in 1554 and 1556 with a new title emphasizing the work's application to contemporary issues: "wherin it may appeare howe men sithens that tyme have gone astray."[85] The year 1555 saw the publication of Fisher's *Treatyse Concernynge the Fruytfull Sayinges of Davyd the Kynge . . . in the Seven Penytencyall Psalmes.* Thus the Marian print history of works by Fisher and More reveals the crystallization of their respective reputations as a holy bishop and a witty humanist.

By 1556, the deaths of Fisher and More had become grist for the mill of the Marian Counter-Reformation, as figures associated with the regime reminded the public of Catholic martyrs to counteract Protestant models of martyrdom. On March 21, 1556, Henry Cole gave a public sermon before Thomas Cranmer's execution that offered a macabre tallying of Catholic and Protestant deaths: "It semed mete, according to the law of equality, that as the deth of the duke of Northumb[erland] of late, made even with Tho[mas] Moore chancellor that died for the church so there shold be one that shold make even with Fisher of Rochest[er] & because that Ridley, Hooper, Ferrar were not able to make even with that man it semed mete, that Cranmer shold be joyned to them to fill up this part of equality."[86] According to Cole's "law of equality," More and Northumberland are equivalent, since each was an important statesman. Fisher's execution must be equaled by the deaths of four bishops, a claim that may possibly reflect his elevation to a cardinalship but could also suggest that More was a less worthy martyr than Fisher. Two polemical works dedicated to Mary in 1556 offered similar assessments of Fisher and More. In *The Displaying of the Protestantes,* Miles Huggarde, Mary's hosier and an influential propagandist, included the two in a list of Englishmen who died for the Catholic faith: "What shall I stande here upon the death of John Fyssher semetyme Byshop of Rochester, a man of notable learning & innocencie of lyfe, or the death of the second Cicero, syr Thomas More, a man endewed with heavenlye eloquence."[87] While Fisher is notable for his learned piety, Huggarde characterizes More for his rhetorical style ("the second Cicero"). Huggarde's description of himself on the title page as "servant to the Quenes majestie" may have given the work additional weight as evidence of the government's opinions, and the treatise was immediately popular, going through two editions in June and July 1556. James Cancellar's *Pathe of Obedience* placed Fisher and More at the head of a similar catalog: "those which have suffered for the unitie of the Catholycke churche of Christe, as dyd that holy father Docter Fysher sometyme Byshop of Rochester, and Sirre Thomas More sumetyme Chaunceler of thys Relme."[88] Cancellar also emphasizes Fisher's devoutness ("holy father"), describing More only in terms of his secular position as "Chaunceler." The work's title page noted Cancellar's position in Mary's Chapel Royal, thus linking Cancellar's views to the regime. These references to Fisher and More reaffirmed Fisher's prominence, suggesting that he was of greater value than More in promoting the Marian Counter-Reformation.

The More clan was probably well aware of these sentiments through its connections to Cole and possibly even Huggarde, who—like Morwen—was associated with Bonner.[89] Scholars have certainly noted that the More family began an aggressive literary campaign to reframe More as a martyr who could benefit the Counter-Reformation.[90] William Roper, Basset's father, wrote a hagiographic manuscript biography of his father-in-law, which family friend Nicholas Harpsfield then used as the basis for his own manuscript biography of More. In May 1557, William Rastell, Basset's cousin, printed More's English *Workes,* a monumental volume in folio format that totaled nearly fifteen hundred pages. Rastell's dedication of the volume to Mary I presented More's works and saintly death as crucial props for the Counter-Reformation. Rastell states that More's writings contain "the trewe doctryne of Christes catholike fayth" and "the confutacion of detestable heresyes," meaning that this publication, "beinge red of many, as it is likely to be, shall much helpe forwarde youre Majesties most godly purpose, in purging this youre realme of all wicked heresies."[91] Rastell also presents More as a proto-saint who serves as a heavenly intercessor on behalf of Mary herself: "now (beynge with almyghtie God, and lyvynge in heaven with hym) . . . [he] ceaseth not to praye to God for the kinges majestie, for your hyghnesse, your subjectes, your realms, and domynions, and for the common welth, and catholyke religion of the same, and for all christen realmes also."[92] Besides providing the Counter-Reformation with practical assistance through his writings, More facilitates the divine implementation of Marian religious policies as well as the refutation of heresy throughout Europe. If Cole, Huggarde, and Cancellar had suggested that More had less worth to the Counter-Reformation than Fisher, Rastell emphasizes the centrality of More's life and death to the key narratives of Mary's religious policies: the eradication of heresy and the restoration of the Roman Catholic Church within England. The material characteristics of the publication further substantiated the significance that Rastell attributed to the volume, as More was the first English author after Chaucer to have his collected works issued in hefty folio format.[93]

The English *Workes* established a new narrative for More's life that undercut the importance of his earlier humanist productions such as *Utopia.* Rastell arranged the volume in a chronological fashion, using the table of contents to mark the increasingly polemical and religious nature of More's works as well as his rise to and resignation of the chancellorship. By moving from rhymes "written by Syr Thomas in his youthe, for hys pastyme" to "certen letters and other thinges which Sir Thomas More wrote while he was prisoner in the towre of London," the volume underscored More's own self-presentation of his trajectory away from worldly affairs and toward spiritual matters.[94] Indeed, while the title page proclaimed that the book's contents would be in More's own English (*The Workes of Sir Thomas More Knyght, Sometyme Lorde*

Chauncellour of England, Wrytten by Him in the Englysh Tonge), Rastell included several short Latin compositions and English translations of Latin texts, such as a brief prayer entitled "A Godly Instruction," More's self-written epitaph, a Tower letter to Antonio Bonvisi, and Basset's translation.[95] Rastell appears to have chosen these texts—and omitted *Utopia*—because they conform to a narrative that emphasizes More's eventual martyrdom. It is well established, for example, that More wrote his own epitaph in order to separate himself from his earlier role as Henry's civil servant: "He therfore irke[d] and wery of worldly busines, giving up his promocions, obtained at last by the incomparable benefite of his most gentil prince (if it please god to favour his enterprise) the thing which from a childe in a maner alway he wished & desired, that he might have some yeres of his life fre, in which he litle & litle withdrawing himself from the busines of this life, might continually remembre the immortalite of the lyfe to come."[96] More's mixture of flattery and spiritual sentiments may seem at odds, but both elements present his resignation as a voluntary withdrawal from "worldly busines" to private contemplation. By praising Henry as a "most gentil prince," More implied that he remained in the king's good graces, leaving only because he had grown "wery" of the "worldly busines" accompanying his "promocions." This trajectory from "worldly" affairs to "immortalite" provided a template for the English *Workes*. Rastell specifically chose to publish Latin texts that could help shape More's saintly legacy, which the liberal thrust of *Utopia* might undermine. Both "A Godly Instruction" and *Of the Sorowe* legitimate More's lack of vocal opposition to Henry by suggesting that fearful sainthood is as valuable to the Catholic cause as bold martyrdom. Furthermore, More's letter to Bonvisi is presented as his final correspondence with those outside his family, as it precedes the last text in the *Workes*, More's farewell letter to Margaret Roper. *Of the Sorowe* is the most significant of these translations, providing an explanation for More's hesitant approach to his own death.[97] As a result, Basset's translation plays an important role in verifying the authenticity of More's saintliness, just as her mother's translation had indicated More's private allegiance to humanist learning.

Unlike the other translations included in the *Workes*, Basset's translation was accompanied by a separate introduction that suggested its importance by establishing her identity and credentials. The title introduces Basset as "one of the gentlewomen of the queenes majesties privie chamber, and nece to the sayde syr Thomas More" (*OS*, 1350; *YE*, 1077).[98] As lady-in-waiting to Mary and wife to James Basset, gentleman-in-waiting to King Philip, Basset held a privileged position at the Marian court. Rastell accordingly prioritizes Basset's role as Mary's lady-in-waiting over her kinship to More, establishing the translation's connection to the regime just as Huggarde and Cancellar had linked their publications to Mary. The intimacy between Basset and the queen evokes Rastell's depiction of the mutual admiration between More and Mary within the dedicatory preface to the *Workes:* "Syr Thomas More . . . whyle he lyved, dyd beare towards your highnesse a speciall zeale, an entier affection, and reverent devocion: and on thother syde lykewyse your grace (as it is well knowen) had towards him in his life time, a benevolent mynde and singular favoure."[99] This portrayal might hint that Mary appointed Basset as one of her ladies-in-waiting in recognition of More's unwavering Catholicism. At the same time, Rastell firmly situates Basset within a private domain at odds with the world of public affairs, much as Hyrde had presented Roper as a praiseworthy wife: "Somewhat I had to doo ere that I could come by thys booke. For the gentlewoman which translated it, semed nothing willing to have it goe abrode, for that (she sayth,) it was firste turned into englishe, but for her owne pastyme and exercise, and so reputeth it farre to[o] symple to come in many handes" (*OS,* 1350; *YE,* 1078). Because Basset appears to define her work as a "pastyme and exercise" meant only for her personal use, Rastell is able to portray her translation as private rather than public. In actuality, Basset had a very real stake in the publication of the *Workes.* The anonymous Latin *Chronicle* of Henry's first divorce claims that the volume was printed "ope et impensis nobilissimae simul ac doctissimae feminae, Thomae Mori ex filia neptis" (with the help and at the cost of a most noble and at the same time most learned woman, a granddaughter of Thomas More by his daughter).[100] Besides providing funding for the book's printing, Basset may have supplied the copies that her mother had preserved of More's writings, including the crucial final Tower letters.[101] Rastell's presentation of Basset's demure refusal of public acknowledgement may not accurately reflect her participation in this venture, but it did frame Basset as an exemplar of female modesty. In addition, Rastell's emphasis on Basset's leisure time characterizes the translation as a private composition, depicting her studious engagement in pious learning during her hours away from Mary's service. As in the case of prefaces to the works of male translators such as Phaer, this description of Basset's "pastyme" suggests that Basset's leisure pursuits complement her official service to Mary. Despite her apparent privacy, Basset takes on a quasi-official role as a proponent of Catholicism.

Rastell had yet another reason for insisting on Basset's modest repudiation of any public agenda or speech, as he positions her translation as a manifestation of More's private, contemplative voice. According to Rastell, the translation does not exhibit Basset's own literary style or voice at all. Rather, her work "goeth so nere sir Thomas Mores own english phrase that the gentlewoman (who for her pastyme translated it) is no nerer to hym in kynred, vertue and litterature, than in hys englishe tongue: so that it myghte seme to have been by hys own pen indyted first, and not at all translated: suche a gyft hath she to folowe her graundfathers vayne in wryting" (*OS*, 1350; *YE*, 1078). This remarkable passage casts Basset not as a translator but as a medium who channels More's indubitable English voice. The prerequisites for Basset's assumption of More's voice are her blood ties ("kynred"), piety ("vertue"), and learning ("litterature"). Just as Basset follows her grandfather's example of Catholic humanism, so she inherits his facility with the "english phrase." As More's granddaughter, Basset is capable of translating the text into her "graundfathers" English, and it is Basset's privacy that allows her translation to become an acceptable and even authentic expression of the contemplative persona More shaped in his final years. Basset's marginal notes participate in creating this illusion that her voice does not exist within the text proper. For example, she calls attention to a particularly creative rendering of the source text: "Whereas the latine texte hath here somnia speculantes Mandragore, I have translated it in englishe, our mindes all occupied wyth mad fantasticall dreames, because Mandragora is an herbe as phisycions saye, that causeth folke to slepe, and therin to have many mad fantastical dreames" (*OS*, 1375F–G; *YE*, 1119).[102] Here Basset demonstrates her facility with both Latin and medical knowledge, a pet discipline of More and Margaret Roper.[103] By scrupulously explaining her reasoning for translating "mandragora" (mandrake) with "mad fantasticall dreames," Basset asserts her faithfulness as a translator and demonstrates that she continues the Morean tradition of educated women. Such meticulous fidelity implicitly limits Basset's authorial role, reinforcing Rastell's claim that the translation should be regarded as a genuine part of More's English *Workes*. Furthermore, by speaking on her own behalf only in the margins of the text, Basset performatively enacts the extreme modesty that Rastell had already attributed to her, so that she both endorses and constructs the apparent privacy of this text.

Basset and Rastell may have felt compelled to validate her translation as More's genuine speech because Basset does not channel More's voice so much as adjust it to fit a familial agenda. In Basset's rendering, *Of the Sorowe* becomes both a theological justification of cautious martyrdom and textual evidence of More's death. As the work's full title indicates—*Of the Sorowe, Werinesse, Feare, and Prayer of Christ before*

Hys Taking (*De tristitia, tedio, pavore, et oratione Christi ante captionem eius*)—More is primarily interested in the question of why Christ felt pain, weariness, and fear in the garden of Gethsemane. More notes that Christ's all-too-human emotions might seem to discount his divinity: "Some man may happly here mervel, how this could be, that our saviour Christ beyng very god equal with his almighty father, could be hevy, sad, & sorowful" (*OS*, 1354C; *YE*, 1083). *Of the Sorowe* answers this question by arguing that two classes of martyrs exist: the bold and the timorous. Christ's anxious questioning of God's will in the garden thus functions as evidence that timorous martyrs justifiably scrutinize God's purpose. In redefining martyrdom through Christ's Passion, More provides scriptural validation for his own careful resistance to Henry's policies. Engaging in translation practices similar to those of her mother, Basset in turn heightens More's defense of his conduct with careful modulations and marginal notes that both corroborate her grandfather's saintly death and indicate that his timorous martyrdom corresponded with Christ's precedent. Basset's translation therefore substantiates the existence of fearful martyrs even as it presents More himself as this kind of martyr.

Basset's deviations from her source text, though small, consistently portray timorous martyrdom, which is conveniently similar to More's own death, as superior to bold martyrdom. More is adamant that both kinds of martyrs are equally worthy of admiration, although he cautions against seeking martyrdom too readily. Yet Basset modifies that sense of parity by implying that bold martyrs suffer only in a physical sense. Citing Christ's statement in Matthew 10:23 regarding persecution—"yf they persecute ye (sayth he) in one citie, geat ye into an other" (*OS*, 1355B; *YE*, 1085)—More asserts that the true test of martyrdom occurs when a Christian must sacrifice either his life or his faith: "Whosoever therefore is broughte to suche a straighte, that nedes he must either endure some paine *in his bodye* [ei], or els forsake god, this man may be right wel assured, that he is by gods owne wil come to suche distresse" (*DtC*, 307; *OS*, 1355E–F; *YE*, 1086).[104] The undeniable need to choose between bodily or spiritual death is the hallmark of a true martyr, and Basset heightens this distinction by translating "ei" (to himself) as "in his bodye." Basset also associates bold martyrs with physical pain, suggesting that these martyrs do not undergo the mental torment experienced by timorous martyrs. More refers to some martyrs as "bold and hardy"; these Christians fit the traditional conception of martyrdom by "joyfullye speed[ing] theim towards their deathe apase" (*OS*, 1370D, B; *YE*, 1110). More's epithet for these martyrs is "alacer" (eager), which Basset translates with the doublet "bold and hardy" as well as the adjective "joyfullye" (*DtC,* 249, 251). By qualifying "bold" with "hardy," Basset links the traditional idea of the martyr's jubilant death with physical endurance. Basset likewise inserts a reference to physicality that underscores More's point that bold martyrs may sacrifice their bodies all too easily: "Christs valiant Champions have . . . of their owne accord, professed themselfes christen men, when no creature required it of them, & of theyre own mindes, offred *their bodies* [se] to martirdome when no man called for them" (*DtC,* 65; *OS,* 1355C; *YE,* 1085). Basset stresses the physical nature of their sacrifice by translating "se" (themselves) as "their bodies," once again demonstrating a crucial opposition between bold and timorous martyrs. Because their "mindes" have no scruples about the rightness of their actions, these bold martyrs are able to offer up "their bodies" to physical torments without any mental anguish. By adding these references to physicality, Basset insinuates that these martyrs suffer only in a bodily manner.

In contrast with this emphasis on the bodily suffering of the bold martyr, Basset's translation stresses the physical and mental pain that timorous martyrs endure. Mental anguish was characteristic of More's ordeal, amply demonstrated by letters written from the Tower and printed by Rastell in the same volume. These "heavy, sorowfull, and timorous" martyrs "*right sore affrayde* [cunctanter et timide], creepe faire and softly" toward death (*DtC,* 249; *OS,* 1370D, B; *YE,* 1110). Here Basset collapses More's doublet "cunctanter et timide" (hesitantly and timidly) into "right sore affrayde," a phrase that insists on the emotional torments undergone by timorous martyrs while eliding the idea of indecisiveness. As a result, Basset removes a moment that might remind the reader of the fact that More's own martyrdom had been criticized as overly hesitant. As if to forestall any further objections to More's cautious behavior, Basset's translation defines timorous martyrdom as a combination of physical and mental suffering, heightening More's contention that Christ exhibited hesitation to provide comfort to later martyrs: "Wherefore forasmuch as Christ dyd foresee, that many ther wold be so tender of body, that . . . they shold fele themselfes so *feareful & faint-herted* [meticulosam], & . . . uppon feare to be enforced *to faynt and geve over* [vincerentur], might mishap wilfully to *yeld & not go through* [se dederent], Christ vouchsaved *therefore I say* [added], to comfort theyr weake spirites with the example of his own sorow, heaviness, werines, & incomparable feare" (*DtC,* 101; *OS,* 1357G–H; *YE,* 1089–90). Here Basset highlights More's emphasis on the mental weakness of these timorous martyrs with a judicious use of amplification: "meticulosam" (fearful) becomes "feareful & faintherted," "vincerentur" (they would be conquered) becomes "be enforced to faynt and geve over," and "sua se sponte dederent" (they would willfully surrender themselves) becomes "mishap wilfully to yeld & not go through." These doublets underscore More's argument that a timorous martyr must conquer the frailties of both flesh and mind. Basset furthermore adds in "therefore I say," drawing the reader's attention to the significance of Christ's intention to use his Passion to legitimate a careful approach to death. It is tempting to identify this "I" as evidence of Basset's authorial voice. Since these words are not in the source text, it might seem that Basset—and not More—is the one speaking so emphatically. Yet Basset's own marginal note on "mandragora" demonstrates her encouragement of the idea that her voice does not exist within the translation proper. This emphatic "I" is neither More nor Basset but the version of More that Rastell's edition works to construct: the martyred More. Basset therefore shapes her source text to fit political circumstances even as she glosses over her manipulation of More's legacy, much as her mother's translation sought to adjust Erasmus's reputation.

Basset's marginal notes function as an even more overt means of heightening the text's relevance to More's final days. Since the treatise argues that those who are "over feareful and faintharted" should consider "this bitter agony of Christe" (*OS,* 1370E–F; *YE,* 1111), the subject matter of *De tristitia* could be taken as an indicator that More qualified as a timorous martyr. Two of Basset's marginal notes make this parallel between More and Christ even more explicit by pointing out the unfinished nature of the text and reinforcing More's martyrdom (see figure 3). In doing so, Basset parlays her capacity to speak for More into a new role as his editor, gaining a greater amount of authorial agency in the process. One note emphasizes More's inability to look over the text, presumably because of the seizure of his writing materials: "I have not translated this place as the latine copye goeth, but as I judge it shoulde be, because my graundfathers copy was for lacke of laysure never wel corrected" (*OS,* 1399E; *YE,* 1157). Here Basset refers to a particularly tricky passage, which both she and the Yale editors rearrange for the sake of clarity: "Whan I consider here these woordes of the Evangelyste that they all forsoke him and ran awaye, I can nowe no more doubte, but that he went to theym all and found theym all a slepe" (*OS,* 1399E; *YE,* 1157; *DtC,* 563). More had placed the biblical quotation at the end of the sentence, an awkwardness that Basset corrects while drawing attention to More's final "lacke of laysure." Basset mentions her correction of another imperfection in the text to similar effect. As the Yale

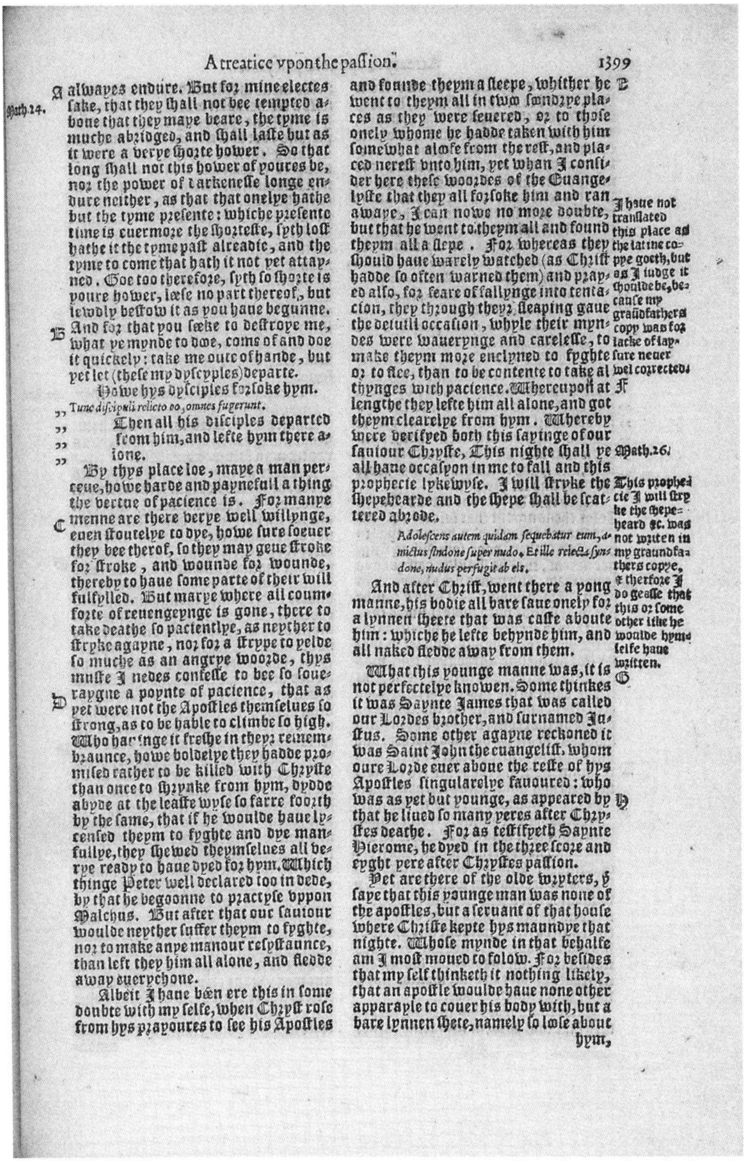

A alwayes endure. But for mine electes sake, that they shall not bee tempted aboue that they maye beare, the tyme is muche abridged, and shall laste but as it were a verye shorte hower. So that long shall not this hower of youres be, nor the power of darkenesse longe endure neither, as that that onelye hathe but the tyme presente: whiche presente time is euermore the shortest, syth lost hathe it the tyme past alreadie, and the tyme to come that hath it not yet attayned. Goe too therefore, syth so shorte is youre hower, lese no part thereof, but lewdly bestow it as you haue begunne. (Math. 24.)

B And for that you seke to destroye me, what ye mynde to doe, come of and doe it quickely: take me oute of hande, but yet let (these my dyscyples) departe.

Howe hys dysciples forsoke hym.

" *Tunc discipuli relicto eo, omnes fugerunt.*

" Then all his disciples departed
" from him, and lefte hym there a-
" lone.

By thys place loe, maye a man perceue, howe harde and paynefull a thing the vertue of pacience is. For manye C menne are there verye well willynge, euen stoutelye to dye, howe sure soeuer they bee therof, so they may geue stroke for stroke, and wounde for wounde, thereby to haue some parte of their will fulfylled. But marye where all coumforte of reuengeynge is gone, there to take deathe so pacientlye, as neyther to stryke agayne, nor for a strype to yelde so muche as an angrye woorde, thys muste I nedes confesse to bee so soueraygne a poynte of pacience, that as D yet were not the Apostles themselues so strong, as to be hable to climbe so high. Who hauinge it freshe in theyr remembraunce, howe boldelye they hadde promised rather to be killed with Chryste than once to shrynke from hym, dydde abyde at the leaste wyse so farre foorth by the same, that if he woulde haue lycensed theym to fyghte and dye manfullye, they shewed theymselues all verye ready to haue dyed for hym. Which thinge Peter well declared too in dede, by that he begoonne to practyse vppon Malchus. But after that our sauiour woulde neyther suffer theym to fyghte, nor to make anye manour resystaunce, than left they him all alone, and fledde away euerychone.

Albeit I haue ben ere this in some doubte with my selfe, when Chryst rose from hys prayoures to see his Apostles and founde theym a sleepe, whither he E went to theym all in two sondrye places as they were seuered, or to those onely whome he hadde taken with him somewhat alofe from the rest, and placed nerest vnto him, yet whan I consider here these woordes of the Euangelyste that they all forsoke him and ran awaye, I can nowe no more doubte, but that he went to theym all and found theym all a slepe. For whereas they should haue warely watched (as Christ hadde so often warned them) and prayed also, for feare of fallynge into tentacion, they through theyr sleaping gaue the deuill occasion, whyle their myndes were wauerynge and carelesse, to make theym more enclyned to fyghte or to flee, than to be contente to take al F thynges with pacience. Whereupon at lengthe they lefte him all alone, and got theym clearelye from hym. Whereby were verifyed both this sayinge of our sauiour Chryste, This nighte shall ye all haue occasyon in me to fall and this prophecie lykewyse. I will stryke the shepehearde and the shepe shall be scattered abrode.

(I haue not translated this place as the latine copye goeth, but as I iudge it shoulde be, because my graundfathers copy was for lacke of laysure neuer wel corrected.)

(Math. 26.)

(This prophecie I will stryke the shepeheard &c. was not writen in my graundfathers copye, & therfore I do gesse that this or some other like he woulde hymselfe haue written.)

Adolescens autem quidam sequebatur eum, amictus sindone super nudo. Et ille reiecta syndone, nudus perfugit ab eis.

And after Christ, went there a yong manne, his bodie all bare saue onely for a lynnen sheete that was caste aboute him: whiche he lefte behynde him, and all naked fledde away from them.

G What this younge manne was, it is not perfectelye knowen. Some thinkes it was Saynte James that was called our Lordes brother, and surnamed Iustus. Some other agayne reckoned it was Saint John the euangelist, whom oure Lorde euer aboue the reste of hys Apostles singularelye fauoured: who was as yet but younge, as appeared by H that he liued so many yeres after Chrystes deathe. For as testifyeth Saynte Hierome, he dyed in the three score and eyght yere after Chrystes passion.

Yet are there of the olde wryters, that saye that this younge man was none of the apostles, but a seruant of that house where Christe kepte hys maundye that nighte. Whose mynde in that behalfe am I most moued to folow. For besides that my self thinketh it nothing likely, that an apostle woulde haue none other apparayle to couer his body with, but a bare lynnen shete, namely so lose about hym,

Figure 3. Page 1399 of *The Workes of Sir Thomas More* (1557), which includes Mary Basset's translation of Thomas More. Reproduced by permission of The Huntington Library, San Marino, California.

edition's facsimile of More's manuscript shows, a gap remains after this sentence: "Whereupon at lengthe they lefte him all alone, and got theym clearelye from hym. Whereby were verifyed both this sayinge of our saviour Chryste, This nighte shall ye all have occasyon in me to fall and this prophecie lykewyse." Basset's translation provides a suitable "prophecie" by citing Jesus's reference to Zechariah 13:7 in Matthew 26:31 and Mark 14:27: "I will stryke the shepehearde and the shepe shall be scattered abrode." Basset explains that she herself has interpolated this phrase: "This prophecie . . . was not writen in my graundfathers copye, & therfore I do geasse that this or some other like he woulde hymselfe have written" (*OS,* 1399F; *YE,* 1157). These lapses in the source text allow Mary Basset to develop her own editorial authority, shown by her repeated use of "I," as she makes revisions denied to her grandfather by his untimely death. The legitimacy of these changes derives from Basset's role, both self-appointed and established by Rastell's paratexts, as a representative of More. Basset must not only write in her grandfather's "english phrase" but also anticipate what he *might* have written ("he woulde hymselfe have written"). This very need for Basset to act as More's editor due to his "lacke of laysure" reinforces the text's partial nature and confirms More's martyrdom. Significantly, the majority of marginal notes in More's *Workes* are didactic in nature, summarizing the gist of a passage or identifying allusions.[105] As a result, Basset's editorial interventions are unprecedented within the *Workes,* further marking the singularity of her role as More's representative and editor.

That Basset's voice exists only on the peripheries of the text she translates may appear to substantiate the idea that translation subordinated the voices of early modern Englishwomen. Yet this marginal space allows Basset an active—and visible—role as a shaper of More's message. Indeed, she colludes with Rastell, who appends a brief note to the end of the text that also notes the work's unfinished nature to gesture at More's martyrdom: "Syr Thomas More wrote no more of this woorke: for . . . sone after was he putte to death" (*OS,* 1404; *YE,* 1165). Even more strikingly, Rastell's preface to the translation parallels More's execution with Christ's Passion: "(eaven when he came to th'exposicion of these wordes, Et injecerunt manus in Jesum) [More] was bereaved and put from hys bookes, pen, inke and paper, and kepte more strayghtly than before, and soone after also was putte to death hymselfe" (*OS,* 1350; *YE,* 1077–78). At the moment that the Roman soldiers lay their hands on Jesus in the garden of Gethsemane ("Et injecerunt manus in Jesum"), so Henry's stricter imprisonment abruptly ends More's narrative. Rastell's use of the intensifiers "also" and "hymselfe" highlights the similarity between the deaths of Thomas More and Jesus Christ, both executed by impious governments. Rastell and Basset each use the paratexts in a similar manner, indicating that Basset appears mute only because she carefully obscures her voice. While this pattern of apparent self-elision allowed Basset's printed text to conform to strictures about women's public speech, Basset also contributed to the Marian Counter-Reformation through this disappearing act, which guaranteed the authenticity of her translation as an expression of More's attitude toward martyrdom.

Conclusions

The printed translations of Margaret Roper and Mary Basset offer a basis for a fresh understanding of the relationship between women, translation, and the domestic sphere. While Hyrde and Rastell characterize both translations as the result of domestic leisure, their descriptions parallel those found in prefaces written by male translators, whose translations evoked a private life that that complemented their public personae as gentlemen and public servants. As an idealized daughter and wife, Margaret Roper used her leisure time to translate Erasmus, and this composition could in turn serve as evidence of the More family's private commitment to humanist study. A lady-in-waiting to Mary I, Mary Basset translated More's *De tristitia* for her own pastime, demonstrating both filial piety and a personal commitment to Catholicism that was congruent with the Marian Counter-Reformation. In addition, Basset's privacy recalled both her mother's example and More's retreat from the world, allowing Basset's translation to pass as More's own words. In categorizing these translations as private compositions, Hyrde and Rastell simultaneously vouchsafed the translators' modesty and politicized their texts. Furthermore, both Roper and Basset demonstrably reshaped their source texts in ways that attempted to alter public views of Erasmus and More, underscoring the translator's ability to intervene in public debates without speaking independently. Even Basset's marginal notes sought to elide her own voice and to substantiate the version of More that her translation presents.

The complex ways in which Hyrde, Roper, Rastell, and Basset negotiated the public and private sphere indicate that we must pay closer attention to apparently formulaic declarations prefacing women's texts if we are to understand better the ways in which these works functioned. Although it is tempting to view male-authored prefaces to women's translations as a form of patriarchal control that elides women's agency, in many cases these prefaces mark the cooperative nature of these enterprises. By offering an interpretive framework for the female translator's work, a male collaborator could suggest that the translator conformed to the stereotypically feminine virtues of silence, chastity, and obedience even as he legitimated a public display of learning that might otherwise seem presumptuous. Hyrde and Rastell may appear to limit and even erase the agency wielded by Roper and Basset, but the ways in which their paratextual frameworks operate in concert with the translations themselves suggest that both editors and translators were working collaboratively on joint projects. If Hyrde and Rastell associated these translations with More's private life, Roper and Basset themselves were responsible for producing the translations that supported such assertions. Besides demonstrating the translators' considerable learning, these works subtly transformed Roper's and Basset's source texts into an outlet for their political aims. As cooperative participants in the fashioning of their public reputations, Roper and Basset eschewed public speech even as they manipulated the public voices of the works' male authors. By collaborating with men who praised their feminine modesty, these women developed a covert form of authorial and political agency thanks to the very prefaces that asserted their domesticity.

CHAPTER TWO

Royal Propaganda

Mary Tudor, Elizabeth Tudor, and the Edwardian Reformation

In 1548, the editors of printed translations by Mary and Elizabeth Tudor made an unprecedented case for the importance of female translators by asserting that the princesses' works were important contributions to governmental religious policy. That January, Mary's partial translation of Erasmus's "Paraphrase . . . upon the Gospell of Sainct John" was published as part of the English *Paraphrases* orchestrated by Katherine Parr. Nicholas Udall's preface to Mary's translation praises both Katherine and Mary for their exemplary devotion to improving the common good through patronage and translation: "Howe happie art thou, o England, for whose behoufe and edifying in Christe, Quenes and Princesses spare not ne ceasse with all earnest endevour and sedulitee to spende their tyme, their wittes, their substaunce, and also their bodyes?"[1] Edward VI had ordered every church in England to purchase and display the *Paraphrases,* and Udall's emphasis on the rank of these royal women offered further evidence of the volume's authority. In March, John Bale edited Elizabeth's translation of Marguerite de Navarre as part of his effort to publish works that legitimated English Protestantism. Like Udall, Bale emphasizes Elizabeth's royal status, remarking that she has "a most vyctoryouse kynge to her father, & a most vertuouse, & lerned kynge agayne to her brother." Bale also presents Elizabeth as a model of learned piety whose work offers a template for the spiritual regeneration of the nation: "They shall not be unwyse, that shall marke herin, what commodyte it is, or what profyght myght growe to a christen commen welthe if youth were thus brought up in vertu & good letters."[2] By stressing the princesses' learning and their role as pious models, Udall and Bale presented Mary and Elizabeth as crucial participants in the Edwardian regime and suggested that they possessed a measure of political agency.

Without intending to do so, Udall and Bale established an enduring model that presented women's translations as an acceptable form of public commentary. As queen, Elizabeth reissued Edward's injunctions requiring all English parishes to display copies of the English *Paraphrases,* meaning that Mary's translation of Erasmus was readily available throughout England even fifty years after its initial publication. Meanwhile, Elizabeth's translation of Marguerite saw four editions during her reign. While only one of these editions reprinted Bale's prefatory material, two editors repurposed Udall's praise of Mary and Katherine for their own intentions. James Cancellar, who had been one of Mary's priests during her reign, borrowed substantially from Udall for his own preface to Elizabeth's Marguerite, perhaps to present Elizabeth in a conservative light: "How happie then is that countrie and people, for whose behoofe and edifying, Queenes and Princes spare not, ne ceasse not, with all earnest indevour and sedulitie to spende their tyme, their wits, their substaunce, and also their bodyes in the studies of noble Sciences?"[3] Cancellar follows Udall and Bale in highlighting Elizabeth's learning by adding the phrase "studies of noble Sciences." Thomas Bentley appropriated Cancellar's version of this sentence in the preface to his *Monument of Matrones* (1582), which reprinted religious texts by women of all ranks, including Elizabeth's Marguerite: "Sundrie right famous Queenes, noble Ladies, virtuous Virgins, and godlie Gentlewomen of al ages . . . for the common benefit of their countrie, have not ceased, and that with all carefull industrie and earnest indevour, most painfullie and diligentlie in great fervencie of the spirit, and zeale of the truth, even from their tender & maidenlie yeeres, to spend their time, their wits, their substance, and also their bodies, in the studies of noble and approoved sciences, and in compiling and translating of sundrie most christian and godlie books."[4] Bentley's reworking reflects the content of the *Monument* by including "noble Ladies" as well as "godlie Gentlewomen," ultimately suggesting that the commonwealth could benefit from the literary labor of women of all ranks. By the 1580s, then, the female translator's work could be construed as a useful contribution to public life.

This chapter will explore the ways that Udall and Bale laid the groundwork for this development by appropriating the Tudor princesses' translations as propaganda for the Edwardian Reformation. Elizabeth composed her translation of Marguerite de Navarre in 1544 as a New Year's gift for Katherine Parr, while Mary undertook her partial translation of Erasmus at Katherine's invitation. Critics generally observe in passing that Udall and Bale commandeered the princesses' texts, but the full significance of these editorial interventions has yet to be recognized, perhaps because of the published versions' apparent subordination to male agendas. Mary's case is particularly striking, as Udall misleadingly claims that her work endorses the Edwardian Reformation. Yet neither Mary nor Elizabeth attempted to control the circulation of these translations after their accessions, and their social prominence may have inspired other female translators to become visible participants in England's religious politics. The Tudor princesses' translations reveal that the female translator could hold a fame of her own that was as important as the reputation of her source text's original author, suggesting that the female translator did not necessarily hide behind the authority of her source text.

Trustworthy Sources: Translation, Fame, and Religious Propaganda

Some translations gained cultural significance due to the fame of the translator, as when Thomas Cranmer, the archbishop of Canterbury, attached his name to a published translation of a continental catechism that aimed to introduce English children to reformist tenets (*Catechismus,* 1548). As Cranmer's dedicatory preface to Edward VI states, "there is nothynge more necessarye . . . then that it myghte be forseen, howe the youthe & tender age of youre lovynge subjectes, maye be brought up and traded in the trewth of Goddes holy worde."[5] The quasi-official nature of this text was further established by the inclusion of Edward's coat of arms on the title page, whose obverse bears a woodcut in which Edward sits on a throne handing a Bible to a bishop, probably Cranmer, as other bishops, priests, aristocrats, and commoners look on. While the political goals of this text are evident, scholars have been perplexed by its uncertain authorship. The catechism freely translates and reshapes Jonas Justus's Latin version of a German catechism, but the text is never acknowledged as a translation. Instead, the title page states that this work was "set forth by the mooste reverende father in God Thomas Archbyshop of Canterbury," and the text itself is accompanied by an announcement that it had been "Oversene and corrected" by Cranmer.[6] D. G. Selwyn has plausibly argued that Cranmer edited a translation composed by one of his associates.[7] The book's foregrounding of Cranmer and Edward, rather than the original author or Cranmer's cotranslator, can be profitably understood in terms of the phenomenon of source credibility outlined by Carl Hovland and other researchers at Yale: "An important factor influencing the effectiveness of a communication is the person or group perceived as originating the communication—and the cues provided as to the trustworthiness, intentions, and affiliations of this source."[8] In other words, audiences are more likely to change their opinions about topical issues when they encounter evidence either issuing from or endorsed by highly credible sources. According to Hovland et al., the most significant elements for source credibility are expertise and trustworthiness.[9] Certainly the paratexts to Cranmer's catechism emphasize the authoritative approval of both Edward and Cranmer, who held expertise and trustworthiness by virtue of their leadership roles within the English church and their perceived interest in bettering it.

As historians have mentioned in passing, translation was a crucial source of religious propaganda in early modern England, and the source credibility attached to translations of famous theologians such as Luther and Calvin helps explain the effectiveness of this activity.[10] Because the translator and the original author could function simultaneously as the source of the text, translation allowed men even of the middling sort to bolster their credibility with readers and to play a part in religious controversies. In many instances, the translator therefore yielded to the original author, whose higher profile could better legitimate the religious views expressed in the text. As an anonymous translator of Pierre du Moulin noted of his decision to withhold his name, "The name of the Author is a sufficient patronage for the booke."[11] Yet in certain cases, such as Cranmer's catechism, the translator's authority could be equivalent to or greater than the original author's reputation. In April 1550, Edward Seymour, the recently disgraced Duke of Somerset, issued an English translation of a letter sent to him by John Calvin. The title page advertised the work's dual authorship, stating that the letter was "delyvered to the sayde Duke, in the time of his trouble, and so translated out of frenshe by the same Duke." Somerset had been ousted as Edward's Lord Protector of the Commonwealth the preceding December, and the translation was printed the day before his release from the Tower of London to mark his imminent reinstatement at court. The work's preface situates the translation within the context of the riots that propelled Somerset's downfall, subtly attesting to Somerset's godly credentials and authority: "Nothing is more odious or destestable afore god then the disobedience of subjectes against their Kynges and Governours."[12] Powerful men such as Somerset turned to translation while in disgrace or exile, perhaps because they no longer wielded a more direct power that was superior to a translator's mediated agency. Somerset, for example, published his translation of Calvin after his power had been diminished in the wake of the coup. Similarly, after John Scory, bishop of Chichester under

Edward, fled into exile to escape the Marian Counter-Reformation, he printed translations of Augustine and Cyprian that advertised his name and former position on their title pages.[13]

Aristocratic women, however, found that taking public credit for printed translations was a convenient means of drawing attention to their own social prestige and furthering the ability of their translations to serve as models of popular devotion. Women could not hold public office, but translation offered an indirect means of participating in public debates. Furthermore, translation implicitly denied contemporary dismissals of women's intellectual inferiority by visibly demonstrating the female translator's learning and hence her expertise. By allowing their translations to be published with full attribution, these female translators could become credible sources regarding piety and doctrine. Margaret Beaufort, the mother of Henry VII and the Countess of Richmond and Derby, influentially established this model by printing translations of two works from French into English: the fourth book of Thomas á Kempis's *Imitatio Christi* (1504) and *The Mirroure of Golde for the Synfull Soule* (1506). Rather than apologizing for Beaufort's foray into the public sphere, these publications drew attention to her authorship to establish their own authority. The preface to the *Mirroure of Golde,* for example, notes that the text was "translated oute of frenche in to Englisshe by the right excellent princesse Margaret moder to oure soverain lorde kinge Henry the .vii. and Countesse of Richemond & derby."[14] This publication also features woodcuts of the Beaufort portcullis and Tudor rose that provide visual representations of Beaufort's high status. After the Tudor princesses' translations were printed in 1548, other aristocratic Englishwomen similarly published translations whose title pages advertised their authorship, suggesting that the translator's identity could be an important selling point. In 1592, Mary Sidney Herbert, who had gained newfound fame as a literary patron after the death of her brother Philip, issued a volume whose title page unapologetically announced that its contents—translations of Philippe Duplessis-Mornay and Robert Garnier—were "done in English by the Countesse of Pembroke."[15] Similarly, Elizabeth Cooke Hoby Russell attempted to shape public perceptions of herself through the title page to a translation of a work by John Ponet (published 1605), which states the text was "translated out of Latin into English by the Right Honorable Lady Elizabeth Russell, Dowager to the Right Honourable the Lord John Russell, Baron, and sonne and heire to Francis Earle of Bedford."[16] As in the case of Beaufort's translations, these publications advertised Sidney Herbert and Russell's rank and fame for godly piety in order to attract readers.

Women from less lofty backgrounds who had developed reputations for outstanding piety also followed this model. As mentioned in chapter 1, Mary Basset, Thomas More's granddaughter, became the first gentlewoman to publish a translation under her name by contributing an English version of More's final Tower treatise to his collected works in 1557. Three years later, Anne Lock Prowse published a translation of Calvin under her initials. By the 1580s, Prowse—now a former Marian exile, a friend of prominent reformer John Knox, and the widow of preacher Edward Dering—had become well known for her Calvinist views. John Field's 1583 edition of a sermon by Knox, which he had received from Prowse, depicts her as a paradigm of religious zeal: "I know you live to your God and as you have in times past; being no young scholler in his schoole, given sufficient testimonie to the Church of God, of your sincere faith and holy profession, when you lived in exile to enjoy it."[17] Perhaps for this reason, Prowse chose to take credit for her 1590 translation of Jean Taffin, further authorizing her message that "hotter" Protestants should maintain their beliefs despite recent attacks (*Of the Markes of the Children of God*).[18] Likewise, Dorcas Martin's 1581 translation of a catechism entitled *An Instruction for Christians Conteining a Fruitfull and Godlie Exercise* was reprinted under her own name in Thomas Bentley's *Monument of Matrones*. The 1581 edition of Martin's translation has been lost, but it is possible that she chose to publish the work with full attribution. Martin had served as a stationer for an illegally printed tract by Thomas Cartwright and supposedly harbored him while he was a fugitive, giving her a heightened fame within London presbyterian circles.[19] These cases suggest that the female translator often had credibility as a source whose authority was as important as that of the original author. In fact, Beaufort's *Mirroure,* Russell's Ponet, and Martin's catechism all failed to mention the original authors of their works, underscoring the potential power that these women had to authorize the texts' reception. These translators did not issue their works under their own names because they could hide behind the original author but rather because they had the social and cultural cachet to serve as pious exemplars.

Appropriating Erasmus: Mary Tudor, Roman Catholicism, and the English *Paraphrases*

Aristocratic women of the early Tudor period often translated devotional texts or became patrons of religious translations to provide models of vernacular piety to literate readers. While their efforts may have influenced popular devotion, these translations also provide an essential context for translations undertaken by Mary Tudor. Two of Mary's relatives—Catherine of Aragon and her great-grandmother Margaret Beaufort—as well as her governess Margaret Pole, Countess of Salisbury, either translated or commissioned translations meant to foster lay spirituality largely aligned with humanist attitudes.[20] During the 1540s, Katherine Parr reworked this model by supporting translations that subtly advanced reformist ideas. When Mary undertook translations of texts by Thomas Aquinas and Erasmus, she therefore asserted her courtly credentials and associated herself with women such as Beaufort and Parr. Even if Mary recognized the differences between Parr and the women who preceded her, the distinctions were to all appearances slight enough that Mary's translations could profitably float between the poles of conservative and reformist orthodoxy during the last decades of Henry's reign.

As in the case of the More women, translation was probably a staple of Mary's education. The historical evidence for her schooling is scanty, but Henry's instructions for Mary's removal to Wales in 1525 state that Pole must "intende to her learninge of Latine tongue & French."[21] Juan Luis Vives proposed in *De ratione studii puerilis epistolae duae* (1523) that Mary use translation to improve her ability to write in Latin: "Let her begin to turn short speeches . . . from English into Latin. At first they should be easy; then, by degrees, more difficult, in which there should occur all kinds and forms of words. Let these partly be serious and religious, and in part joyful and courteous."[22] Giles Du Wés, Mary's French tutor, published a textbook featuring French dialogues with interlinear English translations. Both Vives and Du Wés agreed that Mary's education should feature a strong emphasis on moral and religious instruction. Vives suggested that Mary read classical moralists (Cicero, Seneca), church fathers (Jerome, Augustine), contemporary humanists (Erasmus, More), and Christian poets (Prudentius). Du Wés cited Augustine and Isidore, respectively, in dialogues on peace and the soul, and he devoted three dialogues to the subject of the Mass: its proper attendance, its commemorative nature, and its ceremonies.[23] While there is little evidence that Mary followed either of these programs of study, a 1533 letter from Catherine of Aragon accompanied books by Ludolph of Saxony and Jerome, the latter probably edited by Erasmus, that were calculated to reinforce Mary's piety and virtue: "I will send you 2 bookes in latine. One shalbe De vita Christi, with the declaration of the gospelles. And the other the epistles of St Hierome that he did write alwaies to Paula and Eustochium."[24] After Catherine's death, Mary may have associated humanist learning with her mother, as one of her servingwomen later reported that Mary had turned to "lettres humaines" for consolation in the 1530s.[25]

Whatever role translation may have played in Mary's education, she was familiar with royal and aristocratic women who encouraged translation of religious texts into the vernacular in order to serve pious and political aims associated with humanism. As previously noted, Beaufort initiated this tradition. She had sought spiritual direction from John Fisher, and her translations crafted a vernacular piety that could supplant Lollard sentiments.[26] Besides translating the fourth book of Thomas á Kempis's *Imitatio Christi* from French into English, she commissioned William Atkinson to translate the first three books. This translation brought the *devotio moderna* (modern devotion) to an English lay audience, while Beaufort's contribution, which focused on the Eucharist, subtly advanced new ideas such as frequent communion. Beaufort's *Mirroure of Golde for the Synfull Soule* encouraged readers to prepare for penance by examining their sinfulness. Beaufort thus established a powerful model of the religious authority available to royal women through translation. In the 1520s, Margaret Pole, then Mary's governess, offered English readers another example of aristocratic women's interest in vernacular translation by commissioning Gentian Hervet's translation of Erasmus's *De immensa dei misericordia.* The title page noted that Hervet had completed the work at Pole's "request," and Hervet's dedicatory preface to Pole suggested her interest in popularizing the work: "I thought it shuld be a good dede/if for your ladysships pleasure it were printed & spred abrode."[27] Pole's son Reginald was one of Erasmus's correspondents, and Hervet's translation was part of Thomas Berthelet's 1526 slate of Erasmian publications, possibly indicating that Margaret Pole, like Margaret Roper, hoped to defend Erasmus's reputation. Similarly, Catherine of Aragon asked Thomas Wyatt to translate Petrarch's *De remediis utriusque fortunae,* a series of dialogues with Stoic underpinnings. Wyatt instead translated Plutarch's *Quyete of Mynde,* which similarly offered counsel for those experiencing crises. The publication of this translation under Catherine's aegis in 1528 had political implications given the fact that Henry had initiated divorce proceedings the year before. By the late 1520s, then, women associated with Mary had established the potential effectiveness of translation into English as a means of advancing pious views with a political charge. Mary herself participated in this tradition by becoming the first royal woman to employ humanist principles of translation to turn a text from Latin into English. Her

1527 manuscript translation of a prayer by Thomas Aquinas ("Concede mihi") achieved limited circulation among religious conservatives and may have held political connotations through its demonstration of a humanist education befitting a princess.[28]

The vitality of this tradition during the last decade of Henry's reign is evident in Katherine Parr's use of translation to support religious reform. Perhaps the clearest evidence of this shift in priorities is Katherine's reworking of Thomas à Kempis's *Imitatio*—based on a 1531 translation rather than Beaufort's 1504 version—to create a subtly reformist text: *Prayers or Medytacions* (1545).[29] A year earlier, Katherine had translated John Fisher's *Psalmes or Prayers Taken Out of Holye Scripture* from Latin into English. Published anonymously, this work offered readers a chance to interact with biblical texts, including complete versions of Psalms 22 and 100, despite governmental prohibitions on Bible reading. As a result, Katherine's translation aided Cranmer's attempts to advance vernacular piety with the English litany of 1544.[30] In 1545, Katherine made arrangements for the English translation of five books of Erasmus's Latin *Paraphrases on the New Testament,* assigning books to several well-established scholars: Nicholas Udall ("Luke") and Thomas Key ("Mark"). By asking Mary to translate "John," Katherine acknowledged her long-standing friendship with her stepdaughter and, as Aysha Pollnitz has noted, Mary's restored favor at court.[31] Like Katherine's translation of Fisher's *Psalmes,* the English *Paraphrases* could provide a mediated way for the laity to interact with the Bible and thus encourage greater familiarity with biblical texts. While Katherine's intentions were firmly reformist, this undertaking fit easily within Mary's conservative framework. Vives had recommended Erasmus's *Paraphrases* to Mary as being "useful to piety," and Henry Parker, Lord Morley, had dedicated a translation of Erasmus to Mary.[32] Catherine of Aragon had probably sent Erasmus's edition of Jerome to Mary, and she commissioned Erasmus to write the *Christiani matrimonii institutio* (1526). By agreeing to translate Erasmus's *Paraphrase on John,* Mary pleased Katherine Parr and honored her mother's learned devotion, simultaneously acknowledging her dependent position at court as well as maintaining her identity as Catherine of Aragon's daughter. More important, Mary took part in a tradition sanctioned by other aristocratic women in which translation of religious works into the vernacular was an acceptable means of shaping popular devotion.

As the Edwardian Reformation entered its initial phases, the government co-opted Mary Tudor's partial translation of Erasmus's "Paraphrase . . .

upon the Gospell of Sainct John" to suggest her support for Edward's policies.[33] In July 1547, Somerset and Cranmer issued *Injunctions* that advanced a cautious program of reform, including banning liturgical processions. While Henry VIII had curtailed Bible reading in 1543, the *Injunctions* encouraged literate men and women to read and interpret the English Bible with the aid of Erasmus's English *Paraphrases:* "Thei [priests] shal provide, within three monethes, nexte after this visitacion, one boke of the whole Bible, of the largest volume in English: And within one twelfemonethes, next after the saied visitacion, the Paraphrasis of Erasmus also in englishe upon the Gospelles, & the same sette up in some convenient place, within the sayed Churche, that they have cure of, whereas their parishioners may most commodiously, resorte unto the same, & reade the same." Another injunction explicitly orders uneducated priests to use the Bible and *Paraphrases,* whether in Latin or English, in tandem: "Every Person, Vicar, Curate, Chauntry preeste and stipendarye, beyng under the degree of bachelar of Divinitie, shall provyde, and have of his awne, within three monethes after this visitacion, the New Testament, both in Latyn and in Englysh, with Paraphrasis upon the same of Erasmus, and diligently studye the same, conferringe the one with the other."[34] Taken together, these requirements suggest the regime's interest in familiarizing both its citizens and its priests with a standardized approach to biblical interpretation. The reformist implications of this focus on Bible reading are made clear in the first sermon of Cranmer's *Homilies,* which the *Injunctions* required nonlecturing clergy to read aloud in church: "Let us diligently searche for the welle of life, in the bokes of the new and old Testament, and not ronne to the stinkyng podelles of mennes tradicions, devised by mannes imaginacion, for our justificacion and salvacion."[35] Bible reading, then, was one means of exerting influence on an English populace that was not fully prepared to accept reformation. Cranmer himself certainly viewed the *Paraphrases* as a significant instrument in ensuring religious conformity, as his August 1548 instructions for the visitation of parishes in Canterbury ordered visitors to check whether parishes and priests had purchased and displayed the *Paraphrases.*[36] The English *Paraphrases*—including Mary's portion—were thus vital to the Edwardian Reformation.

To stoke popular support for reform, the *Paraphrases* and several other publications presented the royal family as a credible model of reformed piety. Edward Whitchurch, a longtime collaborator with Edward's official printer Richard Grafton, had taken on a quasi-official role by publishing the *Homilies* (twice in 1547) and *Paraphrases* (1548, 1551).[37] On November 5, 1547, Whitchurch printed his second edition of the *Homilies* even as he saw to press the first edition of Katherine Parr's *The Lamentacion of a Sinner.* William Cecil, master of requests for Somerset, contributed a preface that stressed Katherine's official position as a dowager queen as well as her desire to "remov[e] superstición, wherwith she was smothered, to enbrace trew Religion, wherwith she may revive."[38] Just a day later, Thomas Berthelet, who had been printer to Henry VIII, reissued Parr's *Prayers or Medytacions.* Even if Katherine's reputation was weakened after Henry's death and her swift marriage to Thomas Seymour, these publications could serve as a quasi-official endorsement of the government's religious policies.[39] Meanwhile, Stephen Gardiner, bishop of Winchester, complained to Somerset that the *Injunctions* implied that Edward approved of the *Paraphrases:* "To have such books recommended to the realme in the Kinges name by your Graces direction, me semeth verye weighty, and your Grace not to have bene well handled in it. All the world knoweth the Kinges Highnes him selfe knew not these bookes, and therfore nothing can be ascribed unto hym."[40]

Within this context, Mary Tudor's partial translation of the "Paraphrase . . . upon the Gospell of Sainct John" might appear to provide yet another sign of the royal family's support for religious reform. Katherine wrote Mary in September 1545 or 1547 with a request that the translation might be attributed to her in print:

> Signify whether you wish it to go out most happily into the light under your name, or whether rather by an unknown author. To which work really, in my opinion, you will be seen to do an injury, if you refuse the book to be transmitted to posterity on the authority of your name: for the most accurate translating of which you have undertaken so many labors for the highest good of the commonwealth; and more than these (as is well enough known) you would have undertaken, if the health of your body had permitted. Since no one does not know the amount of sweat that you have laboriously put into this work, I do not see why you should reject the praise that all confer on you deservedly.[41]

Katherine shrewdly notes the value that "the authority" of Mary's "name" will impart to the translation as well as the work's application to current religious policy ("for the highest good of the commonwealth"). Even if Mary were to publish the work anonymously, Katherine asserts that her involvement is well enough known to associate the translation with the princess and, implicitly, with governmental reform ("no one does not know the amount of sweat that you have laboriously put into this work"). Despite Mary's commitment to Catholicism, her connection to the *Paraphrases* could be viewed as evidence of her support for the Edwardian Reformation.

Erasmus's contested reception within England only heightened the chance that Mary's participation in the *Paraphrases* might be read as an endorsement of governmental policies. Pollnitz has convincingly argued that Mary's initial interest in translating Erasmus should be understood in light of Erasmus's conservative reputation during the late Henrician era.[42] Yet as the previous chapter noted, Erasmus had a twofold legacy as an instigator of religious reform and a champion of Roman Catholicism. By the 1540s, exiled reformers were taking advantage of Erasmus's double reputation to advance Protestant sentiments and debate Catholic theology. George Joye included Erasmus in a list of antipapist reformers such as Wycliffe and Luther, while John Bale linked Erasmus with Protestant theologians including Luther, Zwingli, Melanchthon, and Bullinger.[43] Meanwhile, tracts attacking Gardiner cited Erasmus's *Paraphrases* in support of Protestant practices and theology.[44] Reformist interest in Erasmus may explain Gardiner's strenuous objections to the 1547 *Injunctions*. In a letter to Somerset from October 1547, Gardiner claimed that the *Paraphrases* could subvert the realm's civil and ecclesiastical hierarchies: Erasmus "wrote [the *Paraphrases*] above 26 yeres a goo, when his penne was wanton, as the matter is so handled, as being abrode in this realme, were able to minister occasion to evell men to subverte, with religion, the policie and order of the realme."[45] Other religious conservatives may have shared Gardiner's views; while John Craig has found that at least 162 parishes complied with the *Injunctions*, some apparently did not.[46] Certainly Nicholas Udall, the editor of the *Paraphrases*, felt a need to defend biblical study from criticism in a dedicatory preface to Katherine Parr: "The Romish Pharisaicall sort . . . stiere and provoke the indignacion of Princes and Magistrates against the publishing, or againste the true preachers and teachers therof . . . by allegeyng that it wyll moove sedicion and teache errour."[47] Udall's defense of the Bible, and by extension the *Paraphrases*, suggests that official endorsement of this controversial work was inherently polemical.

Indeed, the English *Paraphrases* became one of the most important signs of the royal family's approval of religious reform thanks to the requirement that every church own this volume. Whitchurch and Grafton printed between twenty thousand and thirty thousand copies of the *Paraphrases*, an expensive folio work comprising over a thousand pages.[48] The volume's sheer physical size suggested its significance, which was reiterated by a title page that featured Edward VI's coat of arms at the top of the page and Katherine Parr's arms at the bottom (see figure 4).[49] Nicholas Udall's dedicatory preface of the work to Edward offers further evidence of the king's support for reform by associating ongoing religious changes with Henry VIII's reformation of the English church: "I truste that almightie god . . . wil by his especial grace illumine your herte to procede in the way of trueth which your father hath opened unto you, & will geve you grace althynges to perfeicte which your father moste godly beganne to your handes."[50] Significantly, Udall cites the *Injunctions* as evidence of Edward's interest in religious reform, likening the young king to the biblical reformer Josiah: "it now evidently appereth your Majestee to bee the faithfull Josias, in whose tyme the booke of the law is found out in the house of the Lorde, & by your moste godly injunccions reade in the hearyng of all your people" ("DPE," 6v). Yet while Henry was deeply involved in his religious policies, it was not Edward—but rather his counselors, especially Cranmer—who had composed the *Injunctions.* The *Paraphrases,* as Gardiner had predicted, were presented in Edward's name, but the religious program they fulfilled was not necessarily of his own devising.

Udall also establishes Edward's commitment to religious reform by associating translation of religious texts with improving the Commonwealth. Asserting that vernacular religious texts are an important means of spreading reform, Udall claims that printed devotional texts can reinforce both official religion and the state itself:

> Muche more good, and a muche greater benefite to a common weale dooeth suche an one, as translateth or composeth any fruictefull booke or traictise, whych by goyng abrode thoroughout a whole Royalme maie profite al pastours, curates, studentes, & all people universally: then any man is hable to do by preachyng, teachyng, or geving instruccions to one company alone, or in one place or countrey and no mo, though he should never so rightely, never so diligently, or never so cunnyngly dooe the same. Now besides that suche a translatour travayleth not to hys own private commoditie, but to the behouf and publique use of his countreye. ("DPE," 11v)

Print is powerful by virtue of its ability to be disseminated throughout the land ("going abrode"), which allows published books to exert influence more consistently and widely than a preacher who works "in one place." Furthermore, print can assist with the government's current program of educating both unlearned priests ("pastours, curates") and the

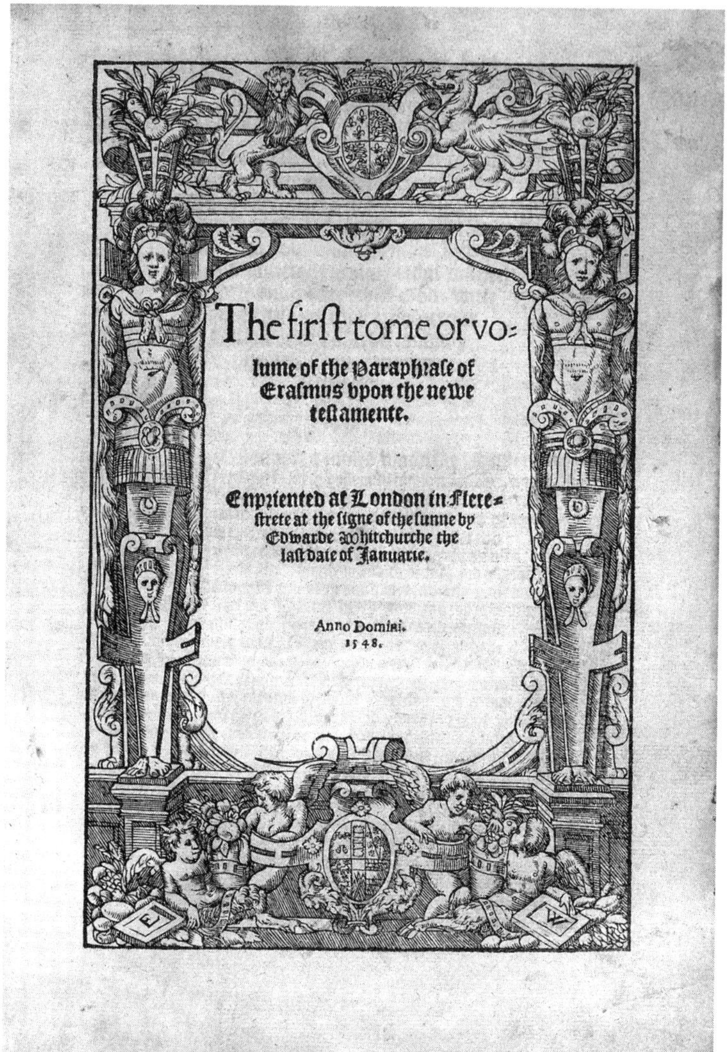
The first tome or vo-
lume of the Paraphrase of
Erasmus vpon the newe
testamente.

Enpriented at London in Flete-
strete at the signe of the sunne by
Edwarde Whitchurche the
last daie of Januarie.

Anno Domini.
1548.

Figure 4. Title page of *The First Tome or Volume of the Paraphrase of Erasmus upon the Newe Testament* (1548), which includes Mary Tudor's translation of Desiderius Erasmus. Reproduced by permission of The Huntington Library, San Marino, California.

laity ("studentes, & al people universally"). Within the context of the Edwardian Reformation, the translator—who can convey foreign Protestant doctrines into English—takes on a public function as a promoter of governmental policy. The English *Paraphrases* offer a concrete example of this paradigm since Udall casts Erasmus as an antipapist reformer: "The trashe & bagguage stuf that through papisticall tradicions had found a waye to crepe in, this man hath sifted out from the right doctrine" ("DPE," 10r).[51] Nevertheless, Udall declares that Edward and Katherine Parr have played a more important role in the English *Paraphrases* than Erasmus himself: "For Erasmus facte dyd helpe onely suche as are seen in latin: the Quenes goodnesse extendeth to the helpe of the unlearned also whiche have more nede of helpyng foreward: and your Majestees benefite it is, that maketh so precious a treasour common to as many as may take profite or fruict therby" ("DPE," 11r). Portraying the royal family as authoritative sources on religious issues, Udall suggests that the source text and original author are less important than its current endorsers.

Similarly, Udall invokes commonwealth ideology to frame Mary's translation of the "Paraphrase . . . upon the Gospell of Sainct John" as an important contribution to current religious policy. Alluding to Mary's public role as Henry's daughter, Udall suggests that her translation is evidence of a praiseworthy desire to serve the state and, by extension, the Edwardian Reformation: "What coulde be a more manifeste argumente of myndyng the publique benefite of her countrey, what coulde bee a more evident profe of her will and desyre to dooe good to her fathers moste dere beloved subjectes, what could be a more plaine declaracion of her most constaunt purpose to promote Goddes worde, and the free grace of his gospell? then so effectually to prosecute the weorke of translatyng whiche she had begoonne."[52] Here Udall presents Mary's unfinished translation as a means of advancing the "good . . . [of] her fathers moste dere beloved subjectes," deceptively claiming that Mary, like Edward, follows her father's reformist interest in "promot[ing] Goddes worde, and the free grace of his gospell." Udall also mentions Mary's rank to authorize her translation and by extension the *Paraphrases* as a model of learned devotion:

> To what learned man maye not the sedulitee of suche a noble princesse bee a spurre and provocacion to employe the talente of his learnyng and knowlage to the publique use and commoditee of his countrey? . . . To what persones (be they never so ignoraunt or unlearned) maie not this moost earnest zele of a princesse of suche

> highe estate, bee an effectuall provocacion and encouragyng to have good mynde and wyll to reade, heare, and enbrace this devout and catholyke Paraphrase so plainly and sensibly translated, and so graciously by her offred, and (as ye would saie) put in all folkes handes to be made familiar unto them? ("DP," *Para,* 2v)

As a "princesse of . . . highe estate," Mary may appear to translate on behalf of "the publique use and commoditee of [her] countrey" and to "offre" the work to readers. In turn, her participation in the *Paraphrases* encourages the country "to reade, heare, and enbrace" the *Paraphrases* and legitimizes the *Injunctions*' requirement that this work be disseminated throughout England ("put in all folkes handes"). Yet as Katherine Parr's letter to Mary indicates, the work had a private origin as a favor to Katherine. While Udall's account is based on truths—Mary was Henry's daughter, Mary did begin a translation of Erasmus's "Paraphrase"—Udall misrepresents these facts to associate Mary with a reformist position at odds with her own views.

It is tempting to speculate that Mary did not finish her translation of Erasmus precisely because of its possible connection to religious reform. Udall notes that Francis Mallet, who had been Katherine Parr's chaplain, completed the translation:

> Whan she had with over peynfull studie and labour of wryting, cast her weake body in a grievous and long syckenesse, yet to the intent that the diligent Englishe people shoulde not bee defrauded of the benefite entended and ment unto them: she committed the same weorke to Maister Frauncisce Malet doctour in the facultee of divinitee with all celeritee and expedicion to be finished and made complete. That in case the kynges majesties moste royall commaundemente by his moste godly injunccions expressed, declared, and published, (that the sayed Paraphrases shoulde within certain monethes bee sette foorthe to the Curates and people of this Realme of Englande) hadde not so prevented her grace, but that she might eftsones have put her fyle to the poolishing thereof. ("DP," *Para,* 2r–2v)

Udall clearly refers to the *Injunctions*' stipulation that both unlearned priests ("Curates") and commoners must own the *Paraphrases* within a year, suggesting that Mary halted work in the months before the text's anticipated publication.[53] While most scholars have taken this illness literally, some have speculated that Mary feigned sickness as a means of distancing herself from the project, and Mary's strategic use of her health to negotiate other situations threatening her faith lends credence to this idea.[54] In 1549, Mary pleaded poor health to argue that she should be allowed to hold Mass, and a year later she pretended to be ill so that she could hear Mass on Christmas.[55] She probably paid careful attention to the *Injunctions* and likely would have recognized their reformist tenor. In fact, Mary apparently wrote Somerset that summer to complain about possible changes to the Henrician church.[56] Yet even if Mary disagreed with the agenda of the English *Paraphrases,* she steered a middle course by allowing the work to carry her name.

This tacit endorsement of the translation may reflect its religious conservatism, which fits uneasily within the agendas of the *Injunctions* and Udall's prefatory remarks. It is impossible to know just how much Mary or Mallett contributed to the finished translation, so the following discussion will refer to the translators jointly in recognition of their collaboration. The translation accurately conveys the sense of Erasmus's original, yet the translators show skill in using doublets to reinforce the work's main points.[57] For example, Erasmus's dedicatory preface to Ferdinand admits that paraphrasing the gospels is problematic because this activity cannot preserve Christ's concise speech: "it is the office of a Paraphrase to expresse that thing that is *brefely spoken, and in fewe words couched* [strictius . . . dictum]."[58] This moment is typical of Mary and Mallett's use of doublets, in this case to highlight Erasmus's emphasis on brevity. As the translators somewhat ironically expand Erasmus's reference to terseness ("strictius dictum"; briefly spoken) with the doublet "brefely spoken, and in fewe wordes couched," they show an awareness that translation, like paraphrase, is a secondary discourse with interpretive potential. In a less neutral moment, the translators expand Erasmus's praise of Charles V, Ferdinand's older brother and Mary's cousin. After Henry's divorce from Catherine of Aragon, Mary had turned to Charles as a protector, which may explain why her translation dwells on his virtues.[59] In comparison with emperors throughout the previous eight hundred years, Charles is "the *moste vertuous* [optimus], if we consider besides his other very imperiall qualities, his fervent *affeccion and zeale* [studium] towardes religion and godlynes" (*PE*, 6; "SJ," 3v–4r). By translating "optimus" (best) as "moste vertuous" and rendering "studium" (zeal) as "affeccion and zeale," the translators emphasized Charles's piety and in turn offered coded support for his devotion to Roman Catholicism. Throughout the translation, Mary and Mallett similarly exercise their interpretive prerogative to exhibit conservative religious views that clash with Udall's prefatory framework.

By its very nature, Erasmus's *Paraphrases* had a complicated relationship with religious reform, and the translators often alter the text to reassert Roman Catholic orthodoxy. For example, Mary and Mallett emphasize traditional devotion to the Virgin Mary throughout the "Paraphrase." The translators render Erasmus's statement that Christ was born "ex homine" (of man; *PE*, 4) with the phrase "of the virgin Marie" ("SJ," 3r), insisting on Mary's part in Jesus's birth. Some religious conservatives had complained that Erasmus's commentary on the wedding at Cana (John 2:1–10) undercut Mary's authority.[60] Mary and Mallett soften Christ's rejection of his mother's power after Mary mentions the lack of wine at the wedding: "Not *utterly denying* [abnegans] hys mother, but declaring that she had litle to doe with the busines he went about, he aunswereth her: woman what have I to doe with the[e]" (*PE*, 66; "SJ," 21v). By translating "non abnegans" (not denying) as "not utterly denying," Mary and Mallett suggest that Mary still possesses some authority despite Christ's rejection. The translators continue to allow Mary slightly more power than she has in their source by highlighting her facilitation of the miraculous transformation of water into wine: "the *godly pitifull* [pia] carefulnes of his mother, did procure that, lest the servauntes lacke of belefe, or their unready service, should be a let wherby that whiche lacked at the feast should not be amended. But how and what time the thing should be dooen, she *holding her peace* [tacita] leaveth it *secretly* [added] to hir sonnes *wil and appointment* [arbitrium]" (*PE*, 66; "SJ," 21v). Mary and Mallett use doublets for "pia" (holy) and "arbitrium" (decision) to underscore Mary's conformity to Christ's will, yet they also give her a covert agency by adding "secretly" and by paraphrastically translating "tacita" (silent) as "holding her peace." The translation thus subtly reflects Roman Catholic views on Mary's elevated rank and intercessory power.

Mary and Mallett also emphasize elements of Erasmus's text that contradict the ecclesiastical structure of both the Henrician and Edwardian churches. Udall's dedicatory preface of the volume to Edward had justified Henry's split with Rome by condemning the pope's usurped authority: "The Romishe Nabugodonozor had by wrestyng and pervertyng the holy scriptures of God to the establishyng and maintenaunce of his usurped supremitie clymed so high: that he . . . moste blasphemously exalted hymselfe above all that is called God" ("DPE," 3r). The translators, however, offer oblique support for the pope's primacy in their portrayal of Peter as Christ's lieutenant on earth, supporting Mary's later statements that she had concealed her personal support for papal authority during Henry's reign.[61] When Christ admonishes Peter for slicing off the soldier's ear in the garden of Gethsemane (John 18:11), he seems to allude to Peter's role as the first pope: "If thou wilt succede *me* [added] as my *vicar* [vices], thou must fight with no other swerd than of Gods woorde" (*PE*, 351; "SJ," 108v). The translation of "vices" (place) as "vicar" may have been suggested by the similarity of the two words, yet the term "God's vicar" traditionally referred to Peter and later popes.[62] The addition of "me" further suggests that Peter took Christ's place as the leader of the earthly church, the basis for later Roman Catholic claims of papal supremacy. A similar moment occurs later in this chapter, when Erasmus describes Peter as one who "should be a *speciall minister* [princeps] *under Christ* [added] of the *holy* [totius] churche" (*PE*, 357; "SJ," 110v). A literal translation of "ecclesiae princeps" (prince of the church) would have had dangerous implications under both Edward and Henry, and the translators understandably skirt Erasmus's insinuation that Peter was the first pope. Yet "speciall" suggests Peter's distinctive position, and the interpolation of "under Christ" implies the lieutenancy suggested by the earlier translation of "vices" as "vicar." Furthermore, rendering "holy" for "totius" (whole) avoids Erasmus's overt reference to Peter's universal authority even as it evokes a "holy churche" distinguishable from other churches through its allegiance to Peter.

The translators further enhanced the text's conservative tone by opting for traditional terms that had already occasioned debate within the sphere of English biblical translation. For example, Mary and Mallett consistently render the word "poenitentia" as "penance" rather than the reformist translation of "repentance." Thomas More had objected to William Tyndale's translation of the Bible in part because his substitution of new words for traditional terms—including "repentance" for "penance"—might encourage heresy. Although "penance" could serve as a synonym for "repentance," Tyndale argued that this term could be viewed as supporting Roman Catholic doctrine: "By this word penanuce/they make the people understonde holy dedes of their enjoynynge/with which they must make satisfaccion unto godwarde for their synnes, when all the scripture preacheth that Christ hath made full satisfaccyon for oure synnes."[63] The potential for this doctrinal use of "penance" is evident within Mary and Mallett's translation of Erasmus's commentary on Christ's judgment of the adulterous woman (John 8:3–11). Erasmus interpreted Christ's interaction with the woman as a model for priests, and Mary and Mallett make a number of changes to this scene that suggest Christ serves as the woman's confessor: "With silence he succoureth her, that was *pulled & hurried to pain* [rapiebatur], to preserve her unto *penaunce* [poenitentiam]: and that *she mighte with due repentaunce bee better advised, and converte to healthe and salvacion* [resipisciet ad salutem]" (*PE*, 187; "SJ," 59r). The translators emphasize the woman's distress by rendering "rapiebatur" (she was seized) as "pulled & hurried to pain," setting the stage for her transformation through penance. In turn, their translation of "resipisciet" (repent) as "she mighte with due repentaunce bee better advised, and converte" emphasizes Christ's role as a counselor who spurs the woman's regeneration, a result that is stressed by their doublet for "salutem" (salvation), "healthe and salvacion." Mary and Mallett further suggest the penitential nature of this moment in their rendering of the woman's final conversation with Christ: "Because *she did not denye, but confessed* [non inficiata est] the thynge that she had committed, she wente awaye justifyed" (*PE*, 190; "SJ," 59v). Here the translators add the idea of confession through their doublet for "inficiatur" (she did not deny), transforming Christ into a protoconfessor who ensures the woman's salvation ("she wente awaye justifyed"). The biblical authorization of auricular confession had been under debate since the 1530s, and the *Six Articles* (1539) characterized confession as essential but not required by God's law.[64] Through their use of traditional terms, Mary and Mallett provided a biblical precedent for this embattled practice. In fact, their preference for "penance" subtly contradicted the biblical passages inserted by Udall throughout the *Paraphrases*, as the Great Bible had followed Tyndale's use of "repentance."

Finally, the translators align Erasmus's text with Roman Catholic doctrine on the Mass, a traditional element that Mary particularly cherished. Mary would lobby unceasingly for the ability to attend Latin Mass after the introduction of English services in 1549, and restoration of the Mass would become central to her reign.[65] As her chaplain, Mallett abetted Mary's resistance to Edwardian policy by conducting Masses for her and her household; he was imprisoned in 1551 for performing Mass while Mary was absent.[66] This devotion to Roman Catholic ceremonies contrasts sharply with Udall's dedicatory preface of the *Paraphrases* to Edward, which claimed that the pope had "infected the clere fountaine of Goddes woorde with the suddes of humaine tradicions, and the dregges of vaine ceremonies" ("DPE," 3r). The central ceremony within Roman Catholicism was the Mass, and Gardiner had complained to Somerset about Erasmus's description of this sacrament as a symbol: "If the Paraphrasis goo abrode, people shalbe lerned to call the Sacrament of the Aultar holibred and a symbole; at whiche newe name manye will marvayle."[67] Alert to these implications, the translators carefully rewrite Erasmus's commentary on Christ's pronouncement that his body would become bread (John 6:52–58): "I shall leave unto you my fleshe and blood as *a hid secret mystery, and mistical token* [mysticum symbolum] of this *copulacion and felowship* [societatis]: which selfe thing although ye do receive it yet will it not profit you unles ye receyve it spiritually" (*PE*, 156; "SJ," 49r). Mary and Mallett eliminate the idea that the Eucharist is a "symbolum" (symbol), instead focusing on the sacred mystery of the Mass ("hid secret mystery and mistical token"). With a second doublet rendering "societatis" (fellowship), the translators heighten the idea that Mass is a transformative experience allowing the communicant to experience God: "copulacion and felowship." When Erasmus describes the Eucharist as a symbol in his paraphrase of John 13, the translators similarly avoid using the English cognate "symbol": "after that laste and misticall supper was prepared, in the whiche the holy *memoriall* [symbolo] of his body and bloude beeing geven, he leafte *unto us* [added] by waye of covenaunte a continuall remembraunce of himselfe" (*PE*, 280; "SJ," 87r). The term "memoriall" evokes the commemorative purpose of Mass, and the translators emphasize the necessity of this ceremony as a performance of God's "covenaunte" with humankind by adding the phrase "unto us." Mary and Mallett thus present the Mass as a sacred rite that infinitely replicates Christ's sacrifice. Such views were decidedly conservative in 1548, as a surge of publications attacking the Mass preceded the 1549 establishment of the Book of Common Prayer.[68]

The conservative nature of the translation helps explain why Mary did not ban the English *Paraphrases* after her accession.[69] For the most part, Mary and Mallett seem to have found Erasmus's doctrine unobjectionable, and their translation subtly transmitted a devotion to Roman Catholicism—including the papacy, traditional ceremonies, and the Mass—that would become central to Mary's attempts to restore English Catholicism. Udall may have attempted to inscribe Mary and her translation within the framework of the Edwardian Reformation, but the translation resisted Udall's characterization through conservative language and small departures from Erasmus's text. Perhaps that is why Mary allowed the published translation to bear her name: despite Udall's prefatory statements, an alert reader might find much to support Roman Catholic practice within the work itself. Ironically, then, the Edwardian regime's attempt to regulate biblical interpretation included a translation that might have directed English men and women toward conservative religious beliefs rather than away from them. When Elizabeth reissued the injunction requiring all English churches to own the English *Paraphrases,* she ensured that Mary's translation would continue to offer justification for Catholic doctrine under the auspices of yet another Protestant government.

Nobility's Godly Fruit: Elizabeth Tudor, John Bale, and Religious Reform Under Edward

During the final years of Henry VIII's reign, Elizabeth Tudor enthusiastically translated works that simultaneously shaped her reputation for learning and reflected an interest in moderate religious reform. In doing so, she followed the example of Katherine Parr, who—as previously discussed—used translation to spread reformist sentiments. Yet Katherine was not the only influence on Elizabeth's early translations, as the royal tutors translated religious works to gain patronage. Mary may also have provided a model for Elizabeth through her translation of Aquinas, which had a limited circulation within courtly circles. Like Mary's Aquinas, Elizabeth's translations displayed her knowledge of foreign languages, yet Elizabeth's productions were more sustained demonstrations of learning than Aquinas's short prayer. By translating at least four works that had discreetly reformist agendas, Elizabeth sought to gain approval from her father and stepmother. Indeed, both her source texts and her translation strategies were carefully chosen—either by Elizabeth or someone else—to appeal to Henry and Katherine's particular interests. Elizabeth thus adapted familial and pedagogical models for the purpose of situating herself within a larger community that was both aristocratic and moderately reformist.

Elizabeth's early translations reflect her rarefied education in Latin, Greek, French, and Italian according to humanist principles. Before 1544, Elizabeth was tutored by Katherine Astley, but after that point her education was handed over to humanist tutors with ties to John Cheke, first Regius Professor of Greek at Cambridge and tutor of Edward VI. William Grindal and later Roger Ascham, both Cheke's students, instructed Elizabeth in Latin and Greek, while Jean Belmaine oversaw French lessons for Elizabeth and Edward.[70] Translation was probably an important component of the royal tutors' pedagogy. Following Belmaine's instructions, Edward translated biblical sentences on idolatry and justification by faith from English into French.[71] Cheke, meanwhile, relied on double translation—the translation of a text from one language into another and then back again—to teach classical languages. Since Elizabeth and Edward likely shared some schooling during their earliest years, Elizabeth may have learned this practice from Cheke himself.[72] Grindal probably used this method with Elizabeth, and Ascham glowingly reported his own success in teaching Elizabeth Latin and Greek through double translation: "Queene Elizabeth . . . by this double translating of Demosthenes and Isocrates dailie without missing everie forenone, and likewise som part of Tullie every afternone, for the space of a yeare or two, hath atteyned to soch a perfite understanding in both the tonges . . . as they be fewe in nomber in both the universities, or els where in England, that be, in both tonges, comparable with her Majestie."[73] Ascham may give himself too much credit for Elizabeth's skills, but his remarks suggest that translation played an important role in her education.[74] In keeping with contemporary educational goals for women, Elizabeth's curriculum also featured an emphasis on piety, particularly along the reformed lines endorsed by her tutors. Ascham, for example, approvingly mentioned to Johann Sturm in 1550 that Elizabeth read Cyprian and Melanchthon.[75] Given this context, the reformist cast of Elizabeth's juvenile translations is unsurprising.

The royal tutors clearly recognized the practical applications of learning foreign languages, as they composed a number of translations that sought patronage by displaying their humanist and even reformist credentials. These men largely chose to translate the church fathers, who were viewed by reformers as witnesses to the primitive Christian church's structure and practices. During Henry's reign, Cheke presented Henry with a manuscript translation of Maximus from Greek to Latin and dedicated to the king two published books containing Latin translations of Greek sermons by Chrysostom: two sermons in 1543 and a further six on providence in 1545. Elizabeth's tutors also showed an understanding of translation's ability to display their learning and religious views. In 1543, Ascham presented John Seton with a Latin translation of Oecumenius's anthology of passages by Eastern church fathers on Philemon. That same year, he gave a Latin translation of Oecumenius's collection on Titus to Edward Lee, archbishop of York, inadvertently offending Lee because the work discussed clerical marriage.[76] In 1553, Jean Belmaine presented Edward VI with a French translation of the Book of Common Prayer, and he later sent Elizabeth his French version of Basil's "On the Solitary Life." Belmaine's dedicatory preface to the former translation emphasizes the gift's religious agenda by praising the Book of Common Prayer as a means of spreading reform: "Que pleust a dieu que tous ceux qui font profession de la Religion chrestienne, et en cherchent la verite, et ceux qui y contredisent (quelque part qu'ilz soient) en eussent chacun un pareil entre mains, en langage tel que bien entendissent, et y prinssent goust; car il estouperait la bouche a plusieurs mesdisans, et aux autres servirait d'une lumiere tresclaire les faisant voir les grans abus" (May it please God that all those who make profession of Christian religion and search for its truth, and those who contradict it, wherever they may be, each one of these may have the same [book] in hand, in such language that they may well understand and develop a taste for it; for it will stop the mouth of many detractors, and to others it will serve as a very bright light making them see great abuses).[77] All of these translators sought patronage by selecting authoritative source texts that conveyed and legitimated their personal support for religious reform.

Elizabeth similarly used translation as a means of currying favor, possibly at the instigation of men such as Belmaine and Grindal, by composing a series of New Year's gifts for her father and stepmother. In 1544, Elizabeth gave Katherine Parr an English translation of Marguerite de Navarre's *Le miroir de l'âme pécheresse* (1531). A year later, Elizabeth presented Katherine with another translation as a New Year's gift, this time turning the first book of John Calvin's *Institution de la religion chrestienne* (1541) from French into English. At the same time, she gave Henry a trilingual translation of Katherine Parr's *Prayers or Meditations* into Latin, French, and Italian. During this period Elizabeth may have also presented Henry with a translation from Latin into French of Erasmus's *Dialogus fidei* (no longer extant).[78] All of these source texts could be associated with Katherine's agenda of moderate reform, but several features differentiate the translations intended for Henry from those given to Katherine.[79] Just as Elizabeth's tutors translated religious works into languages other than English for Henry and other patrons, so Elizabeth demonstrated her scholarly progress through her trilingual version of Parr and her French rendition of Erasmus. Meanwhile, the translations given to Katherine gracefully acknowledge the queen's interest in vernacular translation of religious works. Elizabeth's dedicatory preface to the translation of Marguerite may even compliment Katherine on her recent translation of Fisher by praising "the affectuous wille and fervent zeale, the wich your highnes hath towardes all godly lerning."[80] Elizabeth's translations thus negotiated her precarious position at the late Henrician court, which could be mediated both by her learning and by her ability to associate herself with authoritative figures such as Marguerite and Erasmus.

As with Mary Tudor's Erasmus, Elizabeth's translations gained a new political value during the Edwardian Reformation. In April 1548 John Bale published an edition of Elizabeth's translation of Marguerite de Navarre that definitively established Elizabeth's reformist credentials: *A Godly Medytacyon of the Christen Sowle*. At this time Bale had no official position within the Edwardian church or government, but he did have a long history of writing propaganda on behalf of religious reform. A former Carmelite friar, Bale had composed plays such as *King Johan* to spread support for the royal supremacy during Cromwell's ascendancy.[81] After Cromwell's fall, Bale went into exile on the Continent, where he penned tracts attacking bishops (*Yet a Course at the Romyshe Foxe,* 1543; *The Epistle Exhortatorye,* 1544) and translated a selection of material portraying Martin Luther's final days as saintly (*The True Hystorie of the Christen Departynge . . . of . . . Martyne Luther,* 1546). Bale was particularly interested in drawing connections between the past and present to identify a tradition of distinctively English Protestant thought that would justify religious reform.[82] Besides documenting the case of John Oldcastle, a Lollard who could be viewed as proto-Protestant, Bale also edited the literary remains of Anne Askew, burned during Henry's reign for sacramentarian views that the Eucharist was memorial in nature (*A Brefe Chronycle Concerning . . . the Blessed Martyr of Christ, Sir John Oldecastell,* 1544; *The First Examinacion of Anne Askewe,* 1546; *The Lattre Examinacyon of Anne Askewe,* 1547).[83] By 1546, English authorities had begun to take action against the spread of Bale's publications. That May, the Privy Council ordered the lord mayor of London to question several individuals "touching certain heretike bokes of Bale's making lately broughte in a hoye [boat] of Flaunders."[84] On July 8, 1546, Henry VIII issued a proclamation forbidding anyone to "receive have take or kepe in his or their possession, any maner of booke printed or written in the englishe tongue" by Bale and other reformers; those who already owned these works were instructed to submit their copies for public burning by October 1.[85] On August 4, a Welshman named John Geffrye was duly arrested "for having oonc of Bales bokes, with erronious wourdes by him uttred apon the same," and that fall two dozen of Bale's books were burned by Bonner at Paul's Cross.[86]

Just a few months after that bonfire, the accession of Edward VI and the initial phases of the Edwardian Reformation completely changed Bale's situation. Stephen Gardiner, bishop of Winchester, complained to Somerset on May 21, 1547, about the popularity of Bale's *True Hystorie of . . . Martyne Luther* as well as his edition of Askew, which portrayed Gardiner in an unflattering light. Besides characterizing these books as "very pernicious, sedicious, and slaundrous," Gardiner asserted that Askew's *Examinacyons* would damage Henry VIII's posthumous reputation.[87] On June 6, Gardiner wrote Somerset again about Askew's *Examinacyons,* disingenuously claiming that he was only continuing a past practice of alerting governmental authorities to the spread of dangerous books.[88] In reality, Bale's works appear to have been one of the many flashpoints for religious negotiation between Gardiner and Somerset in the early months of Edward's reign. Contrary to the Henrician precedent, no official condemnation or burning of Bale's works was forthcoming, perhaps because these books were compatible with the regime's use of print as religious propaganda on behalf of reform.[89] By 1548, Bale's reputation was secure enough that several London printers reissued works with relevance to the current religious climate. Anthony Scoloker and William Seres republished the *Epistle Exhortatorye* and Bale's edition of material related to Oldcastle, while Thomas Raynald reprinted Bale's *Actes of Englyshe Votaryes.* Bale himself remained on the Continent until late July of that year, but he continued his earlier efforts with new publications, including an edition of a treatise by John Lambert, another sacramentalist executed by Henry (*A Treatyse . . . Concernynge Hys Opynyon in the Sacrament of the Aultre,* 1548).[90] By the second year of Edward's reign, then, Bale's texts were popular enough to be profitable, and Bale himself was tacitly recognized as an ally by the government.

Bale prepared for his return to England by seeking royal patronage through publications that furthered the agendas of the Edwardian Reformation. In late July, Bale printed a catalog of British authors that explicitly linked his interest in establishing a proto-Protestant history for England with the current politics of the Edwardian regime (*Illustrium majoris Britanniae scriptorum,* 1548). The title page features a woodcut in which Bale kneels as he presents the work to Edward, who sits on a throne of state and holds a scepter (see figure 5). As in the case of the English *Paraphrases,* Edward's coat of arms appears on the title page, suggesting royal approval of Bale's text. Meanwhile, an onlooker lifts the curtain to Edward's right, perhaps representing the larger audience of readers—both English and international—anticipated by Bale's later description of the book as "publico scripto" (public writing).[91] As Bale's dedication of the *Illustrium . . . scriptorum* to Edward VI reveals, he was eager to capitalize on Edward's support for religious reform to advance his own historical and literary agendas. Bale explains that he has written this work so that readers might know "per quos nostra patria ad cognitionem christianae religionis pervenerit, quorum ministerio apud nos defensa ac propagata sit doctrina sacra, quae incrementa, qui progressus fuerint, quae certamina ac mutationes in ea extiterint" (by whom our fatherland came to the knowledge of Christian religion, by whose ministry sacred doctrine was defended and propagated among us, what increases, what advances there were, what contests and changes appeared in it).[92] Bale's presentation of the English church as an institution experiencing a constant state of flux implies that recent reforms are simply another stage in this process of refinement rather than a break

ILLVSTRIVM
MAIORIS BRITANNIAE
SCRIPTORVM, HOC EST, ANGLIAE, CAMBRIAE,
ac Scotiæ Summariū, in quasdam centurias diuisum, cum di-
uersitate doctrinarū atq; annorū recta supputatione per
omnes ætates a Iapheto sanctißimi Noah filio, ad
annum domini. M. D. XLVIII.
AVTORE IOANNE BALAEO SVDOVOLCA.

EXCVDEBATVR PRAESENS OPVS, ANNO A NATIVI-
tate unicæ illius pro peccatis uictimæ, patri in crucem oblatæ, quadragesimo octa
uo supra millesimum & quingentesimum, pridie Calendas Augusti.

Sit lingua mea, calamus scribæ velociter scribentis: ps:45° 2°
Robt wright

Figure 5. Title page of John Bale's *Illustrium majoris Britanniae scriptorum* (1548).

with tradition. Bale praises Edward's involvement in this process by mentioning his repudiation of Catholicism: "cum potentissima Re[gia] Ma[jestas] t[ua] re ipsa ostendat, se veram Dei agnitionem & invocationem, omnibus humanis rebus anteferre, ecclesiam Christi & doctrinam coelestem amare, cuius curam & propugnationem, adversus antiqui serpentis in regno papistico tyrannidem, vere regio animo suscepit" (since your most powerful Royal Majesty in reality shows that you place the true acknowledgment and invocation of God above all human things, that you love the church of Christ and heavenly doctrine, whose care and defense against the tyranny of the old serpent in the papist kingdom, your majesty has truly undertaken with a royal mind).[93] Besides employing the typical abuse of Catholicism found in Protestant propaganda, Bale notes that Edward rejects Catholic customs for religious practices based on the Bible. In Bale's view, the works of earlier English writers offer crucial support for religious change: "Multa in nostrae gentis scriptorum monumentis peti possunt, quae prudenter decerpta, & usurpata ad ecclesiae Christi aedificationem . . . profutura sunt" (Many things can be found in the records of the writers of our race, which wisely plucked and taken will be of use for the building of Christ's church).[94] The *Illustrium . . . scriptorum* thus associates Bale's literary and religious agendas with Edward and the reforms carried out in his name.

A few months before publishing the *Illustrium . . . scriptorum,* Bale had already co-opted the royal family's association with religious reform by editing Elizabeth's translation of Marguerite de Navarre. Bale's access to this text suggests that he may have been in contact with those around Katherine Parr or even Katherine herself, especially as Bale claimed to possess a holograph copy of the manuscript: "She wrote first with her owne hande, moch more finely than I coulde with anye prentynge letter."[95] He had probably attracted the attention of Katherine and her circle through the publication of Anne Askew's *Examinacyons.*[96] Askew's account indicates that Henrician authorities suspected she could supply incriminating evidence regarding the religious beliefs of Katherine's ladies-in-waiting and presumably Katherine herself: "They asked me of my Lady Suffolke [Catherine Brandon], my Lady of Sussex [Anne Radcliffe], my Lady of Hertford [Anne Stanhope], my Lady [Joan] Denny, and my Lady Fitzwilliams [Jane Ormond]. . . . Sayd they unto me, that the kyng was informed that I could name if I would, a great number of my sect."[97] Janel Mueller has recently noted that the title pages for both the *Examinacyons* and Parr's *Lamentacion* employ similar phrasing (both were published "at the instant desire" of friends), indicating that

Katherine was aware of Bale's work as an editor and shared his interest in popularizing vernacular texts that advanced English Protestantism.[98] Bale's edition of Elizabeth's translation may thus have been part of a second push within Katherine's circle to provide the public with formative models of royal women's reformist sentiments, especially since the *Godly Medytacyon* appeared in April 1548, just after Whitchurch reissued Parr's *Lamentacion* on March 28. This agenda may explain why Elizabeth's translation of Marguerite—an example of two royal women's piety—was chosen for publication rather than her rendition of Calvin, arguably a text with stronger reformist associations.[99] Yet Bale's edition was at most a quasi-official publication, without the tacit imprimatur of the Edwardian government. As Udall had done with Mary's Erasmus, Bale would offer the text as evidence of the royal family's endorsement of Protestantism, but Bale also took this opportunity to advance reformist tenets that outpaced the government's cautious reforms. By associating these ideas with Elizabeth, Bale legitimized his view that the Edwardian Reformation should take a less moderate path.

Like Udall, Bale established Elizabeth's credibility as a model of piety for the nation by dwelling upon her education, rank, and commitment to the public good. The title page presented Elizabeth as a reformist with a striking woodcut that implies her personal knowledge of God (see figure 6). Wearing a crown and holding a book, Elizabeth kneels before the resurrected Christ. The connections between Elizabeth's learning and divine knowledge are evident in the juxtaposition of the closed book under her elbow (possibly the translation itself or the Bible) with Christ's extended finger pointing to heaven. Elizabeth's book is furthermore reminiscent of the title page to Askew's *Examinacyons*, which represented Askew holding the Bible to the consternation of the pope. In this case, however, the fact that the book is closed suggests that pious reading is a prerequisite for Elizabeth's privileged contact with Christ. The woodcut also subtly rebuts Catholic reliance on intercessors as Christ lifts his robe to reveal the mark of his crucifixion, presenting Elizabeth as a second Mary Magdalene who learns of Christ's resurrection firsthand. Finally, as Maureen Quilligan has argued, the fractured column in the background may suggest that the Roman Catholic Church is in need of repair.[100] The title page authorizes this implicitly Protestant stance by emphasizing the royal nature of the text. Not only was the work "compyled in frenche by lady Margarete quene of Naverre," but it has also been "aptely translated into Englysh by the ryght vertuouse lady Elyzabeth doughter to our late soverayne Kynge Henri the .viii." A Latin inscription reiterates Elizabeth's royal parentage and associates her rank with her learning

A Godly Medytacy
on of the chriſten ſowle, concer-
ninge a loue towardes God and
hys Chriſte, compyled in frenche by lady
Margarete quene of Nauerre, and apte-
ly tranſlated into Englyſh by the
ryght vertuouſe lady Elyzabeth
doughter to our late ſouerayne
Kynge Henri the. viij.

Inclita filia, ſereniſſimi olim Anglorum
Regis Henrici octaui Elizabeta, tam Græ
cæ quam latine fœliciter in Chriſto
erudita.

Figure 6. Title page of *A Godly Medytacyon of the Christen Sowle* (1548), Elizabeth Tudor's translation of Marguerite de Navarre. Reproduced by permission of The Huntington Library, San Marino, California.

and piety: "Inclita filia, serenissimi olim Anglorum Regis Henrici octavi Elizabeta, tam Graece quam latine foeliciter in Christo erudita" (Elizabeth, celebrated daughter of the fairest King late of England, Henry VIII, happily learned in Christ, both in Greek and Latin). The title page thus establishes Elizabeth as a royal scion whose learned devotion both embodies and authorizes reform.

Much as Udall had done with the English *Paraphrases,* Bale invests Elizabeth's translation with political meaning by placing it within the context of the ongoing Edwardian Reformation. Bale opens the dedicatory preface of the work to Elizabeth with a consideration of nobility, advancing Chrysostom's definition of nobility as a "famouse renome obtayned by longe exercysed vertu" (*M,* 5r) to combat the "monstruouse or . . . prestygyouse nobylyte" claimed by the Roman Catholic Church (*M,* 3r): "The Romysh clergye ymagenynge to exalte themselves above the lewde layte (as they shame not yet to call the worldly powers) have geven it [nobility] in a farre other kynde, to mytars, masses, Cardynall hattes, crosers, cappes, shaven crownes, oyled thombes, syde gownes, furred amyses, monkes cowles, and fryres lowsy coates, becommynge therby pontyfycall lordes, spirytuall sirs, and ghostly fathers" (*M,* 3v). Bale's contemptuous disdain for Catholic ceremony ("masses"), hierarchical authority ("pontyfycall lordes, spirytuall sirs, and ghostly fathers"), and garb ("mytars," "monkes cowles") presents the elements of Roman Catholicism as corrupt impositions upon "the lewde layte." Bale also attacks the doctrine of transubstantiation, which allows the priesthood to elevate itself above God: "A prest maye every day both byget hym [Christ] and beare hym, where as hys mother Marye begate hym . . . but ones" (*M,* 4v). In contrast with this false nobility based on tradition and exterior trappings, Bale asserts that Edward possesses a prestige derived from virtue. Just as Josiah had "destroyed . . . carved ymages" and "restor[ed] agayne the lawes of the lorde" (*M,* 5v–6r), so Edward's reforms hold the promise of reviving English religion: "Most excellent & godly are hys begynnynges reported of the very foren nacyons, callynge hym for hys vertuouse, lerned, and godly prudent youthes sake, the seconde Josias" (*M,* 6r). By praising Edward's foreign reputation as a "seconde Josias," Bale aligns his new definition of virtuous nobility with Edwardian propaganda, including Udall's preface to the *Paraphrases,* that justified religious change by identifying Edward with biblical reformers. Bale in turn attributes reformist sentiments to Elizabeth on the basis of her translation and family, pointing to Elizabeth's writings as evidence that she, like her brother, exemplified Chrysostom's idea of virtuous nobility:

> Of thys Nobylyte, have I no doubt (lady most faythfully studyouse) but that yow are. . . . If questyon were axt me, how I knowe it? my answere wolde be thys. By your godly frute, as the fertyle tre is non other wyse than therby knowne, luce .vi. [Luke 6] I receyved your noble boke, ryght frutefully of yow translated out of the frenche tunge into Englysh. I receyved also your golden sentences out of the sacred scriptures, with no lesse grace than lernynge in foure noble languages, Latyne, Greke, Frenche, & Italyane. (*M*, 7r)

Bale's punning association of the "frute" from the "fertyle tre" in Luke 6:43 with Elizabeth's "fruteful" translation of Marguerite suggests the inherent piety in the princess's literary activities. Bale also finds reformist sentiments in Elizabeth's Latin, French, and Italian versions of the first verse of Psalm 13 ("The fole sayth in hys harte, there is no God," *M*, 41v) and her composition of an adage in Greek ("Feare God, honoure thy parentes, and reverence thy fryndes," *M*, 41v). Bale claims that Elizabeth's Greek sentence is a source of moral guidance surpassing anything offered by Catholic authorities: "Neyther Benedyct nor Bruno, Domynyck nor Frances (whych have of longe yeares bene boasted for the pryncypall patrones of relygyon) ever gave to their superstycyouse bretherne, so pure preceptes of syncere christyanyte" (*M*, 8v). Here Bale leverages Elizabeth's conventional maxim into a condemnation of major monastic institutions: respectively, the Benedictines, Carthusians, Dominicans, and Franciscans. A marginal note on the English version of Psalm 13:1 reinforces this strong anti-Catholic stance by remarking, "Antichrist Hys clergy" (*M*, 41v). In an even more surprising move, Bale interprets Elizabeth's trilingual versions of this verse as a source of reformist doctrine: "Your grace unto us sygnyfye[s], that the baren doctrine & good workes without fayth of the hypocrytes, whych in their uncommaunded latyne ceremonyes serve their bellyes & not Christ, in gredyly devourynge the patrymony of poor wydowes & orphanes are both execrable in themselves, and abhomynable afore God" (*M*, 7v–8r). As we will see, Elizabeth's translation does indicate her enthusiasm for justification by faith alone, but it does not explicitly condemn Catholic "doctrine" or "good workes." Furthermore, England still used "latyne ceremonyes," and while Cranmer's *Homilies* had asserted justification by faith alone, this development had been introduced with little fanfare to reduce conservative opposition. Bale therefore portrays Elizabeth as supporting reforms that were more overtly reformist than the theological position of the current English church.

After attributing his own views to Elizabeth, Bale characterizes her translation as a means of public service that is reminiscent of Udall's prefaces to the *Paraphrases*. Once again, Bale reframes Elizabeth's translation so that it serves his aims, this time by skewing the circumstances of the text's production:

> Chefely have she done it for her owne exercyse in the frenche tunge, besydes the spirytuall exercyse of her innar sowle with God. . . . And thynkynge that other myght do the same, of a most fre christen harte, she maketh it here commen unto them, not beynge a nigarde over the treasure of God. . . . She have not done herin, as ded the relygyouse and anoynted hypocrytes in monasteryes, co[n]vents and colleges, in spearynge theyr lybraryes from men studyouse, and in reservynge the treasure contayned in their bokes, to most vyle dust and wormes. (*M*, 40r)

By describing the translation as a private endeavor ("her owne exercyse," "her innar sowle"), Bale follows the humanist precedent of associating translation with leisure time, conveniently glossing over the work's original purpose as a New Year's gift for Katherine Parr. At the same time, Bale suggests that this translation genuinely represents Elizabeth's private religious views and her rejection of Catholicism. While Catholic scholars have hoarded their learning in "monasteryes, co[n]vents, and colleges," Elizabeth hopes to make her knowledge "commen" to spread "the treasure of God." Of course, this program sounds very similar to Bale's own publication agendas, and Elizabeth's lack of interest in this scheme is suggested by her failure to print other translations. Bale, however, presents himself as abetting Elizabeth's plans by publishing her work: "Thys one coppye of yours have I brought into a nombre to th'intent that many hungry sowles by the inestymable treasure contayned therin, maye be swetely refreshed" (*M*, 9v). While Bale may co-opt Elizabeth's translation for his own purposes, he also suggests that she has legitimate agency as a model of reformed piety ("*she* maketh it here commen," "*She* have not done herin," "so do *she* agayne most frely dystrybute it"). As a member of the royal family, Elizabeth seems to function as a symbol of the Edwardian Reformation and to provide a pattern of reformed sentiment for the nation.

Bale's edition of the translation differs from Elizabeth's presentation copy (titled *The Miroir or Glasse of the Synnefull Soule*) in substantive ways that reinforce the reformist agenda of his paratexts. As Janel Mueller and Joshua Scodel's edition of the presentation copy shows, Elizabeth freely translates Marguerite de Navarre's poem into prose while condensing the poem's repetitive language and imagery, removing its highly sensual language, and lessening the speaker's self-abasement.[101] Three major patterns of revision can be identified within Bale's version. First, a systematic set of revisions smooths out Elizabeth's phrasing so that the text is both more elegant and easier to read. A second group of changes realigns the translation with the French source, adding in some of the lines omitted in the presentation copy and rendering some terms more literally. To take one small example, Elizabeth tends to render Marguerite's "Brief" (in short) paraphrastically: "Now to speke shorte." Bale's edition retains the paraphrasis but employs an English cognate for "brief": "Now brevely to conclude."[102] A third kind of revision inserts material that is not found in the source text but that advances the agendas expressed in Bale's preface. For example, Bale's edition reworks Marguerite's preface to the reader so that it more obviously seeks a public audience: "If thu do throughly reade thys worke (*dere frynde in the lorde*) [added] marke rather the matter than the homely speache therof, consyderynge it is the *stodye* [worke] of a woman. . ." (*G*, 44; *M*, 10r). Besides adding a direct address to the reader that implies Elizabeth welcomed the text's publication ("dere frynde in the lorde"), this version replaces "worke," which nicely renders "l'ouvraige," with "stodye," a term that reiterates Bale's praise of Elizabeth's learning (*Ma*, p. 165, line 4). Mueller and Scodel speculate that Bale was responsible for all of these alterations, but the second and third revision strategies appear opposed to each other. If Bale was truly interested in realigning Elizabeth's translation with her French source text so exactingly, then it seems improbable that he would have interpolated new material without any basis in the source text. It may be more likely that Elizabeth or Katherine revised the text so that it better followed the French, especially given Elizabeth's acknowledgement of the work's defects in her preface to Katherine. Bale seems a probable candidate for the third set of revisions, although the extent of his editorial interventions cannot be definitively proven. Certainly scholars have suspected that Bale reworked Askew's *Examinacyons,* and he may have seen fit to alter Elizabeth's text as well.[103] While the translation has most frequently been read for psychological insight into Elizabeth's relationship with her parents, the textual variants in Bale's edition suggest the significance of the text's doctrinal implications for ongoing debates over the Edwardian Reformation.[104]

At first glance, the *Miroir* might seem to be a less than ideal text to support Bale's position, since the poem is not militantly reformist. In fact, the moderate nature of Elizabeth's source text was better suited for the context of Henry's final years, when his eclectic approach to religious policy made an openly reformist stance untenable.[105] As Renja Salminen notes, Marguerite's poem does not overtly attack the Roman Catholic Church or its practices: "La reine ne l'a pas composé dans l'intention de se déclarer sectatrice de la Réforme. Le texte dans son ensemble, dans son esprit, ne contient rien qui soit de caractère militant, rien qui s'oppose directement . . . la foi catholique" (The queen did not write it with the intention of declaring herself a partisan of the Reformation. The text in its entirety, in its spirit, contains nothing that is of a militant nature, nothing that is directly opposed to the Catholic faith).[106] Nevertheless, Salminen observes that Marguerite does subtly undermine Catholic practices that reformists hoped to alter or eliminate.[107] For example, Marguerite refutes the idea that saintly intercession can lead to salvation: "There is neyther man sainte, or els aungell, for whom the harte of a sinner will chaunge" (*G,* 54). Perhaps in agreement with this idea, Elizabeth removes a later reference to saints, rendering "sainctz et Prophetes" (saints and Prophets; *Ma,* p. 176, line 271) as "holy prophettes" (*G,* 60). While this shift in meaning may be an accidental result of Elizabeth's tendency to collapse Marguerite's doublets, it does strengthen the reformist underpinnings of the text. Along similar lines, Marguerite criticizes excessive veneration of the Virgin Mary: "If any man shuld thinke to geve the[e] greater prayse *than god hymselfe hath done* [added], it were a blasphemy. For there is no suche prayse as the same is wich cometh frome god. Also hast thou had so stedfaste, and constante a fayth, that by grace she [i.e., faith] had the power *to make the[e] godly* [deifier]" (*G,* 62; *Ma,* p. 177, lines 307–11). Elizabeth glosses Marguerite's lines by adding "than god hymselfe hath done," effectively reiterating Marguerite's point about God's primacy in contrast with Mary. Furthermore, Elizabeth's translation of "deifier" (to become a god) as "make godly" may follow her systematic elimination of Marguerite's language of deification, but this rendering also removes any implication that Mary deserved special exaltation. Bale's edition heightens this tendency to de-emphasize Mary by adding the intensifier "fule" to blasphemy: "if any man shulde thynke to geve the[e] greatter prayse than God hymselfe hath done, it were a *fule* blasphemye" (*M,* 16v). A marginal citation of Luke 1, referencing Gabriel's praise of Mary, drives home the point. Both the presentation copy and Bale's edition thus offer a slightly more incisive attack on Catholic veneration of saints and the Virgin Mary.

Elizabeth is even more proactive in emphasizing the text's incorporation of two key reformist tenets: biblical study and justification by faith.[108] Marguerite initially rejects God's call on the grounds that the

Bible might be nonsense: "tous ces motz ne voulois escouter/Mais encores je venois . . . doubter,/Si c'estoit vous: ou si par adventure/Ce n'estoit riens, qu'une simple escripture" (I did not want to hear all these words/But still I came to doubt,/If it was you: or if by chance/It was nothing, except a foolish writing; *Ma,* p. 191, lines 725–28). Elizabeth removes the suggestion that the Bible is meaningless by failing to translate "n'estoit riens" (it was nothing): "I wolde not harke unto all these wordes: For i douted whether it were thou, or els a symple writtinge, that so sayd" (*G,* 84). Bale's version makes several small alterations: "Alas unto all these swete wordes wolde I not harken. For I doubted whether it were thu, or els a fabyllouse writynge that so sayde" (*M,* 24v). Besides emphasizing the Bible's significance by modifying "wordes" with the adjective "swete," Bale also substitutes "fabyllouse" for "simple," simultaneously suggesting the miraculous nature of the Bible and eliminating the negative connotations of "simple."[109] Bale's edition also interpolates material that harks back to his prefatory critique of Roman Catholicism: "Often tymes have I with the[e] broken covenaunte. And partly for that my poore sowle was to[o] moche fed with *evyll* [yll] breade or dampnable doctryne *of hypocrytes* [added], I despysed such socoure and *ghostly* [added] physyck *in Gods worde* [added], as wolde have holpe me" (*G,* 52, 54; *M,* 13r). Bale's addition of "hypocrytes" directly relates to his introductory attack on the "baren doctryne & good workes without fayth of the hypocrytes" (*M,* 7v). A further link to Bale's preface can be discerned in the insertion of "ghostly" and "in Gods worde," interpolations that cast Marguerite's text as an exemplar of the spiritual solace found through biblical study and that sharply contrast "evyll breade," presumably the transubstantiation that occurs in the Mass. The published version of Elizabeth's translation takes on a more polemical cast that supports Bale's position on Bible reading and transubstantiation, even though the English church had not yet renounced transubstantiation.

Bale's edition may add in material that radicalizes Elizabeth's translation, but his preface accurately portrays the princess as a supporter of justification by faith. Elizabeth explicitly praises this element of Marguerite's poem while dedicating her work to Katherine Parr: "She (beholding and comtempling what she is) doth perceyve how, of herselfe, and of her owne strenght, she can do nothing that good is, or prevayleth for her salvacion: onles it be through the grace of god" (*G,* 42). Throughout the translation, Elizabeth departs from her source text to emphasize the soul's inability to better itself. For example, she underscores Marguerite's statement that God alone spurs her spiritual regeneration: "He doth not tary tyll i humbly do praye hym, or that (seyng my *hell and damnacion* [enfer]) i do cry upon hym: for with hys spirite, he doth make a wailinge withyne my hart, *greater than i, or any man, can declare* [grand inenarrablement], wich asketh the gifte, wherof the vertue is unknowen to my lytell power" (*G,* 50; *Ma,* p. 169, lines 81–86). Elizabeth rarely employs doublets to translate single words, so her rendering of "hell" ("enfer") as "hell and damnacion" is particularly significant. By qualifying "hell" with "damnacion," Elizabeth suggests that the speaker cannot save herself despite her recognition of her own "damnacion." Her paraphrastic translation of "largely indescribable" ("grand inenarrablement") as "greater than i, or any man, can declare" further indicates the weakness of humankind in comparison with God, who is responsible for the inexpressible "wailinge" experienced by the speaker. Elizabeth also makes a small but illuminating change to Marguerite's later denial of human merit: "I coulde never se[e] that any man, by merite, and payne, coulde vainquishe helle, save onely he, wich hath made such assaute through charite (he being *humbled to the crosse* [que mort humilié])" (*G,* 112; *Ma,* p. 208, lines 1232–35). Elizabeth translates "that died humbled" ("que mort humilié") as "humbled to the crosse," more vividly implying that Christ's sacrifice was sufficient to redeem all humankind. Bale's edition in turn emphasizes this point through several additions: "I coulde never yet se[e], that anye man by meryte or payne *takynge,* coulde *ever* yet vanquyshe that helle, save only he whyche *ded the great* assaulte through hys *unspeakable* charyte, whan he humbled hym selfe to the crosse" (*M,* 34r). With the participle "takynge" Bale evokes and dismisses human agency, even as the addition of "ever," "great," and "unspeakable" reaffirms Christ's power. Bale thus underscores the translation's reformist stance on the contentious issue of merit.

Elizabeth's translation also directly comments on the power of faith to save humankind, further strengthening its implicit endorsement of reformist theology. Indeed, Elizabeth makes it clear that only a certain kind of faith is sufficient for salvation, perhaps obliquely referring to the competing claims of reformers and Catholics. Marguerite asserts that faith proceeds from God and so can protect the soul from harm: "Y a il riens, qui me puisse plus nuire,/Si Dieu me vault par Foy à luy conduire?/J'entens la Foy toute telle, qu'il fault,/Digne d'avoir le nom du don d'enhault" (Is there anything, that can harm me any more,/If God is able to lead me to him by Faith?/I mean all such Faith as is necessary,/Worthy to have the name of the gift from on high; *Ma,* p. 209, lines 1279–82). Elizabeth reworks this passage so that it suggests that a particular sort of faith is necessary for salvation: "Is there any thing, than that can hurte me, if god be willinge through fayth, to drawe me unto hym: I meane, *fayth suche as we must have for to obtayne the right highe gifte from above*" (*G,* 114). Bale's edition moves even further away from the French in highlighting this point: "Is there anye thynge can *pull me backe* if God be wyllynge through his *gyfte of* faythe to drawe me to hym? I meane suche faythe as we must nedes have to obtayne the *hygh graces* from above" (*M,* 35r). By replacing "hurte" with "pull me backe," Bale suggests the impossibility of losing God's grace after faith has been imparted to the soul. His addition of "gyfte" and substitution of "hygh graces" for "right highe gifte" stress the idea that grace is the source of salvation rather than man's merits. Bale also alters Marguerite's concluding thoughts on the efficacy of faith: "Fayth joyned with the truthe, bryngeth fourth hope, wherby perfyght charyte is engendered. And charyte is God, as thu knowist. If we have charyte, than we have also God therwith. Than is God in us, and we are in hym. *And all thys cometh through the benefyte of faythe. For he dwellith in all men whych have true faythe*" (*M,* 38r). In Elizabeth's presentation copy, the final sentences follow Marguerite's poem fairly closely: "Than is god in us, and all we are in hym, and he in all men. If we have hym through fayth" (*G,* 122). Marguerite had also concluded by focusing on faith: "Il est en nous, et trestous en luy sommes./Tous sont en luy et luy en tous les hommes./Si nous l'avons par Foy" (He is in us, and all of us are in him,/All are in him and he in all men./If we have him through faith; *Ma,* p. 214, lines 1419–21). Besides emphasizing justification by faith yet again, Bale removes the modifier "all" and adds new material that is less inclusive than Marguerite's or Elizabeth's versions. As a result, the published version's focus on "true faythe" evokes the division between reformists and Roman Catholics.

Bale's paratexts and alterations to the *Godly Medytacyon* may cast Elizabeth as a Protestant reformer who supports vernacular church services and denies the doctrine of transubstantiation, yet her translation itself is moderate in nature. Elizabeth does show a marked interest in several reformist tenets (Bible reading and justification by faith) and potentially rejects veneration of saints, but she largely follows the unobtrusive reformist agendas of her source text. It is likely that the more polemical alterations of her translation reflect Bale's attempts to reshape the text so that it better conforms to his anti-Catholic views. Yet while Bale may be disingenuous about the purpose and, at times, the theology of Elizabeth's translation, his revisions often have some basis in Elizabeth's own renderings of Marguerite. By publicizing Elizabeth's translation activities, Bale also helped her establish a reputation for learned piety that would serve Elizabeth in good stead as she negotiated the bitter controversies over religious reform during her reign. Elizabeth's interest in furthering this godly persona may account for her tacit acceptance of four separate republications of this translation during her reign. Bale's version was reissued by Roger Ward (1590), and new editions were printed by James Cancellar (1568; c. 1580) and Thomas Bentley (1582).[110] If Bale had positioned her translation in the vanguard of the Edwardian Reformation, by 1590 the *Godly Medytacyon* must have seemed fairly conservative in contrast with the agendas of "hotter" Protestants. Even if Bale's edition used Elizabeth's fame to advance an agenda that she may not have personally endorsed, the text nevertheless planted the seeds for her later self-fashioning as a godly queen.

Conclusions

Nicholas Udall and John Bale commandeered the Tudor princesses' translations for their own purposes, but their editorial interventions helped establish learned women's ability to participate in public debates over religion. Both editors relied upon the translators' rank and education to portray Mary and Elizabeth as models of piety whose labor was intended for the public good. Examination of the translations themselves reveals the varying extent to which these texts conform to their respective editorial frameworks, explaining why Mary and Elizabeth tacitly accepted the circulation of their work. Mary and Mallett took care to emphasize the conservative nature of their source text, particularly with regard to traditional practices such as penance, rites, and papal authority. Mary's translation thus covertly advanced a conservative religious agenda that was compatible with her reputation for Catholic orthodoxy under Edward. Meanwhile, Bale's presentation of Elizabeth as a reformer was consistent with the religious sympathies suggested by her translation of Marguerite de Navarre, which shows a uniform interest in biblical reading and justification by faith. Elizabeth's translation does not indicate that she was in the vanguard of Edwardian reformers, despite Bale's claims that her work supported the abolishment of Latin services and other Catholic innovations. Even so, the Elizabethan settlement matched Bale's thinking on these points, and his sentiments would eventually seem moderate in contrast with the militant Protestantism of Elizabeth's reign. The republication of Bale's edition in 1590 therefore underscored Elizabeth's own self-presentation as an arbiter of religious compromise. Whether or not Mary and Elizabeth agreed with their editors' views, they benefited from Udall and Bale's representations of their piety. Perhaps in recognition of this outcome, both queens rewarded their editors: Udall became headmaster of the Westminster School under Mary, while Elizabeth attempted to restore Bale's library to him and made him a prebendary in Canterbury Cathedral.

Yet these translations are also important as potential catalysts for the increasing prominence of the female translator after the Edwardian period. Margaret Beaufort's pioneering translations had already suggested that aristocratic women could use translation to influence popular piety, but in the forty years between her publications and those of the Tudor princesses, no other woman published a translation under her own name—not even Katherine Parr during her marriage to Henry. In the wake of Mary's and Elizabeth's editions, women became considerably more willing to attach their names to printed translations, and these works adopted the rhetoric of public service used by Udall and Bale. The publication of the Tudor princesses' translations helped spur these developments by placing Mary's and Elizabeth's writings within the politicized context of religious reform, offering a model to the nation of the worth that a learned woman's translation could hold. A close examination of these appropriations of the Tudor princesses' translations reveals the complicated negotiations that allowed women to participate in the public sphere. While the editors of translations by Margaret Roper and Mary Basset may have worked carefully with these women to achieve a shared goal, Udall and Bale imposed their own agendas upon the translations of Mary and Elizabeth regardless of whether the translators agreed with those purposes. Yet by presenting the Tudor princesses as legitimate contributors to the public good, Udall and Bale paradoxically encouraged other Englishwomen to translate works that might give them a voice within religious debates. As women such as Mary Sidney Herbert followed this model by taking public credit for their translations, they shaped their own reputations for learned piety in a proactive manner.

CHAPTER THREE

Princely Counsel

Mary Sidney Herbert, Elizabeth I, and International Protestantism

In late December 1545, Elizabeth Tudor marked the New Year's festivities by presenting her father, Henry VIII, and her stepmother, Katherine Parr, with a complementary pair of manuscript translations. For her father, Elizabeth had translated Parr's *Prayers or Meditations* (1544) from English into Latin, French, and Italian; for Katherine, she had turned the first book of Calvin's *Institution de la religion chrestienne* (1541) from French into English. As the previous chapter demonstrated, the source texts for these translations were carefully selected to demonstrate Elizabeth's humanist education. Yet the material characteristics of these presentation copies also offered Elizabeth another means of self-fashioning. Elizabeth had embroidered matching covers that handsomely displayed her skill in the traditionally feminine art of needlework.[1] The background to the cover of her translation of Parr is worked in a scarlet stitch laced with silver thread, a striking background for monograms in light blue and heavy silver thread that are the center of attention: the intertwined letters of both parents' names with an *H* for "Henry" both above and below.[2] Four pansies at the corners worked in dark and light yellow indicate the learned work within by punning on *pensées* (thoughts).[3] The cover for her translation of Calvin mirrors that of the Parr, except that Elizabeth reverses the colors (using a blue background with red monograms) and substitutes a *K* for "Katherine" above and below the central monogram. While these embroidered bindings highlighted Elizabeth's facility with needlework, her use of gold and silver thread implied that the gift had special value. Furthermore, Elizabeth transcribed the texts in a beautiful italic hand associated with humanist learning.[4] These translations therefore exhibited Elizabeth's mastery of aristocratic skills as well as her unusual erudition.

Yet Elizabeth's translations of Parr and Calvin were not merely decorative, as she took advantage of the mediatory nature of this activity to position herself as an intercessor between these texts' original authors and their dedicatees. In the dedicatory preface of Parr's *Prayers* presented to Henry, Elizabeth confidently states, "I do not doubt, indeed, that your fatherly goodness and royal prudence . . . will judge that this divine work, which is to be esteemed of more value because it has been assembled by the most serene queen, your spouse, ought to be held in slightly greater regard because it has been translated by your daughter."[5] Of course, Henry could already read Parr's *Prayers* in English, but Elizabeth carefully aligns herself with her stepmother here, appealing to her father's devotion to Katherine as a means of legitimating her work and of negotiating her own relationship with him. While the dedicatory preface accompanying her translation of Calvin fails to mention the author's name (perhaps in recognition of Henry's conservative religious views), Elizabeth nonetheless praises Calvin in a manner that privileges the text and consequently its translator: "Seeing the source from which this book came forth, the majesty of the matter surpasses all human eloquence, being privileged and having such force within it that a single sentence has power to ravish, inspire, and give knowledge to the most stupid and ignorant beings alive, in what way God wishes to be known, seen, and heard."[6] The multiple authorial positions inherent in translation allowed Elizabeth, as translator, to share in both the texts' authorship and, in turn, the authors' prestige. Only recently reintroduced into the line of succession and rehabilitated at court, Elizabeth utilized the material and literary aspects of her translations to evoke her education and navigate her liminal status at court.

This chapter will consider the ways that manuscript translations by two women, Mary Sidney Herbert and Elizabeth I, represented the female translator as a counselor. Both male and female courtiers frequently presented manuscript translations to powerful patrons on occasions such as New Year's Day, hoping to curry favor and advance their political agendas. Presentation copies of translations tangibly demonstrated the translator's erudition even as lavish material features such as decorative hands, colored or precious ink, illuminations, and elaborate bindings reinforced the value of that learning. In dedicatory prefaces, translators suggested that the texts had political or religious value, drawing on the reputation of their sources to authorize their own agendas. The cultural capital inherent in translation—that is, knowledge of foreign languages—could thus be leveraged into a form of social capital that legitimated the political and religious stances of the translator. This process of self-authorization is significant for redressing one of the primary critical complaints regarding early modern English-women's translations: the translator's apparent subordination to the (generally) male author of her source text.[7] Sidney Herbert and Elizabeth took advantage of the authority associated with their sources to compose manuscript translations that established their own political wisdom during times of crisis. While Sidney Herbert's *Psalmes* covertly advised Elizabeth on diplomatic relations with Spain, Elizabeth translated Boethius as a form of self-counsel after Henry IV of France became Catholic. If the act of translation itself displayed the female translator's erudition, the authorial multiplicity involved in translation permitted her to exploit the authority of her source text and, as a result, to cultivate her own political and religious agency. The ways that Sidney Herbert and Elizabeth bent their source material to their own purposes suggest new paradigms for thinking about the female translator's relationship to both the work's original author and the resulting translation.

The Treasures of Knowledge: Manuscript Translations and Cultural Capital

Manuscript translations played an important, but largely unremarked, role in the culture of gift exchange that operated at the Tudor court. Each New Year, members of the court presented one another with costly gifts, including jewels and clothing, that created political ties and reinforced patronage networks.[8] Courtiers with advanced linguistic skills gave patrons translations of texts that sought to transform their knowledge into a form of social capital. While dedicating his translation of Gregory Nazianzen's "On the Theophany" (1560) from Greek to Latin to Elizabeth I, Anthony Cooke presents his work as a worthy alternative to typical New Year's gifts: "I sende your highnes this remembraunce of the newe yere not of golde or silver, whereof ye have plentie as apperteineth, and I litle in comparison and yet with that readie to serve, but suche as I thinke more fitt for you to receive and for me to give having respecte to the treasoure of knowledge that dothe more excell, wherewith god hath plentifully endowed you."[9] Pierre Bourdieu's concept of cultural capital is a useful tool for understanding Cooke's presentation of his translation's value. Bourdieu defines cultural capital as "the cultural goods transmitted by the different family P[edagogic] A[ctions]"; that is, individuals obtain cultural capital through schooling ("pedagogic actions") that provides them with "cultural goods."[10] While Cooke possesses an embodied cultural capital by virtue of his education, his translation of Nazianzen transforms that capital into an objectified state: the manuscript itself. Yet as Bourdieu observes, objectified cultural capital has power "only insofar as it is appropriated by agents and implemented and invested as a weapon and a stake in the struggles which go on in the fields of cultural production . . . and, beyond them, in the field of the social classes."[11] By composing dedicatory prefaces to a patron, translators, in Bourdieu's terms, "implemented and invested" their work within contemporary issues. As the previous chapter demonstrated, both Elizabeth and her brother Edward VI, whom Cooke himself had tutored, received advanced humanist educations from tutors who leaned toward religious reform. Consequently, Elizabeth's education had included study of church fathers such as Cyprian, and Cooke's suggestion that Nazianzen is a fit addition to this "treasoure of knowledge" evokes the religious imperatives that informed her scholarship. For men and women at the Tudor court, manuscript circulation of translations functioned similarly as a means of self-authorization, as the translator's preface converted his or her linguistic knowledge into a source of cultural or political commentary.

Male translators of religious works often framed their translations as direct interventions in ongoing spiritual controversies, parlaying the prestige of their own educations and the reputations of the original authors into a source of authorization for their counsel. In 1541, Cooke presented Henry VIII with a translation of Cyprian's "On the Lord's Prayer" from Latin into English. By praising the king's recent breach with Rome, Cooke reveals his own support for Henry's religious reforms: "Where ye founde them [the English] overwhelmed with most deepe darkenes of ignorance . . . [you] hathe delyvered them from all that mysery most sagely and honorably, and caused them to be fedde with spirituall ffoode, that ys the worde of God, and the trewe knowledg of his Lawe." After highlighting Cyprian's adherence to biblical tenets, Cooke depicts his translation as a means of reforming English attitudes toward prayer: "This Sermon often redde of the multitude, I put no doubtes wolde be a greate occasyon to set prayer in his olde place agayne."[12] Similarly, Henry Parker, Lord Morley, presented Henry with a translation of Paolo Giovio's "Comentarys of the Turke," so "that your hyghe wysdome myght counsell with other Christen kynges for a remedye agaynste so perlouse an ennemye to oure feythe."[13] In 1574, John Rainolds dedicated his translation of Plutarch's "How to Profit by One's Enemies" to Elizabeth, praising her for reforming the English church ("Christianam fidem propagasti, Pontificias faeces ejecisti"; You have propagated the Christian faith, you have cast out the pontifical mire) and describing Plutarch's text as especially fit for a Christian prince: "Nullum autem occurrit, aut brevitate aptius, ut ad Reginam; aut usu commodius, ut ad Christianam" (Moreover nothing presented itself either more fitting in brevity, as for a queen, nor more convenient in use, as for a Christian one).[14] Rainolds, a staunch Calvinist, gestures at the application of Plutarch's treatise to the external enemies Elizabeth faced, including Catholic powers such as Spain, while perhaps even encouraging her to undertake further religious reform. Male translators could therefore advance their political and religious agendas by counseling the ruler on how best to govern. While printed translations also often served an advisory function (as in the case of Thomas Wilson's English translations of Demosthenes, which warned Elizabeth to act against Philip of Spain), manuscript translations had a singularity that enhanced their value, which was also signaled by material markers such as bindings, calligraphy, and illumination. Due to their externalization of the text's value, presentation copies of manuscript translations uniquely conveyed the cultural capital symbolized by the act of translation.

Female translators also presented patrons with translations as New Year's gifts to evoke their education and to establish their own religious credentials in relation to contemporary politics. As the previous chapter noted, Elizabeth Tudor presented Katherine Parr with an English translation of Marguerite de Navarre's *Le miroir de l'âme pécheresse* (*The Glasse of the Synnefull Soule,* 1544) from French verse into English prose. Around 1547, she also gave Edward VI a Latin translation of an Italian sermon by Bernardino Ochino ("Che cosa è Christo"). As in the case of Elizabeth's translation of Parr, the material nature of these manuscripts signaled the inherent value of the texts themselves. Elizabeth's rendering of Navarre still retains her intricately embroidered cover, featuring Parr's initials worked in silver and gold thread within a larger pattern of lovers' knots. While Elizabeth's Ochino has lost its cover, she transcribed the text in a decorative italic hand further ornamented by red ruling and capitals. The dedicatory prefaces to these texts asserted the devotional value of the translations, demonstrating how the cultural capital Elizabeth had gained from her education could be applied to her reader's spiritual welfare. Of course, Elizabeth was in her teens when she translated these works, and she probably did not have complete control over the choice of her source texts or even the composition of the dedicatory prefaces. Anne Lake Prescott has argued, for example, that Marguerite de Navarre's text was assigned to Elizabeth by a tutor or perhaps even Parr herself.[15] Meanwhile, Janel Mueller and Joshua Scodel contend that Elizabeth's tutor Jean Belmaine was responsible for suggesting that Elizabeth translate Calvin and for overseeing her preface to this work.[16] Elizabeth's Ochino is less clearly associated with her schoolroom, yet this work follows a similar template. Elizabeth had depicted her translation of Calvin as an appropriate tribute to Parr's interest in religious reform, aiming to advance the queen's "fervent zeal and perfect love . . . towards the selfsame God who created all things."[17] Elizabeth's Ochino shows that she continued to use translation to demonstrate her religious views, for she concludes her dedication of this translation to Edward by praising Ochino's Protestantism: "if nothing else commended the work, the reputation of the writer would adorn it enough: who, expelled from his homeland on account of religion and Christ, is driven to lead his life in foreign places and among unknown men."[18] Thomas Cranmer had recruited Ochino and other Continental reformers in order to advance the Edwardian Reformation, and Elizabeth's reference to Ochino's exile shows her tacit approval of this effort. By the time Elizabeth composed her translation of Ochino, then, she was well aware of the ways in which translation could signal the translator's political and religious stances.

As Elizabeth's careful portrayal of Calvin and Ochino suggests, while women's translations frequently had as much political resonance as those of male translators, female translators gestured at that potential in a much more subtle way than their male counterparts. If women were traditionally barred from the masculine public sphere, then they could not serve as political counselors in any official sense. Nevertheless, women often acted as unofficial counselors, and piety provided a culturally approved platform for their political intervention, particularly given Protestant emphasis on the spiritual equality of men and women.[19] Rather than providing specific advice to their dedicatees, female translators—like Elizabeth—evoke a shared religious viewpoint that subtly invests their translations with contemporary meaning. For example, Jessica L. Malay has shown that Jane Seager's 1589 presentation of an English translation of Filipo Barbieri's *Sibyllarum de Christo vaticinia* to Elizabeth took advantage of the millenarian associations of Sibyls to advance a militantly Protestant agenda, yet Seager only obliquely refers to religious matters by pointing out that her source text's "divine prophesies" are appropriate for Elizabeth as "cheife Defendress" of the Christian "faith."[20] Likewise, during Edward's reign Mary Basset presented Mary Tudor with an English and Latin translation of Eusebius that praised the work's depiction of church history to support Mary's defiance of current religious reforms: "Well maye I in dede, and with good right call thys storye notable, syth (onely scrypture excepted) no one worcke ys ther, that entreateth of more high, more pleasaunt, more profytable matters or thinges more mete and worthye to be redd, studyed, and knowen of every good chrysten man and woman."[21] Female translators also intervened in courtly intrigue, albeit obliquely. In 1550 Mildred Cooke Cecil presented Anne Seymour, Duchess of Somerset, with an English translation of Basil the Great's homily on Deuteronomy 15:9 ("Homilia in illud, Attende tibi ipsi"). The duchess and her husband were enmeshed in a web of courtly conspiracy and could have benefited greatly from the homily's admonitions to beware hidden enemies, yet Cecil's dedication underplays this coded message by concentrating instead on the duchess's reformist interest in church fathers such as Basil: "I trust the Author whose commendation my wordes can smally enlarge, will cleame suche favor that my labor commyng in his companye be thought as welcome for his sake."[22] While these translations offer political and religious counsel, the translators present themselves as fellow believers rather than advisers. By suggesting a shared religious viewpoint that was relevant to the current political climate, female translators actualized the cultural capital inherent in their knowledge of foreign languages. As a result, these women could function as sources of approved religious and political commentary, becoming in effect unofficial counselors.

Revising Philip Sidney's Legacy: Mary Sidney Herbert's *Psalmes* and Anglo-Spanish Relations

For Philip Sidney and Mary Sidney Herbert, translation was a natural outgrowth of their support for international Protestantism. As an activity that bridged cultural and linguistic divides, translation of foreign Protestant texts into English revealed common political and religious interests that might help strengthen English support for beleaguered Dutch and French Protestants. After Philip Sidney's death, Mary Sidney Herbert turned to translation to fashion herself as a political counselor who could extend her brother's legacy to contemporary events. While critics have recognized that these translation projects were spurred by Sidney's death, little attention has been paid to their connections with Sidney's own turn to translation of Huguenot texts during his final years. Like her brother, Mary Sidney Herbert translated religious works with political ramifications that demonstrated her knowledge of foreign languages

(French, Italian, Latin), using her cultural capital to advance the international Protestant cause. Among these translations, the presentation copy of the Sidney Psalter is notable for its attempt to realize that capital in relation to Elizabeth herself. Scholars have already shown that Sidney Herbert became her brother's representative and developed her own literary abilities by finishing the Sidney Psalter, but the unique presentation copy prepared for Elizabeth's intended visit to Wilton gestured at the political ramifications of translation to offer the queen advice consonant with the Sidney family's agendas.[23] Mary Sidney Herbert's translations, then, did not simply memorialize or mourn her brother: they developed her political credibility by building on contemporary perceptions of Philip Sidney's own translations.

Philip Sidney's translations of religious works were directly related to his attempts to develop diplomatic alliances between England and Continental Protestants.[24] In 1572, Sidney represented his uncle Robert Dudley, Earl of Leicester and leader of the militant Protestant faction at court, on a minor embassy to France, where he met Hubert Languet and Philippe de Mornay (known as Duplessis-Mornay), both Huguenots and proponents of cementing ties among Protestants of all nationalities. Sidney's sympathies with this circle may have been further reinforced after he witnessed the Saint Bartholomew's Day massacre in which Catholic mobs indiscriminately murdered Huguenots. From this point, Sidney actively worked to further Languet's idea that Protestants throughout Europe should join forces against Catholic countries, particularly Spain. In a 1577 Continental embassy, Sidney tried unsuccessfully to lay the groundwork for a league of Protestant countries, and he died in 1586 while participating in an English military campaign aiding Dutch Protestants who opposed Spanish control of the Netherlands. During his final years, Sidney imitated and translated French Huguenot works that later appeared to offer literary evidence of his political and religious sympathies: Clément Marot and Théodore de Bèze's *Les Pseaumes de David* (1562), Duplessis-Mornay's *De la verité de la religion chrestienne* (1581), and Guillaume de Salluste Du Bartas's *La sepmaine ou création du monde* (1578).[25] Sidney's translations of Du Bartas and Duplessis-Mornay were clearly linked to the Languet circle and its ideals. Duplessis-Mornay may have introduced Sidney to Du Bartas's work, since Du Bartas and Duplessis-Mornay admired each other.[26] Meanwhile, the Languet circle made a concerted effort during the early 1580s to disseminate Duplessis-Mornay's work internationally through translation. Lucas de Heere translated Duplessis-Mornay's *Traicté de l'église* (1579) into Dutch (*Tractaet ofte handelinge van de Kercke*, 1580), and in 1581

Duplessis-Mornay himself translated *De la verité* into Latin at the urging of Languet (*De veritate religionis Christianae*).[27] Alan Sinfield has noted that *De la verité* had an anti-Catholic agenda, which may explain the Languet circle's interest in translating this work.[28]

During the final years of his life, Sidney undertook a related project, creating versifications of the Bible's first forty-three psalms in imitation of the Marot-Bèze Psalter popular among French Huguenots.[29] While Sidney's interest may have been sparked by his familiarity with the Huguenots, who sang psalms as battle hymns, Sidney had closer models for the politicization of psalms, which had become linked with English religious reform during the Henrician era.[30] Both Thomas Wyatt and Henry Howard, Earl of Surrey, had turned to the psalms as a means of veiled political commentary during imprisonment.[31] Similarly, two of Sidney's Dudley uncles—John Dudley, Earl of Warwick, and Robert Dudley—composed adaptations of psalms that may have served as a means of political protest while the two were imprisoned in the Tower of London after their father's 1553 attempt to crown Lady Jane Grey.[32] Certainly John Dudley's version of Psalm 55 could easily be read as a commentary on his incarceration: "Breake downe the wicked swarminge flockes/that at mye fall rejoyce/whose cruell ravening myndes/to work my bane are bent." Robert Dudley's version of Psalm 94 pointedly criticizes "those hawltie men" who "so lordlye us disdayne" and laments his lack of allies: "When the wicked rulde/and bare the swaye by might/No one wolde preace to take my parte/or once defend my right."[33] As a typical devotional exercise, psalm reading and translation might seem innocuous enough, yet within the English tradition pioneered by Wyatt, psalms functioned simultaneously as a display of Protestant credentials and as a political statement. Sidney's own interest in the politicization of the psalms can be glimpsed in his sources. Besides drawing from the Book of Common Prayer, he turned to versions associated with religious reform: Marot-Bèze, the Geneva Bible, and Bèze's *Psalmorum Davidis* (1580).[34] All of Sidney's translations, then, bear the mark of his religious and political agendas, particularly his deep interest in advancing the ideal of international Protestantism associated with Languet.

Sidney may have died before capitalizing on the possible applications of these works, but his contemporaries were not hesitant to exploit their latent potential. In 1587 Arthur Golding dedicated his own supposed completion of Sidney's unfinished Duplessis-Mornay to Leicester, reminding readers that Sidney died "of manly wounds received in service of his Prince, in defence of persons oppressed, in maintenance of the only true Catholick & Christian Religion."[35] This elegiac evocation of Sidney's saintly death on the battlefields of the Netherlands informs Golding's presentation of the unfinished translation itself as part of Sidney's militant Protestantism, a "peece of service which he had intended to the Muses or rather to Christes Church and his native Countrie."[36] Fulke Greville, one of the greatest proponents of Sidney's reputation as a Protestant martyr, also viewed Sidney's translations as evidence of his religious sympathies. In November 1586, Greville wrote to Sir Francis Walsingham to block the publication of Sidney's *Old Arcadia* and, very probably, Golding's forthcoming translation of Duplessis-Mornay: "He hathe most excellently translated among divers other notable workes monsieur du plessis book against atheisme, which is since donn by an other, so as bothe in respect of the love betwen plessis & him besyds other affinities in ther courses but espetially sir philips uncomparable Judgement, I think fit ther be made a stey of that mercenary book to[o] that sir philip might have all thos religous honors which ar worthely dew to his lyfe & deathe, many other works as bartas his semeyne, 40 of the spalms [*sic*] translated in to myter . . . requyre the care of his frends."[37] Greville suggests that Golding's imminent publication is an affront to Sidney's martyrlike death even as he evokes the shared piety of Duplessis-Mornay and Sidney by mentioning their "affinities." As these reactions suggest, contemporaries retroactively perceived Sidney's religious translations as evidence of his devotion to the Protestant cause and, in turn, as part of his legacy as a Protestant martyr.

When Mary Sidney Herbert chose to translate religious works into English, she participated in a political activity that extended her brother's legacy. While critics once saw Sidney Herbert's translations as the products of her mourning for Philip Sidney and other family members, recent work has emphasized the political connotations of these texts, especially the 1592 publication of her translations of Duplessis-Mornay's *A Discourse of Life and Death* (*Excellent discourse de la vie et de la mort,* 1575) and Robert Garnier's *Antonius* (*Marc Antoine,* 1585).[38] Margaret Hannay has observed that Sidney Herbert's translation of Duplessis-Mornay evokes Philip Sidney's Continental contacts.[39] More recently, Danielle Clarke has contended that Sidney Herbert's *Antonius* relayed her concerns about the English succession, while Victor Skretkowicz has situated the publication of these works in relation to Duplessis-Mornay's 1592 embassy, which sought Elizabeth's financial and military support for the civil war between Henry IV of France and his Catholic subjects.[40] Strikingly, the volume's title page identifies Sidney Herbert as the translator without any prefatory disclaimers of modesty, serving as a reminder of the Sidney family's religious and political views. By turning to translation in the wake of her brother's death, then, Mary Sidney Herbert undertook a politicized activity that developed her own authority as an advocate of international Protestantism.

Elizabeth's proposed visit to Wilton during the summer of 1599 gave Sidney Herbert a special opportunity to apply the cultural capital of translation to a recent development within English foreign policy: the potential end of England's military involvement in the Netherlands. Critics have noted that the Psalter has political relevance to the international Protestantism espoused by the Sidney family, yet the question of why Sidney Herbert would want to present the work—first drafted by 1594—to the queen in 1599 remains unanswered.[41] During this summer, Elizabeth was poised to begin peace negotiations with Spain, represented by Archduke Albert, signaling a possible shift in Anglo-Spanish relations that had obvious relevance to the Sidney family. Elizabeth had long supported Dutch Protestants in their efforts to end Spanish control of the Netherlands, and France had served as a crucial ally in this enterprise. Yet in May 1598, Henry IV negotiated peace with Spain in the Treaty of Vervins, forcing his Dutch and English allies to decide whether they should continue to wage war against Spain.[42] While the Cecil faction maintained that Elizabeth should pursue peace with Spain, Robert Devereux, Earl of Essex, argued that the war should continue, most infamously in his manuscript letter to Francis Bacon, which saw scribal publication in 1598. For Essex, religion was a key factor in determining English foreign policy: "It is with out all doubt that there can be no peace concluded, except popish religion, be either universally established, or else freely exercised in the townes and provinces where nowe it is banished, Allowe the first, that they banish Gods true service, to bring in idolatrie, the[y] leave truth to receive falshood. . . . Allowe the second you bring in a pluralitie of religions, which is no lesse crime."[43] Characteristically, Elizabeth chose a middle course, lowering England's financial support for the war in a December 1598 treaty that arranged for the Dutch to repay some of their debts to England and to assume financial responsibility for English troops serving in the Netherlands.[44] Elizabeth also successfully argued that the six-month grace period granted to her by Vervins for negotiations with Spain should be extended until Albert returned to the Netherlands with his new bride, the Infanta Isabella. The archduke was not expected to return until late 1599, making that summer an ideal time to petition the queen on behalf of the Dutch.

Letters from Robert Sidney indicate that he—and very likely his sister as well—supported Essex's advocacy of continued military involvement in the Netherlands. On January 25, 1598, Sidney wrote to Essex with an update about the movements of the Dutch envoys heading to the Vervins negotiations, expressing his hope that Elizabeth would not abandon the Dutch: "If they can persuade the King of France and her Majesty to continue the war, it is that which they most desire. If they cannot, yet surely they will go on and once more, of themselves, sustain the weight of the King of Spain's forces. But I trust her Majesty will not forsake them, nor enter into a peace with him of whom she can expect no faith."[45] Sidney's distrust of the Spanish king ("him of whom she can expect no faith") is further evidenced by another letter reminding Essex of the precedent of 1588, when Spain used peace talks as a diversionary tactic even as it prepared its armada: "An army there is surely there in providing, and such as cannot be but to our cost, except that our reasons this year can prove of more force than they did the year '88."[46] Sidney was not alone in worrying about another armada. Even Elizabeth attempted to use these fears as a bargaining chip in the Vervins negotiations, instructing Robert Cecil to inform Henry IV of recent rumors: "Wee are still in eminent expectation of invasion by the Spaniard (a matter wherwith the whole world is filled)."[47] Yet Robert Sidney eventually resigned himself to the idea of peace with Spain, writing to Robert Cecil on April 26, 1599, about his absence from his command at Flushing: "Perhaps the Queen may think it right for me to be at Flushing because of the treaty of peace now on hand. Last year I was noted to have opposed it to my power. . . . But I know I can neither further nor hinder it. If I am bidden, I can say my opinion and follow what the Queen shall command."[48] Sidney's grudging acceptance of the situation probably reflected the waning fortunes of Essex—who had alienated the queen in June 1598 by reaching for his sword after she boxed his ears—and, in consequence, anti-Spanish policy. By March 1599 Essex had left for Ireland to deal with the insurrection led by the Earl of Tyrone and thus was preoccupied with more immediate concerns than the Spanish. Mary Sidney Herbert was probably aware of the precarious state of the Dutch cause, as Robert Sidney visited her at Wilton on May 31, just a month after his pragmatic letter to Cecil.[49] The queen's proposed visit to Wilton that summer would give Sidney Herbert an opportunity to remind Elizabeth of the Sidney family's fervent anti-Spanish stance. Not only was Wilton itself strongly linked to Philip Sidney, who had retired there while in disgrace with Elizabeth, but the *Psalmes* would be an ideal text, coauthored with her brother and, as an imitation of Marot-Bèze, easily linked to the Protestant cause for which Sidney had died.

Mary Sidney Herbert oversaw the preparation of a presentation copy whose aesthetic appeal would immediately indicate the special value of the *Psalmes* and, as a result, hint at its political capital. William A. Ringler Jr. proposed MS A as the presentation copy, an identification made probable by its unique material features.[50] John Davies of Hereford transcribed the poems in a distinctive calligraphic hand, florid with ornamental otiose strokes that elevate the text above a merely functional purpose. Davies enhances the work's decorative charm and suggests its value by using gold ink for most capital letters and by gilding the lobes and clubs of lowercase letters such as *d, b, f,* and *h*. The manuscript also has a complex scheme of red ruling that indicates the overall emphasis placed on presentation by creating multiple inset panels. Not only is every page ruled lengthwise and widthwise along each side to create a large rectangle, but each psalm's Latin incipit and number are separately underlined in red. Further ruling along the left side of every page sets off the initial capital letter of each verse, already highlighted in gold, from the psalm itself by creating a sizable margin of up to an inch and a half. Meanwhile, every psalm is boxed in with red ruling above its first line and below its last line. This intricate system of ruling situates the psalms within substantial empty spaces, indicating little need to be concerned with wasting paper. The work's original binding of crimson velvet, now lost, must have only further accentuated the overall presentation.[51] The elaborate hand, striking gold ink, and complex ruling ultimately create a larger effect of lavishness that reflects the value of the work itself, a text initially composed by a king and now presented to a queen. As the accompanying dedicatory poem "Even Now That Care" notes, the Psalter was particularly appropriate to Elizabeth, perhaps especially so given Sidney Herbert's possible belief that Elizabeth herself had translated Psalm 13: "A King should onely to a Queene bee sent."[52] The text's material features thus insist upon the regal nature of this gift, suggesting that this unique copy of the *Psalmes* was well worth a queen's attention.

The prefatory poems written by Sidney Herbert accentuate the cultural capital implied by these unique features by first connecting the work to English Protestantism and then more specifically to Philip Sidney. While the first leaves of MS A have been torn out, scholars agree that the text was most likely prefaced by two poems extant in MS J, a copy of MS A: "Even Now" and "To the Angell Spirit."[53] The first of these poems, "Even Now," simultaneously politicizes the Psalter and appeals to Elizabeth's well-known interest in translation by describing the text as a naturalized English citizen with a new set of clothing, imagery associated with translation:

> . . . hee [Philip] did warpe, I weav'd this webb to end;
> the stuffe not ours, our worke no curious thing,
> Wherein yet well wee thought the Psalmist King
> Now English denizend, though Hebrue borne,
> woold to thy musicke undispleased sing,
> Oft having worse, without repining worne.
> (*PTC,* pp. 102–3, lines 27–32)

Sidney Herbert pointedly disclaims responsibility for the content of the Psalter: "the stuffe not ours." She and Philip have merely fashioned the shape, or English form, which is depicted as "A liverie robe to bee bestowed by thee [Elizabeth]" (*PTC,* p. 103, line 34). This elaborate metaphor presents the Psalter as "liverie" for David, now an Englishman who sings in the queen's service. Similarly, in "Angell Spirit" Sidney Herbert notes that "heavens King may daigne his owne transform'd/in substance no, but superficiall tire" (*PTC,* p. 110, lines 8–9). Although critics have noted Sidney Herbert's use of translation imagery, its full importance has yet to be explored, perhaps because of the tendency to categorize the *Psalmes* in terms that emphasize her creativity.[54] Neither Sidney nor Sidney Herbert followed modern translation practices, as both drew upon sources in French, Latin, and English rather than the Hebrew primary source text.[55] Nevertheless, as Hannibal Hamlin has pointed out, modern conceptions of translation do not apply particularly well to early modern psalms, which blurred the line between translation and paraphrase.[56] Certainly, title pages for metrical psalms by authors such as Francis Bacon suggest that the term "translation" could be applied even to the act of versifying psalms.[57] If some manuscripts of the Sidney Psalter refer to the work as being "translated" or "metaphrased" (that is, "to translate, esp. in verse"), both John Donne and John Harington punningly referred to the *Psalmes* as translations.[58] Donne's laudatory poem describes the Sidneys as "translators" now "translated" to heaven, while Harington's "In Prayse of Two Worthy Translations" praises both Mary, Countess of Shrewsbury, and Sidney Herbert: "A Colledge this translates, the tother Psalms."[59] Sidney Herbert's own use of imagery associated with translation in these dedicatory poems may have been calculated to appeal specifically to Elizabeth, whose reputation for Protestant piety had been established by Bale's publication of her translation of Marguerite de Navarre.

"Even Now That Care" offers a more specific political context for the psalms by alluding to contemporary European history. The poem opens by questioning whether Elizabeth has leisure for "receiving Rimes," given the current political climate:

One instant will, or willing can shee lose
I say not reading, but receiving Rimes,
On whom in chiefe dependeth to dispose
what Europe acts in theise most active times?
(*PTC*, p. 102, lines 5–8)

Sidney Herbert's use of polyptoton ("acts," "active") helps cast the queen as a Protestant monarch since "active" suggested the action-oriented stance of militant Protestants (*PTC*, p. 100). These lines may more pointedly refer to the aftermath of Vervins, when Elizabeth's decision regarding Spain would determine "what Europe acts." The third stanza, which answers this initial question, is evocative of the lull in negotiations during the archduke's absence: "Cares though still great, cannot bee greatest still,/Busines most ebb, though Leasure never flowe" (*PTC*, p. 102, lines 17–18). Sidney Herbert presents the Psalter as fit reading for such an "ebb" in "Busines" by noting the parallels between the careers of David and Elizabeth: "ev'n thy Rule is painted in his Raigne" (*PTC*, p. 104, line 65). Just as David withstood heathen enemies, so Elizabeth has triumphed over Catholic "foes of heav'n" (*PTC*, p. 104, line 70), including the Spanish Armada: "The very windes did on thy partie blowe/and rocks in armes thy foe men eft defie" (*PTC*, p. 104, lines 77–78).[60] Given ongoing fears of another armada mentioned by Robert Sidney and Elizabeth herself in 1598 and 1599, this allusion to the armada may have evoked the consequences of peace talks with Spain. The poem concludes with an idealized description of Elizabeth dictating European policy:

Kings on a Queene enforst their states to lay;
Main-lands for Empire waiting on an Ile;
Men drawne by worth a woman to obay;
one moving all, herself unmov'd the while:
Truthes restitution, vanitie exile,
wealth sprung of want, warr held without annoye.
(*PTC*, p. 104, lines 81–86)

While Elizabeth "mov[es] all," bringing "Kings" and "Main-lands" to "obay" her power, England itself experiences prosperity even as it conducts "warr . . . without annoye," perhaps a reference to England's engagement in military actions outside its borders, as in the Netherlands. "Even Now" thus places the Psalter within the political discourse cultivated by Sidney, offering an argument that England should continue its active opposition to Spain and, as a result, its support of international Protestantism.

The second prefatory poem, "Angell Spirit," provides further justification for anti-Spanish policies by invoking Philip Sidney himself. Although "Even Now That Care" clearly presents the Psalter to Elizabeth, "Angell Spirit" indicates that the work possesses a second dedicatee: "To thee pure sprite, to thee alone's addres't/this coupled worke" (*PTC,* p. 110, lines 1–2). This initial description of Philip as a "pure sprite" offers a punning reference to both his virtue as well as his demise, as without a body he is now only "sprite," or spirit. Given the legendary status of Sidney's death, this opening reference conjures up his reputation as a Protestant martyr, which is reinforced by the third stanza's lamentation of his untimely end: "Had that soule which honor brought to rest/too soone not left and reft the world of all/what man could showe" (*PTC,* p. 110, lines 15–17). The "honor" of Sidney's death in turn allows him to reap a heavenly reward that further politicizes the *Psalmes* to follow:

> Thy Angells soule with highest Angells plac't
> There blessed sings enjoying heav'n-delights
>   thy Makers praise: as farr from earthy tast
>   as here thy workes so worthilie embrac't
> By all of worth, where never Envie bites.
> (*PTC,* p. 111, lines 59–63)

As Hannay has noted, these lines may obliquely refer to Elizabeth's refusal to support Sidney's political career due to her concerns over his flourishing international reputation.[61] Although this "Envie" prevented Sidney from advancement on earth, no such limitation bars his progress in heaven, where his "Angells soule" fittingly enjoys the sphere of "highest Angells." Sidney Herbert thus obliquely chides Elizabeth for hindering her brother's career by giving way to "Envie." In doing so, she presents the Psalter as evidence of the "worth" Sidney held while alive, linking the text to his thwarted political ambitions. Finally, Sidney Herbert positions herself as the current public representative of Sidney's pro-Protestant politics, signing the work, "By the Sister of that Incomporable Sidney" (*PTC,* p. 112). "Angell Spirit" therefore links Philip Sidney's dashed political hopes to the Psalter, transferring Sidney's cachet to Sidney Herbert as the completer of her brother's unfinished work.

Rumors about the "Invisible Armada" of 1599 led Elizabeth to cancel her planned visit to Wilton, and MS A in turn remained there. While Sidney Herbert continued to update the manuscript, Davies never finished the elaborate system of ruling and gilding that distinguishes the majority of this copy. As a result, comparison of MS A's physical characteristics with the textual transmission of the Psalter reveals that Sidney Herbert was still revising the conclusions to five of her brother's Psalms while Davies prepared the presentation copy. The creation of MS A required several stages: after the psalms had been transcribed, Davies returned to the text to add in numbers, Latin incipits, gold capitals, and gilding.[62] The ruling of the psalm's numbers, incipits, and concluding lines must have also occurred during this second stage. Psalms 16, 22, 23, and 26 all end with final stanzas that lack concluding ruling and gilding, suggesting that Davies was unable to transcribe these psalms in their entirety during both the first and second stages.[63] He may not have completed these embellishments because Elizabeth's canceled visit had altered the text's purpose. In fact, Psalm 16 concludes not in Davies's calligraphy but with a more utilitarian hand also tentatively ascribed to Davies.[64] The textual transmission of the Psalter offers further evidence that these psalms remained incomplete up to this point. Sidney Herbert made three rounds of revisions to the Psalter, and MS A and its copies F and J represent the second round.[65] Tellingly, the manuscripts preserving the first set of revisions, now known as the δ tradition, generally omit the revised conclusions found in MS A or offer preliminary versions of these stanzas, indicating that these changes were part of the second round of revisions.[66] Yet most of Sidney Herbert's secondary revisions are incorporated seamlessly into MS A, implying that these changes to Psalms 16, 22, 23, and 26 occurred fairly late in the revision process. Additional support for this conclusion can be found in MS B, Samuel Woodford's partial copy of Sidney Herbert's working papers.[67] The final stanzas of these psalms were crossed out, with an accompanying note instructing that space be left for corrections: "Leave roome for this staff" (Psalm 16), "leave space for this" (Psalm 22), "leave space for six lines" (Psalm 23), and "Leave space" (Psalm 26).[68] While transcribing MS A, Davies did just that, copying and gilding the earlier portions of these psalms but leaving space for new versions of the final stanzas to be inserted. Psalm 1 also belongs to this group of unfinished psalms as it is missing in the δ tradition but preserved in MS J, a copy of MS A. Significantly, MS B contains a notation indicating that this psalm was not finished, "these altered. Q[uaere]."[69] Thus Mary Sidney Herbert was in the process of finishing the final stanzas of Psalms 1, 16, 22, 23, and 26 while Davies was copying MS A. She probably revised these psalms because they ended with incomplete stanzas, which she had already decided not to use in her own work.[70] Scholars have primarily considered Sidney Herbert's revisions of her brother's psalms in terms of her development of poetic abilities.[71] These later revisions, however, underscore the political sentiments expressed in "Even Now" and "Angell Spirit," reframing Philip Sidney's psalms as a source of counsel applicable to current English relations with Spain.

As the commentary in the Geneva and Bishops' Bibles indicates, early modern readers viewed Psalm 1 as an introduction to the entire Book of Psalms, which meant that this psalm had special significance. Philip Sidney's original version of verses 4 through 6 offered a loose paraphrase focusing on the psychology of the wicked:

> Such blessings shall not wycked wretches see:
>   But lyke vyle chaffe with winde shal scattred be.
> For neither shall the men in sin delighted
>   Consist, when they to highest doome are cited,
> Ne yet shall suffred be a place to take,
>   Wher godly men do their assembly make.
>
> For God doth know, and knowing doth approve,
>   The trade of them, that just proceeding love;
> But they that sinne, in sinfull breast do cherish;
>   The way they go shal be their way to perish.[72]

Sidney's version melded Marot and Bèze ("Such blessings" approximates "telles vertus"), the Book of Common Prayer ("they are lyke the chaffe which the wynde scattereth away"), and Bèze's *Psalmorum* ("Consist" renders "consistent" while "approve" translates "approbat").[73] Sidney Herbert, in contrast, grounds her revisions in the Calvinist-oriented Geneva Bible:

> Not soe the wicked; Butt like chaff with wind
>   scatt'red, shall neither stay in Judgment find
> nor with the just, bee in their meetings placed:
>   for good mens waies by God are knowne & graced.
> Butt who from Justice sinnfully doe stray,
>   the way they goe, shall be their ruins way.[74]

This revision carefully compresses Sidney's original, condensing his portrayal of the Lord's approval of "godly men" to refocus the psalm's conclusion on God's just punishment of sinners. By beginning the stanza with the negative adverb "not," Sidney Herbert simultaneously echoes the Geneva Bible's phrasing ("The wicked are not so") and more strongly emphasizes the psalm's turn from the virtuous man to the evildoer than

Sidney had done.[75] Sidney Herbert may have found the Geneva Bible a particularly apt source because of its emphasis on the eventual downfall of the "wicked." The Geneva Bible's argument to Psalm 1, for example, states "that the wicked contemners of God, thogh they seme for a while happie, yet at length shal come to miserable destruction." Sidney Herbert's interest in this interpretation of the psalm can be seen in her echo of the Geneva Bible's version of verse 5 ("the wicked shal not stand in the Judgement"), as the marginal note for "Judgement" explains that the wicked will "tremble, when they fele Gods wrath." Since "Even now" had paralleled David's enemies with the "foes of heav'n" that threatened Elizabeth, the "wicked" men of this first psalm could possibly include Catholic Spain. The skillful enjambment separating "wind" and "scatt'red" offers a visual demonstration of the wicked man's inability to endure God's "Judgment" even as it might evoke the description of the Spanish Armada's fate in "Even Now": "The very windes did on thy partie blowe" (*PTC,* p. 104, line 77). Within the context provided by the prefatory poems, Psalm 1's concluding lines may serve as a warning against allying with God's foes, especially as "stray" echoes Sidney's praise of the virtuous man's rejection of poor advice at the Psalm's start: "He blessed is, who neither loosely treads/The straying stepps as wicked Counsel leades."[76] Sidney Herbert thus alters her brother's version of this psalm so that it offers coded political guidance about the dangers of joining forces with the wicked, whose destruction is inevitably assured.

The new version of Psalm 26 provides another warning about evil counsel with additional poignancy due to its potential link to Sidney's stunted courtly career, which "Angell Spirit" had attributed to "Envie." Sidney's versions of verses 4 and 5 could be read as a personal rejection of courtly vanity: "I did not them frequent/Who be to vaineness bent,/Nor kept with base dissemblers company."[77] Similarly, his rendering of verses 10 through 12 emphasizes David's rejection of corruption:

> Whose hands do handle nought,
> But led by wicked thought
> That hand whose strength should help of bribes is full.
> But in integrity
> My stepps shall guided be,
> Then me redeem Lord then be mercifull.
> Even truth that for me sayes
> My foot on justice stayes,
> And tongue is prest to publish out thy prayse.[78]

While Sidney largely relied on the Book of Common Prayer and the Geneva Bible for this versification, he also included several elements from Bèze: "wicked thought" derives from "male cogitata" while "integrity" translates "integer."[79] Sidney Herbert uses Bèze even more extensively, basing her version on the 1580 English translation by Anthony Gilby:

> With handes of wicked shifts
> with right hands stain'd with gifts
> But while I walk in my unspotted waies
> redeeme and show mee grace
> so I in publique place
> Sett on plaine ground will thee Jehovah praise.[80]

While "wicked shifts" rephrases Gilby's "wicked devises," "publique place" also originates in his translation: "I . . . will magnifie thy name in the publique congregations."[81] Furthermore, Sidney Herbert probably derives "stain'd" from Gilby's translation of Bèze's argument:

> It is a very hard thing in the court to retain true Religion & uprightnesse of life & conversation chiefly when wicked men do reigne, and their flatterers do rage partly open by violence, partly by false accusations, & an other sort doth sing in their eares that they must frame their wits to serve all turns and purposes, even as the fish called Polipus doth change himself into the colour of the stone whereunto he cleaveth. . . . But David . . . still continueth to abhorre the councels & the examples of the wicked.[82]

In paraphrastically translating the Greek proverb "Take the mind of a polyp," Gilby adds new information about the chameleonic nature of this fish. His source text reads, "ac quibusdam etiam prophanum illud proverbium specie prudentiae occinentibus, polypodos noon esche [*sic*]" (and also some crying that pagan proverb with the semblance of wisdom, "take the mind of the polyp").[83] As Gilby's focus on color is not found in any of Sidney Herbert's other known sources, his simile may explain her use of "stain'd," a clever pun on two of the verb's meanings: "to alter the colour of" and "To defile or corrupt morally."[84] If Bèze's argument suggests that "stain'd" had political connotations as a symbol for the changeability of the immoral courtier, the substitution of "gifts" (taken from the Book of Common Prayer) for "bribes" evokes the politicized sphere of Tudor gift exchange. These oblique references to courtly corruption reframe Sidney's marginalization at court as a sign of his righteousness even as they reinforce the warning contained in Psalm 1 regarding evil counselors. If David—and implicitly Philip Sidney—is a model for Elizabeth, then this psalm suggests that she should reject courtly guile and embrace an unpopular but godly course, a sentiment with personal and political relevance given the militant stance of "Even Now."

Sidney Herbert's revision of Psalm 23 also takes advantage of the Psalter's authorial multiplicity to reiterate Sidney's saintly legacy as depicted in "Angell Spirit."[85] Sidney had elaborated on the metaphors of hospitality implicit in verses 5 and 6:

> With oyle Thou dost anoynt my head,
> And so my cup dost fill
> That it doth spill.
> Thus thus shall all my days be fede,
> This mercy is so sure
> It shall endure,
> And long yea long abide I shall,
> There where the Lord of all
> Doth hold his hall.[86]

As before, Sidney relies on sources associated with Calvinism while composing his version. Besides following the phrasing of the Geneva Bible ("thou doest anoint mine head with oyle"), he may draw upon Bèze, who alone among his sources explicitly develops the theme of hospitality: "The . . . similitude is taken from them that keepe good hospitalitie, which most liberally receive those travellers that come unto them."[87] Sidney Herbert retains this elaboration while also adding fresh material from Bèze that subtly reshapes the psalm's conclusion:

> Thou oil'st my head thou fill'st my cupp:
> nay more thou endlesse good,
> shalt give me food,
> To thee, I say, ascended up,
> where thou the lord of all,
> dost hold thy hall.[88]

Sidney Herbert probably drew upon Bèze's argument in substituting "To thee I say ascended up," a description of heavenly translation, for "abide I shall," a reference to living in the house of the Lord. Of her known sources, only Bèze specifically mentions this idea of climbing to heaven:

"It teacheth us that wee ought to rise [assurgere] from those transitorie benefites to those everlasting and heavenly blessinges."[89] While referring to this idea in a highly compressed manner, Sidney Herbert uses the past participle "ascended." Since this tense could suggest that the speaker's flight has already taken place, Sidney Herbert's revision may have evoked "Angell Spirit" and its description of Sidney's place in heaven: "Thy Angells soule with highest Angells plac't/There blessed sings enjoying heav'n-delights/thy Makers praise" (*PTC,* p. 111, lines 59–61). This new conclusion to Psalm 23 allows the voices of David and Philip Sidney to coexist, reinforcing the paratextual depiction of Sidney's heavenly reward as a Protestant martyr who had died while fighting against Spain and for the Dutch.

Within the context established by MS A, Sidney Herbert's revisions could be read as promoting the political aims of the Sidney family, particularly its support of international Protestantism. While Essex had turned his attention to Ireland and Robert Sidney had diffidently accepted the idea of peace with Spain, Sidney Herbert offered a warning that reiterated their earlier concerns about allying with England's foes even as she reminded Elizabeth of her family's sacrifices for this cause. Indeed, the Psalter provided a particularly convenient means of commenting on England's foreign policy due to the apparent connection between Philip Sidney's translations of Protestant texts and his death in the Netherlands. The authorial multiplicity of the work—whose authors include God, David, Sidney, and Sidney Herbert—thus allowed Sidney Herbert to portray the Psalter as an important source of godly political counsel. Addressed to Elizabeth during a delay in negotiations with Spain, the Sidney Psalter encouraged the queen to identify with the militant Protestantism of its authors and to maintain the anti-Catholic stance of her earlier years.

Book and Scepter: Elizabeth's Boethius and the Conversion of Henry IV

As queen, Elizabeth I received numerous dedications of manuscript and print translations that participated in the courtly system of gift exchange. Although Elizabeth herself had little need for patronage at this point, she continued to compose translations that displayed her linguistic abilities. Yet instead of translating Protestant vernacular works, Elizabeth turned to Latin texts reminiscent of her humanist education: Boethius, Cicero, Horace, Plutarch (via Erasmus's Latin translation), Pseudo-Seneca,

Sallust, and Seneca. Elizabeth thus utilized classical literature to display a humanist education typically associated with men, both counteracting stereotypes of feminine weakness and demonstrating her ability to govern.[90] Elizabeth's later translations, however, require further scrutiny on their own terms, for Elizabeth used this activity in a distinctive manner separate from the translation practices of her courtiers: to construct her public and private personae as a queen and a woman. It is a critical commonplace that Elizabeth and her subjects adroitly adapted the medieval conception of the king's two bodies to counter misgivings about her gender.[91] As judges in a 1561 court case stated, "the King has in him two Bodies, *viz.* a Body natural, and a Body politic. His Body natural (if it be considered in itself) is a Body mortal, subject to all Infirmities that come by Nature or Accident. . . . But his Body politic is a Body that cannot be seen or handled, consisting of Policy and Government, . . . and this Body is utterly void of Infancy, and old Age, and other natural Defects."[92] Common wisdom held that women—as the "weaker" sex—should be ruled by men, making Elizabeth's role as queen both anomalous and potentially subversive. Yet Elizabeth's body politic was free from all "Infirmities" present in her body natural, presumably including her femininity, as Elizabeth herself suggested in her famous speech at Tilbury: "I know I have the body but of a weak and feeble woman, but I have the heart and stomach of a king and of a king of England too."[93] As Carole Levin's insightful account of this phenomenon reveals, the queen and her advisers also performatively displayed the queen's "weak" body natural for political purposes such as explaining her refusal to marry.[94] Elizabeth's later translations can further advance our understanding of her deployment of the king's two bodies. Never meant for public circulation and therefore ostensibly private, Elizabeth's translations showed her personal interest in the continued acquisition of cultural capital. Yet the link between translation and political commentary meant that Elizabeth's efforts could be viewed as a form of self-counsel. Her translations therefore became a pivot point around which her personae as private woman and queen moved. As Elizabeth schooled her body natural with translation, itself a humanist pedagogical tool, she positioned herself as a counselor worthy of governing the body politic.

Throughout her reign, Elizabeth allowed select members of her court to become spectators of her ongoing self-education by participating in learned activities that were apparently private yet that provided the raw materials for her pose as a knowledgeable queen. For example, Roger Ascham begins *The Scholemaster* (1570) with an account of his ongoing reading with the queen in 1563, long after he had formally ceased to be her tutor: "After dinner I went up to read with the Queenes Majestie. We red than togither in the Greke tonge, as I well remember, that noble Oration of Demosthenes against Aeschines, for his false dealing in his Ambassage to king Philip of Macedonie. Syr Rich[ard] Sackvile came up sone after: and finding me in hir Majesties privie chamber, he tooke me by the hand."[95] Ascham's anecdote depicts Elizabeth sharing her personal enjoyment in classical literature with the tutor of her school days in her "privie chamber," the queen's private room within her castle at Windsor as well as the very center of her court. Although Ascham presents reading as evidence of Elizabeth's personal inclinations, Sackville's interruption is a reminder that this room was also a public area occupied by her privy counselors and ladies-in-waiting, among others.[96] By reading classical texts with Ascham, Elizabeth could adroitly use the privacy suggested by her privy chamber to indicate her personal grounding in humanist ideals. Even as late as 1601, Elizabeth was publicly reading Latin, although she required some assistance with vocabulary.[97] During these nominally private displays, Elizabeth reverted to the subordinate position of a student, schooling her body natural with classical texts deemed relevant to governance.[98]

In her official capacity as queen, Elizabeth drew on the cultural capital acquired through this private study to establish her own political power as an adviser and ruler. In 1563 she published her *Sententiae,* a collection of concise maxims from classical writers, church fathers, and the Bible that she had arranged thematically around topical subjects including rule, counsel, and war. Not only did Elizabeth's *Sententiae* gesture at the queen's learning, but it also suggested that that knowledge could be utilized within her day-to-day governing.[99] Furthermore, Elizabeth incorporated classical quotations into letters and speeches to fashion herself as a counselor worthy of respect. In 1564 Elizabeth gave a Latin oration at Cambridge that began with a modest deprecation of her femininity: "Feminine modesty, most faithful subjects and most celebrated university, prohibits the delivery of a rude and uncultivated speech in such a gathering of most learned men." Elizabeth then revealed her own erudition by citing Demosthenes as a precedent for her royal authority: "The words of superiors, as Demosthenes said, are as the books of their inferiors, and the example of a prince has the force of law."[100] Similarly, Elizabeth warned James VI of Scotland in 1583 about his councillors' treachery in a letter that alluded to Isocrates: "I would Isocrates' noble lesson were not forgotten, that wills the Emperor his sovereign to make his words of more account than other men their oaths, as meetest ensigns to show the truest badge of a Prince's arms."[101] Susan Frye has persuasively noted that this allusion allowed Elizabeth to occupy a doubly male position as James's "schoolmaster" and fellow "prince."[102] Perhaps most famously, Elizabeth deftly proved her competence in 1597 with an impromptu Latin rebuke of a Polish ambassador, Paul Dzialynski, thereby asserting her own ability to rule.[103] Throughout her reign, then, Elizabeth consistently used her knowledge of classical languages as a basis for presenting herself as a prince with masculine learning.

Elizabeth's translations, like her reading and citation of classical authors, symbolized her personal interest in humanist knowledge that could be applied to governing the realm. Indeed, the material features and limited circulation of her later translations characterize these works as private productions linked to Elizabeth's personal, rather than royal, inclinations. Unlike Elizabeth's early translations, the majority of her later translations were not presentation copies bestowed as gifts. Only two translations can be definitively identified as presents: two letters given to her godson, John Harington (Seneca's *Epistula* 170 and Cicero's *Ad familiaries* 2.6). Neither of these texts survives in manuscript, but scholars have speculated that her translation of *Pro Marcello* was presented to an unknown Oxford don during the queen's 1592 visit.[104] *Pro Marcello,* like Elizabeth's other extant holograph translations from this period, differs considerably from the lavish presentation of her early translations. Rather than the neat italic of Elizabeth's earlier presentation copies, these texts are written in her late italic hand, a loose scrawl. The presentational value of Elizabeth's *Pro Marcello* is limited to two features: her holograph handwriting and a royal watermark (the monogram *ER* surrounded by knotwork and surmounted by a crown). Rather than demonstrating the importance of her work through features such as decorative handwriting, ruling, and embroidery, Elizabeth's *Pro Marcello* gains worth in its appearance of being dashed off during a fleeting moment of spare time. Extant holograph copies of Elizabeth's Boethius, Horace, and Plutarch are similarly functional rather than ornamental. Of these, Elizabeth's Boethius is a foul copy in a particularly messy state (see figure 7). The queen dictated the majority of this translation to Thomas Windebank, her secretary, adding the work's verse sections in her own hand and occasionally correcting Windebank's transcription. Although the text is composed on paper bearing royal watermarks, Windebank used a variety of papers cut to different sizes, further suggesting the text's improvisatory and private nature. As a result of these physical characteristics, scholars have generally read Elizabeth's later translations as personal efforts intended for her eyes alone.

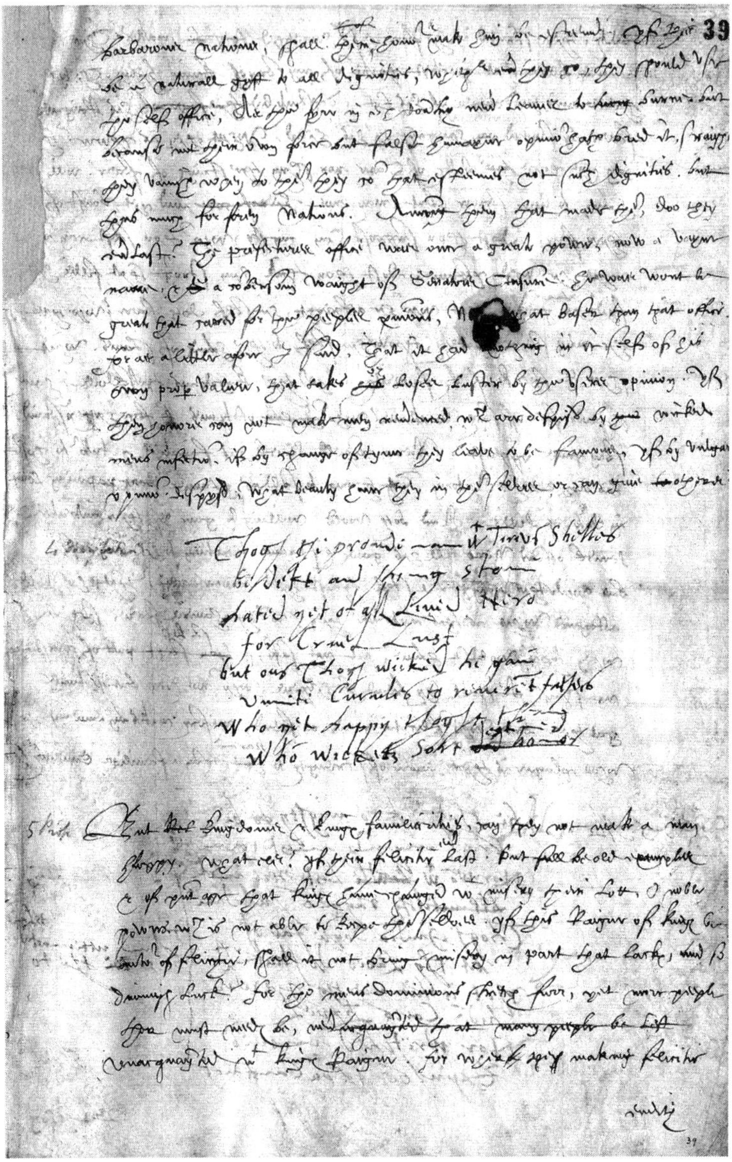

Figure 7. Folio 39 recto of *The Consolation of Philosophy* (1593), Elizabeth I's translation of Boethius. The National Archives of the UK: State Papers 12/289, 39r.

Nonetheless, contemporary responses to Elizabeth's translations indicate that courtiers knew of her translations and—in some cases—read them. In 1591, Henry Savile hyperbolically described the queen's work as "most rare and excellent translations of Histories (if I may call them translations, which have so infinitelie exceded the originals)."[105] Although Savile's praise does not provide definitive proof that he read the queen's translations, others certainly did. Windebank, for example, both wrote the Boethius at the queen's dictation and complied with Elizabeth's directive to make fair copies of the Boethius, Horace, and Plutarch.[106] Even if Elizabeth did not intend Windebank's fair copies to circulate, her secretary was an eyewitness of and possible informant about the queen's translation activities to the court at large. Elizabeth may have presented her translations of Cicero and Seneca to John Harington and possibly an Oxford don, but she was also eager to control the circulation of her work. On August 24, 1593, Robert Devereux, Earl of Essex, wrote a letter to Francis Bacon that referred to Elizabeth's translations: "I told her [Elizabeth] that [the position] I sought for you was not so much your good, though it were a thing I would seek extremely and please myself in obtaining, as for her honour, that those excellent translations of hers might be known to them who could best judge of them."[107] Although it is impossible to determine which "translations" Essex mentions, this letter provides a tantalizing glimpse into how courtiers approached and utilized her translations. At this time, Essex was unsuccessfully seeking to elevate Bacon into the vacant position of attorney general. Apparently Essex had received Elizabeth's translations and forwarded them to Bacon, setting the ground for Bacon to flatter Elizabeth or even assert his familiarity with her to others. However, Essex's reference to the queen's "honour" suggests that Elizabeth was none too pleased with this tactic. Essex's letter supports Leah Marcus's assertion that Elizabeth translated "to be publicly known to be translating" rather than to share her work, so that translation became "a form of political assertion."[108] Elizabeth's translations were another means of demonstrating the cultural capital that she had gained through her humanist education and on which she drew in her role as queen. By translating works intended primarily for her own eyes, Elizabeth reworked the paradigm in which courtiers like Mary Sidney Herbert advised their social superiors through elaborate presentation copies of their translations. Instead of advising others, Elizabeth counseled herself through classical books whose wisdom validated her ability to rule England.

In 1593, Elizabeth embarked on a translation of Boethius's *De consolatione philosophiae* (*The Consolation of Philosophy*, c. 524 CE) in response to the conversion of Henry IV, king of France, from Protestantism to Catholicism.[109] This translation both evoked Elizabeth's personal grief at Henry's actions and suggested that her humanist training was a necessary means of mitigating her response. Boethius remained a popular text in the humanist curriculum because humanist scholars valued the work for its philosophical worth.[110] As a result, the *Consolation* was well suited to serve as a reminder of Elizabeth's education. Boethius composed this text in prose and meter to console his own grief as he awaited execution on false charges of treason. To Elizabeth's contemporaries, Boethius's exploration of sorrow suited the queen's mind-set in the wake of Henry's change of religion. In 1615, William Camden claimed that Elizabeth's translation of Boethius was one means of dealing with her personal sorrow: "In this her griefe shee sought comfort out of the holy Scriptures, the writings of the holy Fathers, and frequent conferences with the Archbishop, and whether out of the Philosophers also I know not. Sure I am that at this time, she daily turned over Boetius his books, *De Consolatione,* and translated them handsomely into the English tongue."[111] Windebank composed a set of memoranda to the translation, indicating that Elizabeth completed the work in a remarkable twenty-four to twenty-seven hours from October 10 through November 5 or 8, just as she was deciding whether to continue providing military aid to Henry.[112] In the wake of Windebank's dating and Camden's account, critics have generally read Elizabeth's translation as a personal meditation on the tragedy of Henry's actions, focusing solely on the correspondence between the grief felt by Elizabeth and Boethius. Yet *The Consolation of Philosophy* is a dialogue between the characters of Boethius and Lady Philosophy, and their conversation mirrors Elizabeth's canny deployment of her two bodies to address the political crisis sparked by Henry's conversion.[113] Between July and November, Elizabeth privately grieved over Henry's choice to abandon Protestantism, even as she publicly gave him pragmatic counsel on a military strategy that she viewed as misguided. In doing so, Elizabeth used her apparent personal grief over the situation as a means of explaining her increasing lack of support for Henry. The characters of Boethius's text had relevance to this distinction between Elizabeth's twofold position as a private woman and a queen. Lady Philosophy, a female ruler who counsels Boethius to accept heavenly truth as he awaits execution, parallels Elizabeth's self-appointed role as Henry's preceptor. Meanwhile, Elizabeth's distress over Henry's Catholicism corresponds to Boethius's despair over the impermanence of worldly goods and honors. As Elizabeth dictated the text to Windebank, she alternately took on the role of mourner and counselor, creating a split form of self-representation that transformed her personal emotions into philosophical justification for abandoning Henry.

The relationship between Elizabeth and Henry had been cordial up to this point, allowing England and France to build an alliance that provided a counterbalance to Spanish power within Europe. Due to their shared religious beliefs, Elizabeth had supported Henry even before his 1589 accession to the French throne, and once Henry become mired in a civil war against the Catholic League that was also sponsored by Spain, Elizabeth offered both financial and military aid for Henry's cause. Despite Elizabeth's own distaste for war, English involvement in the French civil wars allowed the queen to support the Huguenots and to keep the Spanish at bay. After four years of civil war, however, Henry converted to Catholicism on July 13, 1593, a move that appeased the majority of his subjects and, more important, allowed Henry to retain his crown.[114] Elizabeth and her courtiers had received reports hinting at Henry's possible change of religion as early as May 1592, and English opinion of the best strategy to take was divided.[115] On July 10 William Cecil, Lord Burghley, drew up several minutes exploring potential responses to the king's rumored shift to Catholicism, recommending that Elizabeth focus on defending Brittany from the Spanish, since that would be an ideal spot to launch an invasion of England. Yet he also noted that the queen "can not accord with the Fr[ench] kyng in such bondes of amety as she hath doone," as the Pope was "hir Ma[jesty]s mortall ennemy."[116] Burghley's recommendation, then, offered a middle course that limited English aid to France even while it protected English interests. Elizabeth followed Burghley's counsel, first threatening to remove her troops from areas outside Brittany on August 24 even as Henry called for more soldiers. That October, while the queen continued to think about recalling English forces from the majority of France, someone—perhaps Essex, who was a staunch supporter of Henry's cause—drew up a memorandum endorsing continued intervention for both political and religious reasons: besides preventing an alliance between the French and Spanish, Elizabeth could take the moral high road as a defender of the faith. After painting a grim picture of the Huguenot soldiers' likely persecution or extermination at the hands of Catholics, the writer concludes with a dire warning: "How greatlie they wilbe at this time disconforted to see the Q[ueen] of Englande withdrawe her succours, even at the time that they expected by the contenaunce thereof to have obtained good Conditions for their safties, I leave to the imaginacion of the wisest."[117] Despite these concerns, Elizabeth finally confirmed her decision to recall English troops from France (excluding Brittany) on November 13.[118]

Between July and November, Elizabeth manipulated the duality between her body natural and her body politic to frame her growing disinterest in aiding Henry as a spiritual and political necessity. While Elizabeth's unofficial letters to France dwelled on her deep personal grief, her official letters to Henry presented Elizabeth as a shrewd political counselor. Elizabeth's first letter to Henry after learning of his decision opens with a theatrical lamentation whose anaphoric repetition highlights the queen's pain: "Ah que douleurs, O quelz regretz, O que gemissementz Je sentoys en mon Asme par le sonn de telles Nouvelles que Morlains m'a compté" (Ah what griefs, O what regrets, O what groanings felt I in my soul at the sound of such news as Morlains has told me).[119] After this point, however, Elizabeth confined her personal grief to unofficial correspondence that nevertheless continued to exert political pressure. In July, Elizabeth wrote to Henri de la Tour, Duc de Bouillon and a fellow Protestant, to commiserate "ce disgracee accident de la perversion de vostre Maistre" (this disgraceful accident of the perversion of your Master): "Dieu tournera, s'il luy plaist, ses misericordes yeux à si signale offense, et de sa bonte, non par merite, supportera la foiblesse d'un si monstreux acte" (God will turn, if it pleases him, his merciful eyes to such a remarkable insult, and of his goodness, not by merit, will endure the weakness of such a monstrous act). Besides condemning Henry's conversion, Elizabeth endorses Protestant theology by denying that God will forgive this act due to any "merite" (merit) on Henry's part. Notably, Elizabeth concludes the letter by slipping into Latin: "je me trouve si à fyn de mon françois que je ne sçay que dire si non avertat Deus malum a quo lavabo manus meas" (I find myself so at the end of my French that I do not know what to say *except may God avert the evil from which I will wash my hands*).[120] Here Elizabeth's strong emotions, evident in her description of this change in religion as a "perversion" and "disgraceful accident," appear to put her at a loss for French words, causing her to take refuge in Latin. Yet as Elizabeth moves into Latin, itself a diplomatic language, she threatens to withdraw English support of Henry by signaling her willingness to "wash [her] hands" of this "evil." Even more significant, a day after Elizabeth recalled English troops with the exception of those in Brittany, she wrote yet another despairing letter to Henry's sister, Catherine of Navarre: "Si mon papier eust le tamt resemblant a mon coeur, Je ne le vous oserois presenter, le couleur noir sc[a]yant trop mal aux jeunes gents" (If my paper had any resemblance to my heart, I would not dare to present it to you, knowing that the color black is too much disliked by young people).[121] While this and other protestations of sorrow contextualized and mitigated

Elizabeth's decision to limit English aid to Henry, her official correspondence portrayed the queen as a pragmatic counselor with a political rationale for disavowing Henry's cause. For example, in a letter to Henry from October 7, 1593, Elizabeth notes that she only conveys "vos plus necessaires advis" (your most necessary advice) before alluding to Matthew 7:20 to warn him against counselors offering poor military advice: "Voyez les par leurs fruictz; et, par la, Jugez en quelle Racine ilz meritent avoir aux Jardins de vos plaisirs" (See them by their fruits; and, by that, judge what root they deserve to have in the gardens of your pleasures).[122] By indicating her personal grief in private letters and sharing her queenly counsel in official correspondence, Elizabeth deftly invoked her two bodies to legitimate her decreasing support for Henry.

Elizabeth never mentions Boethius in her official correspondence, yet her translation of this text created another venue for performing the public and private personae that she was using to deal with Henry's actions. Furthermore, by translating Boethius, Elizabeth applied her humanist education to the issues raised by Henry's Catholicism and transformed her knowledge of Latin into philosophical guidance that might support her final decision. While the text's depiction of the fictional Boethius allowed Elizabeth to explore her personal grief, the figure of Lady Philosophy permitted her to assume the role of a counselor with access to divine knowledge. Elizabeth generally provides a close rendering of Boethius's language, yet she also adapts the text to her own purposes through subtle alterations to its content and style. The resulting translation suggests that Elizabeth was well aware that this work had relevance to her current position vis-à-vis Henry. Elizabeth's portrayal of Boethius, for example, heightens his grief while eliding his initial mental stupefaction, making the character a more suitable stand-in for the queen. If Elizabeth's initial letter in the wake of Henry's change of religion had strategically used repetition to convey her mental distress, her translation likewise utilizes poetic language to emphasize the sorrow experienced by Boethius. For example, her rendering of Lady Philosophy's initial description of Boethius employs sound devices and small shifts in meaning to heighten the text's presentation of his grief: Boethius "downe Lies, of mindz Light *bereved* [effeto],/With brused Nek by overhevy Chaines/A bowed Lowe Looke."[123] Elizabeth renders "effeto" (exhausted) as "bereaved," a participle that punningly reinforces Boethius's despondency in its signification of loss. Furthermore, Elizabeth's use of alliteration and consonance in the phrase "bowed Lowe Looke" gives this passage a halting quality that matches Boethius's despair. At the same time, Elizabeth carefully omits moments in which Boethius demonstrates complete mental bewilderment. Boethius introduces the previous verses as Lady Philosophy's comment on "mentis perturbatione" (the disturbance of his mind), but Elizabeth renders this phrase as "my mynds pane," replacing his distraction with another reference to grief (*T,* 78; *CP,* book 1, prose 1.51).[124] Likewise, when Boethius first sees Lady Philosophy, he states, "I was stupefied" (obstipui; *CP,* book 1, prose 1.46), yet no equivalent to "obstipui" appears in Elizabeth's translation of this moment (*T,* 76–78). As a result, Elizabeth presents Boethius as a character deeply affected, but not weakened, by grief, paralleling her own display of sorrow and disdain in response to Henry's Catholicism.

Just as Elizabeth's official correspondence with Henry presented the queen as a counselor, so she alters the character of Lady Philosophy to heighten her regal bearing and pedagogical role. Lady Philosophy enters bearing symbols relevant to Elizabeth's own self-presentation as a learned queen: "Her right hand held a booke the Left a sceptar" (*T,* 76). While translating Boethius's description of Lady Philosophy, Elizabeth makes several small alterations emphasizing the way in which Lady Philosophy's heavenly knowledge (the "booke") provides the basis for her power (the "sceptar"): "Over my hed to stand a Woman did apeare Of *stately face* [reverendi vultus] with flaming yees [eyes] of insight above the Comun worth of men" (*T,* 74; *CP,* book 1, prose 1.2–5). By translating "reverendi vultus" (a face to be revered) with the phrase "stately face," Elizabeth indicates Lady Philosophy's nobility and also constructs a sequence of alliterative "s" and "f" sounds that links Lady Philosophy's rule ("stately face") with her heavenly knowledge ("flaming yees of insight above the Comun worth of men"). Elizabeth more overtly presents Lady Philosophy as a ruler analogous to herself by translating Boethius's description of her "imperiosae auctoritatis" (mighty authority) as "imperius rule" (*T,* 76; *CP,* book 1, prose 1.46). If Lady Philosophy's divine knowledge legitimates her power, it also allows her to act as a counselor during Boethius's time of need, and Elizabeth carefully emphasizes Lady Philosophy's role as an instructor in divine learning. When Boethius calls Lady Philosophy "magistra," Elizabeth initially translates this term as "maistres" (*T,* 82; *CP,* book 1, prose 3.7), but in a later revision she substitutes the word "pedag[og]ue," a gender-neutral term that lacks the erotic connotations of "mistress" even as it emphasizes Lady Philosophy's pedagogical purpose.[125] Elizabeth also represents Lady Philosophy as a counselor whose heavenly precepts trump the secular advice provided by the Muses. When Lady Philosophy first arrives, she orders the Muses to leave Boethius to her healing care, causing the Muses' exodus: "The Checked rabel with Looke downe Cast with Wo, with blusche

Confessing shame, doleful out of doores the[y] Went, but I Whose sight drowned in teares Was dim[m]ed, Could not knowe What she Was" (*T,* 76; *CP,* book 3, prose 1.42–45). Perhaps taking inspiration from the repeated use of "m" and "s" sounds in "lacrimis mersa" (drowned in tears), Elizabeth crafts an alliterative pattern of "d" sounds emphasizing the source text's suggestion that secular literature (represented by the Muses) cannot provide consolation for such deep-rooted sadness ("doleful out of doores," "drowned in teares Was dim[m]ed"). Thus Elizabeth presents Lady Philosophy as both a powerful female ruler and a counselor, creating a figure parallel to her own self-construction as an adviser to Henry.

The lessons that Boethius learns from Lady Philosophy also relate to Elizabeth's French correspondence, particularly her warnings to Henry about the dangers of renouncing Protestantism solely for worldly gain. In her first letter to Henry after his conversion, Elizabeth asks a rhetorical question that implicitly urges Henry to reconsider his decision: "Mon dieu est il possible que mondain respect aulcun deut effacer le terreur que la crainte Divine nous menace" (My God, is it possible that any worldly respect should efface the terror with which the fear of God threatens us)."[126] Throughout *The Consolation of Philosophy,* Boethius learns to recognize that true happiness accompanies spiritual, rather than earthly, advantages. Elizabeth explicitly extends this message to royal power by making several crucial alterations to Lady Philosophy's comments on kings: "But Kingdomes and Kinges familiarities, can they Not make a Man *happy* [potentem]. What els? yf their felicitie ever Last. But full be old examples and of present age that kinges have changed With *Misery* [calamitate] their Lott. . . . Thus Must it Needes follow that *greatest* [majorem] portion of Myserye Kinges have" (*T,* 194; *CP,* book 3, prose 5.1–5, 13–15). By translating "potentem" (powerful) as "happy," Elizabeth links this passage with Lady Philosophy's larger message about the false happiness of earthly things. Elizabeth then contrasts this emotion by translating "calamitate" (misfortune) as "Misery," anticipating the statement that kings have "the greatest portion of Myserye." As a result, Elizabeth's use of the term "happy" creates a trajectory in which rulers experience a fleeting happiness that must end with "misery," thereby insisting on the fickle nature of worldly joy. Indeed, Elizabeth heightens this idea by substituting a superlative ("greatest") for the comparative adjective "majorem" (greater) in the phrase "greatest portion of Myserye Kinges have." Likewise, Elizabeth reinforces Boethius's rejection of earthly glory: "Thou thyself knowest that *No ambition* [minimum ambitionem] of mortall thinges did Rule Us[.] *We were Not guided by the pride of Any Mortall glory* [added]" (*T,* 160; *CP,* book 2, prose 7.1–2). While Boethius had registered his distaste for glory by stating that he had "minimum ambitionem" (little ambition), Elizabeth makes Boethius's disinterest more absolute by rendering this phrase as "no ambition." Furthermore, she adds a recapitulation of the idea ("We were Not guided by the pride of Any Mortall glory"), thereby suggesting that both "mortall things" and "Mortall glory" are unimportant. As a result, both Boethius and Lady Philosophy agree that worldly success has little significance, an opinion concurring with Elizabeth's pointed reminder to Henry that spiritual matters should precede political maneuvering.

While Lady Philosophy presents religious truth as the source of human happiness, Elizabeth's translation is infused with a subtle Protestantism suggesting that reformed faith alone can lead to true felicity. As before, this tweaking of Boethius's message corresponds with Elizabeth's response to Henry's decision. Before learning that Henry had fully committed himself to Catholicism, Elizabeth had hoped to convince him of the superiority of Protestantism by emphasizing its undeniable truth. Instructions approved by Elizabeth and given to Sir Thomas Wilkes on July 14 ordered her ambassador to remind Henry of his past allegiance to Protestantism: "It shall please him to understand that in no wise we can allow, nor thinke it Good before God, that for any worldly respectes, or any cunning persuasions, he should yeld to chaunge his Conscience, & opinion in Religion from the truth wherein he hath bin brought up from his Youth."[127] Just as Wilkes's instructions present Protestantism as the only path to salvation ("the truth"), so Elizabeth puts Protestant code words in Lady Philosophy's mouth in order to align the text's piety with Protestantism. For example, Elizabeth adds a Protestant tinge to Lady Philosophy's contrast between good and evil: "See you Not in What a *great* [quanto] slowe [slough], Wicked thinges be Wrapt in, and With how *great* [qua] a light, *godlynes* [probitas] shynes" (*T,* 270; *CP,* book 4, prose 3.1–2). Notably, Elizabeth translates both "quanto" (how much) and "qua" (what) as "great," using the rhetorical device of antithesis to contrast the "great slowe" of wickedness and the "great . . . light" of "godlynes." As Mueller and Scodel observe, this moment is also one of several in which Elizabeth inserts a reference to reformed piety into her translation by translating "probitas" (goodness) as "godlynes."[128] Similarly, Elizabeth adds a Protestant tone when Lady Philosophy notes the debasement inherent in abandoning "probitas": "since that *true pietie alone* [sola probitas] May lift Up a man, it followes that Whom wickednes hath throwen downe from state of Man, hath cast him downe beneth the Merit of Man" (*T,* 272; *CP,* book 4, prose 3.51–54). By rendering "sola probitas" (only goodness) with "true pietie alone," Elizabeth not only indicates the primacy of Protestantism but also implies that deviating from reformed faith leads to complete degeneration ("beneth the Merit of Man"). Elizabeth's version of the text specifically comments on those who decide to abandon the truth and thus suffer this debasement, taking a path that Henry will presumably also follow thanks to his conversion. In the source text, Lady Philosophy states, "The fortune of those who indeed are either in possession of virtue, or making progress in it, or attaining to it, whatever that fortune may be, is all good, but for those who persevere in wickedness every kind of fortune is very bad" (*CP*, book 4, prose 7.33–37). Elizabeth's version, however, limits Lady Philosophy's comments to those who are aware of truth and ignore it, a category that would presumably include Henry: "Worsse is the state of them that be eyther in the possibilitie, or in the advaunce or obtayning of Vertue And yet byde in their iniquitie" (*T*, 312). While lapsed Protestants such as Henry have the "possibilitie" to "advaunce" or "obtain . . . virtue," they willingly "byde in . . . iniquitie" by refusing to reject Catholicism. Thus Elizabeth's alterations of the text add a Protestant slant that may have allowed her to meditate on Henry's rejection of Protestant truth. In turn, the text reinforces her own predisposition, as demonstrated in her instructions to Wilkes and her July 13 letter to Henry, to view his change of religion as a cynical political game.

As Elizabeth negotiated with Henry, translating Boethius's *Consolation of Philosophy* offered a potentially useful means of converting the cultural capital of her education (specifically her knowledge of Latin) into a source of relevant spiritual and political counsel. Though this translation was not necessarily meant to be circulated among Elizabeth's subjects, it gave the queen an unofficial means of enacting the personae that she was already deploying to address the political dilemma created by Henry's newfound Catholicism. Through the figure of Boethius, Elizabeth could express her grief at Henry's decision even as she reinforced her own predisposition to abandon Henry's cause by translating Lady Philosophy's advice to put spiritual matters above political affairs. Furthermore, this translation offers a glimpse into the myriad small ways in which could Elizabeth manipulate her image. As Elizabeth dictated her text to Windebank, she demonstrated her learning, and in the process of translation, she altered the text in a manner that applied her classical education to the political crisis at hand. Yet because the translation was ultimately not meant for public consumption, Elizabeth limited her work to an audience of two: herself and Windebank. As Camden's account reveals, contemporaries could interpret even Elizabeth's private autodidacticism as a political activity. By using translation to channel the grief of her weaker body natural into a source of counsel applicable to her body politic, Elizabeth considered the ramifications of her final decision to revoke English troops from France. In the process, she may have found a model that reinforced her self-presentation as both a private woman who reacted emotionally to Henry's Catholicism and as a pragmatic queen who refused to continue supporting a losing battle.

Conclusions

The cultural and social capital inherent in the manuscript translations of Mary Sidney Herbert and Elizabeth I shows that women could use unique copies of their translations to fashion themselves as political counselors. The Sidney Psalter circulated fairly widely, but the presentation copy prepared for Elizabeth bore special political significance. Sidney Herbert's paratextual poems emphasized the potential applications of the Psalter by reminding Elizabeth of Philip Sidney's legacy and by situating the psalms within the context of Anglo-Spanish relations. In describing the Sidney Psalter with the language of translation, Sidney Herbert associated the work with the posthumous politicization of Philip Sidney's translations, and she also carefully revised the conclusions of several psalms originally written by Sidney in ways that may have been applicable to the current political landscape. These alterations indicate that far from slavishly submitting to male authority, Sidney Herbert coopted her brother's literary and political legacies to serve her own ends. Elizabeth, meanwhile, was well aware of the potential uses of manuscript presentation copies of translations, as in her youth she had given lavish copies of her religious translations to powerful relatives at court: Henry VIII, Katherine Parr, and Edward VI. After becoming queen, Elizabeth modified this precedent by composing utilitarian translations of Latin works to remind her courtiers of her unusual humanist training and to assert her status as a learned prince. The very lack of polish in these later translations suggested the queen's profitable use of leisure time, allowing her to practice a form of self-counsel legitimating political decisions that might otherwise be dismissed as the caprices of her weak body natural. In the case of Elizabeth's Boethius, the doubled subject positions of the source text mirror the queen's deployment of her two bodies as she negotiated the political fallout from the French king Henry IV's conversion to Catholicism. By aligning herself both with Boethius and Lady Philosophy, Elizabeth could display the humanist credentials associated with her body politic and find support for a decision that was not uniformly popular among her Privy Council.

These case studies suggest the need for new critical models that better reflect the ways that women interacted with authoritative source texts, particularly as translators. Female translators had the ability to endorse or alter the ideas put forward by their sources and to shape the ways in which the original author was received or interpreted. While this interpretive potential may have been circumscribed at times, it nonetheless permitted female translators a means of developing their own credibility as learned counselors with the ability to convey approved wisdom to their readers. The linguistic skills required of any translator meant that this activity allowed the female translator a unique means of demonstrating the cultural capital imparted by her education. As an executive author recognized for her role in producing the final text, a female translator could transform that cultural capital into social capital with public implications by linking the text and its author with contemporary political or religious agendas. Through translation, women might therefore associate themselves with respected source texts to substantiate their own views on political, religious, and literary matters. While it might be tempting to view translation as an activity that automatically subordinated women to patriarchal power, the cases of Sidney Herbert and Elizabeth reveal that when female translators turned to highly esteemed works, they could use the resulting authorial multiplicity to enhance their own reputations, political influence, and religious credentials.

CHAPTER FOUR

Anonymous Representatives

Mary Percy, Potentiana Deacon, and Monastic Spirituality

In 1632, an English translation of Saint François de Sales's *Delicious Entertainments of the Soule* appeared, attributed on the title page only to "a Dame of Our Ladies of comfort of the order of S[aint] Bennet in Cambray." The anonymity of the translator, a member of the English Benedictine convent in Cambrai, met the heightened verbal chastity expected of enclosed nuns. More important, this refusal to take public credit for her work signaled the translator's incorporation within the collective identity of her house. Such self-abnegation conformed to the strictures of monastic life, particularly the vows of poverty, obedience, and chastity. The Benedictine *Rule,* for example, praises obedience as the cornerstone of the Benedictine virtue of humility, noting that the nuns "ought to have neither bodyes nor wills at their owne disposing."[1] The constitutions of the Cambrai house cite this admonition as a rationale for the elimination of personal property in favor of communal ownership: it is "strictlie forbidden, to give, take, lend, send, beg, aske, receave, or [ex] chang directlie or indirectlie, in there persons or names; much or little; neither cloathes, monney, letters, tokens, gifts, for anie thing whatsoever," so that "whatsoever is gotten or given to the Monastarie, must be appropriated to the wholl communitie."[2] As this prohibition on personal belongings suggests, within the communal framework of the convent, all individual labor, including literary production, became part of the house's collective goods. By withholding her identity, the anonymous translator of the *Delicious Entertainments* performed this renunciation of personal property. Yet the translator could have achieved this goal without identifying herself as a member of the Cambrai convent, which suggests that the implications of her anonymity require closer scrutiny. By revealing her religious affiliation, this anonymous "Dame" gestured at the corporate nature of the Cambrai convent and consequently transformed herself into an unnamed representative of her house to the outside world.

The critical history of the *Delicious Entertainments* reveals that this apparent evocation of the Cambrai convent's piety was not as straightforward as it might seem. Like other English convents on the Continent, the Cambrai Benedictines experienced discord over Ignatian spiritual direction. Many convents relied upon Jesuit confessors, who adapted the *Spiritual Exercises*—which Ignatius of Loyola developed to help male spiritual directors guide their male penitents—for this new setting. The *Spiritual Exercises* and other Ignatian meditative treatises aimed to stir the penitent to action, whether internal or external, through examination of conscience, guided contemplations, and methodical set prayers, such as using all the senses to re-create pivotal biblical moments.[3] Some nuns found these practices conducive to mystical experiences, as when Lucy (Elizabeth) Knatchbull of the Brussels and Ghent Benedictines used the self-examination sparked by the *Spiritual Exercises* to enter her own contemplative raptures.[4] Yet Father Augustine (David) Baker OSB, the unofficial spiritual director of the Cambrai house, believed that the action-oriented, prescriptive spirituality of the Jesuits was inappropriate for the meditative life of nuns: "The exercises of those men cannot be trulie Contemplative and spirituall, nor they be internall and Contemplative livers: But their exercises and living must be in the active life."[5] Baker instead advocated an individualized spirituality based on following God's internal directions rather than a spiritual director: "Nor doth God use to illuminate anie man fullie to the purpose; I meane as to the guidance of another, but illuminateth the soule herself."[6] Baker's approach prevailed among the Cambrai Benedictines, and A. F. Allison and D. M. Rogers tentatively attributed the translation to Agnes (Grace) More, another Cambrai nun who translated a mystical treatise compatible with Baker's philosophy.[7] Nevertheless, a catalog of the house's library drawn up by Baker himself definitively attributes a manuscript copy of the translation to "D[ame] Potentiana a religious of this house."[8] Potentiana (Elizabeth) Deacon rejected Baker's approach to mysticism in favor of Ignatian prayer, and her recent editors Jos Blom and Frans Blom have observed that the *Delicious Entertainments* is at odds with the house's mainstream practices.[9] Deacon's apparent representation of her convent's piety was therefore an assertive attempt to manage outside perceptions of the house. By naming herself only as "a Dame of our Ladies of comfort," Deacon implied that her rejection of contemplative mysticism—a minority viewpoint within the house—truly reflected the convent's attitudes. While Deacon's preferred spirituality held little sway within her convent, anonymity gave her a potential opportunity to shape public views of the Cambrai nuns.

This chapter will consider the ways that anonymity could evoke collective identity by examining Deacon's *Delicious Entertainments* as well as an anonymously published translation by Mary Percy of the Brussels Benedictines. Scholars such as Marcy North have already shown that anonymity was a vital and complex form of authorship with substantial advantages for authors and printmakers alike.[10] In the cases of Deacon and Percy, anonymity might seem to suggest that both women were doubly subject to patriarchal authority, hampered by enclosure as well as early modern prescriptions limiting women's public speech. Nevertheless, anonymity did much more than simply permit Deacon and Percy to fend off criticism: it also allowed their publications to represent their convents at large and to influence public views about English monasticism. After Jesuit priests encouraged postulants to leave the Brussels convent, Percy translated a mystical treatise written by an Ignatian priest and his penitent that implicitly legitimated the place of Ignatian spirituality within the cloister. Deacon followed Percy's example by translating the *Delicious Entertainments,* which advocated Ignatian piety for cloistered women even as the Cambrai convent faced an investigation into the orthodoxy of its spirituality. Anonymity might seem to elide the agency of the translator and foreground the text's original author, yet these cases reveal that it could serve as a form of corporate authorship that empowered the translator to speak on behalf of her larger religious community.

Collective Voices: Anonymous Translation and Dissident Religious Groups

Members of dissident religious groups often found anonymous translation a potent means of defining their faction's views. In 1560, a group of English exiles in Geneva published a translation of the Bible that sought to influence the direction of the nascent Elizabethan church. By crafting prefatory material that employed a communal voice, the exiles positioned themselves as a unified front dedicated to the cause of Calvinism. The translation's associations with Geneva were highlighted on both the title page and in the dedicatory epistle to Elizabeth I written by her "humble subjects of the English Churche at Geneva." This dedication collectively urged Elizabeth to purify the English church in the manner of biblical reformers: "When we . . . consider earnestly how muche greater charge God hath laid upon you in making you a builder of his spiritual Temple, we can not but partely feare, knowing the crafte and force of Satan our spiritual enemie, and the weakenes and unabilitie of this our nature: and partely be fervent in our prayers toward God that he wolde bring to perfection this noble worke . . . and therefore we indevour our selves by all meanes to ayde, & to bestowe our whole force under your graces standard."[11] By speaking in the first person plural voice ("we"), the preface invokes the broader community of Geneva exiles to suggest their shared support for further church reform as well as their willingness to assist this project. This use of collective authorship also sidestepped Elizabeth's hostile attitude toward the Geneva community. John Calvin had dedicated his revised commentary on Isaiah to Elizabeth in 1559, but he informed William Cecil that his work had been poorly received: "The messenger to whom I had given my commentaries on Isaiah to be offered to the queen, brought me back word, that my homage was rather distasteful to her majesty, because she had been offended with me on account of certain writings that had been published in this city."[12] These offensive "writings" were Christopher Goodman's *How Superior Powers Oght to Be Obeyd* and John Knox's *The First Blast of the Trumpet against the Monstruous Regiment of Women,* which attacked female rulers. By assuming a communal voice, the paratexts to the Geneva Bible framed this text as the shared labor of a community characterized by a commitment to reform rather than by its controversial leaders.

Gayatri Chakravorty Spivak's discussion of the political agency inherent in collectivity illuminates the full ramifications of this communal voice: "Agency presumes collectivity, which is where a group acts by synecdoche: the part that seems to agree is taken to stand for the whole. I put aside the surplus of my subjectivity and metonymise myself, count myself as the part by which I am connected to the particular predicament so that I can claim collectivity, and engage in action validated by that very collective."[13] According to this idea, a member of a group can gain power simply by identifying him- or herself as such, which in turn suggests that this individual represents the larger collective entity. Of course, complete unity within any group is unlikely, as Spivak's phrasing indicates ("seems to imply"), meaning that any synecdochic representation of a collective is inherently illusory. Spivak further notes that leaders are more likely to have the potential for gaining agency as synecdoches of their organizations or communities: "In general, the leaders of collectivities . . . have the right to the metonym/synecdoche complex. That the rank and file do not, sometimes gets overlooked."[14] Elizabeth's reaction to Calvin's dedication indicates the way that leaders could serve as synecdoches for their communities. Goodman's tract had advertised both his name and his location in Geneva, thus apparently voicing the opinions of the Geneva exiles. While Knox's treatise was published anonymously, its authorship was well known to Elizabeth. Yet since these books were associated with specific figures, they were all the easier for others in Geneva to deny, and Calvin assured Cecil that he did not share Knox's views. The anonymous but collective voice of the Geneva Bible, however, removed such specificity to represent the entire community, even though the work was composed by its leaders (primarily William Whittingham). The Bible thus gained an authorial fluidity more potent than if it had been identified as the work of Whittingham.

During the early modern period, translators of subversive religious texts often used anonymity to hide their identity, but some took on a synecdochic role by identifying themselves solely as members of well-defined religious institutions or groups. As the case of the Geneva Bible indicates, one form of collective anonymity occurred when group leaders spoke anonymously for their entire community. Likewise, the Douai-Rheims Bible adopts a collective voice that portrays the text as the work of a specific religious community, this time Roman Catholic: the English College at Douai (and temporarily Rheims). The title pages for the 1582 New Testament and the 1609 Old Testament attribute the work to the English College itself, rather than Gregory Martin, the main translator, and the prefaces to both are written in a corporate voice. The preface to the Old Testament, for example, alludes to the severe financial troubles that the college had recently experienced: "You wil hereby . . . perceive our fervent good wil, ever to serve you, in that we have brought forth this Tome, in these hardest times, of above fourtie yeares, since this College was most happely begune."[15] By drawing attention to the communal nature of the college, the preface suggests this institution's fervent dedication to advancing the English mission at all costs. Members of Catholic religious orders also took on a synecdochic authority by publishing anonymous translations that nevertheless identified the translator's religious affiliation. John Wilson, a secular priest, issued most of these publications during his tenure as supervisor of the Jesuit press at the English College in Saint Omer from 1608 to 1635. Title pages to anonymous translations of works by Carthusian and Franciscan monks noted that the translators were of the same order as the original authors, thus familiarizing readers in England—where monasticism had no visible presence—with the spiritual approaches of these orders.[16] A number of anonymous translations bore a phrase that must have seemed commonplace by the end of Wilson's career: "translated into English by a father of the Society of Jesus."

Jesuit translators frequently chose Ignatian source texts that could aid the English mission but also raised the profile of their order as purveyors of cutting-edge spiritual practices: Robert Bellarmino, SJ; Vincenzo Bruno, SJ; Ignatius of Loyola, SJ; and Teresa of Avila.[17] By 1620 Wilson had also dedicated anonymous translations by Thomas Everard, SJ, to the abbesses of the four English convents then in operation (the Brussels Benedictines, the Louvain Augustinians, the Lisbon Bridgettines, and the Gravelines Poor Clares).[18] These publications invoked the synecdochic role of both the anonymous Jesuit translator and the abbesses to suggest that Ignatian spirituality was compatible with monasticism.

Like these men, female translators used anonymity in a synecdochic fashion. Yet since women generally held unofficial leadership roles within religious groups, only nuns exercised the collective anonymity evident in the Geneva and Douai-Rheims Bibles. Some women identified themselves as members of religious communities by dedicating translations to patrons who were well known for their distinctive piety. In 1560 Anne Lock, herself a Geneva exile and a close friend of Knox, published a translation of Calvin under her initials, addressing the work to a woman who had also experienced substantial travails while in exile: Katherine Bertie, Duchess of Suffolk. By claiming personal knowledge of Bertie's exemplary Protestant piety, Lock indicates her own participation in reformist circles: "How [God] is continually to be thanked, your graces profession of his worde, your abidyng in the same, the godly conversation that I have sene in you, do prove that your selfe do better understand & practise than I can admonishe you."[19] Elizabeth Cary, who had recently converted to Catholicism, dedicated her anonymous 1630 translation of Jacques Davy Du Perron to Queen Henrietta Maria, the highest-ranking Catholic woman in the country. In the preface to the reader, Cary withheld her name even as she revealed her gender: "I desire to have noe more guest at of me, but that I am a Catholique, and a Woman: the first serves for mine honor, and the second, for my excuse." Nevertheless, the dedicatory preface to Henrietta Maria approvingly mentioned the queen's fervent Catholicism, positioning the unknown female translator within her coterie of Catholic noblewomen: "You are a Catholicke, and a zealous one, and therefore fittest to receive the dedication of a Catholicke-worke."[20] As a result, Cary's translation suggested that support for Catholicism extended throughout the aristocracy and royal family.

Catholic women who were members of religious orders were in a better position to follow the example of their male counterparts, as they could identify themselves as members of their orders or particular houses. Catherine Magdalen (Elizabeth) Evelinge, a Poor Clare, created a unique form of authorship that is comparable to synecdochic anonymity by ascribing two printed translations to Magdalen of St Austin (Catherine) Bentley, another nun at her house. These misattributions allowed Evelinge to influence public views of Franciscan piety even as she humbly conformed to her order's emphasis on poverty by divesting herself of authorship.[21] The synecdochic potential of these translations is evident in Evelinge's 1635 translation of Saint Clare's life, which contains a dedicatory preface to Henrietta Maria written in the collective voice of "The English poore-Clares of Aire": "We will therefore, ever pray the only Ruler of Princes, which hath set a Diademe of pure gold upon your head, to prevent you with the blessings of his goodnes, and grant unto your Majestie a long and prosperous joynt-reigne with our Soveraigne Liege-Lord, King Charles, and a glorious Race from your Royall loynes to the Crowne."[22] As portress and a founding member of the Aire convent, Evelinge held a leadership role within the house that may have empowered her to speak for the community. In doing so, she suggested their shared zeal for the birth of a Catholic heir ("a glorious Race") who could consolidate Catholic influence in England and presumably lead to the nation's conversion. For some secular and monastic women, anonymous translation did not just serve as a means of preserving verbal chastity. Rather, these translators renounced their individual identities to shape perceptions of their religious circles or communities, using the collectivity implied by synecdoche to enter the public sphere and claim a mediated form of authority.

God's Currency: Mary Percy, Ignatian Mysticism, and English Monasticism

Like many other English Catholics who knew foreign languages, Mary Percy and several of her confessors—John Gerard, SJ; Richard Gibbons, SJ; Anthony Hoskins, SJ; and Robert Chambers—turned to translation to promulgate and defend Roman Catholicism after Elizabeth's accession. With the exception of Mary's brief reign, England had little exposure to the Counter-Reformation, and translation allowed Catholics to import innovative theology and devotional practices from the Continent. Such publications were all the more important as a means of sustaining Catholic identity since the furtive and unsettled nature of the English mission meant that many English Catholics had limited access to priests. The translations emerging from Percy's circle offered political and spiritual guidance for English Catholics, frequently employing synecdochic authorship to suggest that these works bore the imprimatur of a specific religious order or community. These apparent endorsements strengthened the polemical nature of the translations themselves, which consistently sought to influence the religious views of English readers, whether in England or abroad.

Both Gerard and Gibbons published anonymous translations implying that Jesuit priests supported English nuns and, in particular, the Brussels Benedictines. Gerard helped Percy leave England to become a nun, and he showed a special interest in the Benedictine convent that she founded at Brussels in 1598.[23] That same year, a secret press in London issued Gerard's anonymous translation of *The Spiritual Conflict,* a popular spiritual work by Lorenzo Scupoli, CR. A preface by Jerome, Count of Portia, dedicates the treatise to nuns at a Venetian convent, portraying the cloister as an important arena of spiritual warfare and in turn reminding English readers of the prestige of nuns: "By our Lord you are called and particularly chosen to this no lesse glorious, then hard conflict. We declare not here how to vanquish cities, but how to overcome our will."[24] If Gerard's translation may have offered oblique support for Percy's enterprise, a woodcut of the Jesuit insignia IHS on the title page linked English Jesuits with monastic women's spirituality.[25] Gibbons conducted a retreat for Mary Percy in 1597, and he later published a translation of *The Virgin Maries Life* (1604) by Luca Pinelli, SJ, that openly linked the Brussels convent with Jesuit piety.[26] While Gibbons signed the work only with his initials, the title page advertised that this work was originally composed by "the Reverend father Lucas Pinelli of the Societie of Jesus." Gibbons dedicated his translation to Abbess Joanna Berkeley, indicating that she would recognize the value of Ignatian piety: "I have beene so bould, Religious and vertuous Madame, as to direct this litle booke to you, and make you a present ther of, as one worthie to receave & keepe such a jewel. . . . I know right wel, how much more you doe value and esteeme spiritual, then temporal treasures."[27] Besides suggesting the cachet attached to nuns' piety, the translations of Gerard and Gibbons encouraged readers to associate female monasticism with Ignatian spirituality.

Hoskins, vice-prefect of the English Jesuits in Flanders as well as an extraordinary confessor at the Brussels Benedictines, used anonymous translations to intervene in political controversies that adversely affected Jesuits. With *The Apologies of the Most Christian Kinges of France and Navar* (1611), Hoskins hoped to rebut the "almost daily Libels against the Society of Jesus, concerning the killing of Tyrants; and namely of the death of the most Christian King Henry the fourth."[28] Hoskins countered these "Libels" by translating several brief documents exonerating the Jesuits by Henry IV, Louis XIII, and others. This translation was published under the initials *H. I.*, but its openly pro-Jesuit stance left no question about the translator's views. Hoskins also participated in the international controversy over the oath of allegiance, which James I required his subjects to swear in the wake of the Gunpowder Plot, with *A Briefe and Cleare Declaration of Sundry Pointes Absolutely Dislyked in the Lately Enacted Oath of Allegiance* (1611). This anonymous work supplied a summary and partial translation of a 1611 treatise by Leonardus Lessius, SJ, that had been printed at Saint Omer before being banned by Rome. Hoskins explains that he has prepared this text in haste so that readers can learn that "the feare which Catholickes have of offending the Majestie of Allmighty God, and their care of preserving their Consciences from violating the fayth which they professe, is the only cause that moveth them to declyne in some sort from the exact performance of his Majesties Commaundement."[29] Finally, Hoskins indirectly addressed the Gunpowder Plot by dedicating an edition of Thomas à Kempis's *The Following of Christ* (1613) to Elizabeth Vaux, a benefactor of the Brussels convent who aided Gerard after the Gunpowder Plot and suffered imprisonment from 1611 to 1613. Hoskins's preface artfully alludes to Vaux's imprisonment by praising the solace found in Kempis's text: "It raiseth up to cheerefull confidence the debased head, and placeth in a Throne of endles Honour those who in this world doe seeme imprisoned in the blacke cloud of disgrace."[30] A woodcut of the Jesuit insignia on the title page suggested the text's Ignatian ties, perhaps to remind readers of the society's reputation for spiritual counsel. While Hoskins's translations did not always reveal his religious affiliation, they consistently attempted to influence the ways that English readers viewed Jesuits.

Finally, Robert Chambers, a secular priest and ordinary confessor at the Brussels convent, interceded in English politics by publishing a translation that petitioned James I to lessen persecution of Catholics after the Gunpowder Plot: *Miracles Lately Wrought by the Intercession of the Glorious Virgin Marie, at Mont-aigu* (1606). The title page identifies Chambers by name and office, drawing on the reputation of the Brussels Benedictines to establish the translator's authority among English Catholics: "Translated . . . by M[aster] Robert Chambers Priest, and confessor of the English Religious Dames in the Citie of Bruxelles." In a lengthy dedicatory preface to James, Chambers defends the validity of miracles by citing sources ranging from the Bible to Augustine to Foxe's

Actes and Monuments. Similarly, Chambers's epistle to the reader argues for the legitimacy of pilgrimage, images, adoration of saints, and intercessory prayers. Chambers also appealed directly to James on behalf of English Catholics by evoking the international outrage that followed the execution of his mother Mary, Queen of Scots: "All the world could not but have justly condemned that person as very injurious to your Majestie, who ever should have dared to have had as much as a thought that your Highnes would ever (I do not say) commaund, but so much as permitt that the Catholiks, your mothers chiefest if not her onely frendes, should be any wayes molested, and much lesse indamaged, impoverished, imprisoned, condemned and put to death for the profession of her faith."[31] Chambers's institutional credentials probably enhanced the legitimacy of his doctrinal and polemical agendas among English Catholics. When Mary Percy collaborated with Hoskins on a translation of her own, she must have been well aware of the ways that translation could serve Catholic interests, particularly through authorial poses that invoked the translator's larger religious community.

As increasing numbers of Englishwomen joined or founded convents on the Continent, Mary Percy offered a blueprint for monastic spirituality that combined mysticism and Ignatian methods by publishing her translation of *An Abridgment of Christian Perfection* (1612). Percy's interest in Ignatian piety was largely representative of spiritual preferences at the Brussels convent, which had benefited tremendously from the assistance of English Jesuits. William Holt, SJ, vice-prefect of the English Jesuits in Flanders, convinced Percy to found a convent for Englishwomen rather than join a preexisting continental house. Holt then facilitated the convent's foundation by seeking approval from local rulers Archduke Albert and Archduchess Isabella, locating an appropriate building, identifying a suitable first abbess (Joanna Berkeley), and raising money.[32] Robert Persons, SJ, obtained papal approval for the foundation, and William Baldwin, SJ, Holt's successor as vice-prefect, arranged for Philip III of Spain to pay a monthly pension to the house.[33] Although Ignatius forbade the Society from serving as ordinary confessors to convents, English Jesuits acted as extraordinary confessors for Brussels nuns to supplement the ordinary confessor appointed by the archbishop of Mechelen.[34] While the ordinary confessor performed the weekly Mass and oversaw confessions, the nuns had recourse to Jesuit priests for the *Spiritual Exercises* as well as individual guidance for spiritual difficulties. Unsurprisingly, the Brussels house attracted many novices who were strongly devoted to Ignatian piety. Mary (Jane) Lovell, who entered the house as a novice in 1608, was described by the intelligencer Thomas Edmondes as "the most passyonate besotted poore woman that ever was with the opinyon of the Jesuitte."[35] Many early entrants had Jesuit relations, and the house became a refuge for women with connections to the Gunpowder Plot, including Magdalen (Elizabeth) Digby, sister of Everard Digby, and Mary Roper, niece of Elizabeth Vaux.

Yet in 1609, Abbess Berkeley found herself at odds with Baldwin, a conflict that threatened the house's close relationship with Jesuit priests. On April 13, 1609, Edmondes reported that Lovell, then a postulant, was having difficulty conforming to monastic life: "The Ladie Lovell is very much distracted whether she should resolve to persever in the course of a Nunne . . . for that she doth not only very ill brooke the severities of that lyfe, but also the disagreements which have bin betweene her & the Abbesse, for seeking to reclayme her haultie humor. . . . She is become almost desperate, & the Jesuittes are noe lesse troubled to keepe her from relenting to avoyd the geiving of scandal."[36] Edmondes claimed that the Jesuits were only interested in maintaining control of Lovell's money, but even so his report reveals the deep concerns Jesuits had about Lovell's future in the house. Baldwin may therefore have encouraged a letter that Berkeley sent to the archbishop of Mechelen on March 31 requesting that Percy and several unnamed postulants be allowed to found a new house: "Cum . . . Congregationem hanc nostrum annis aliquot numero crescente defectu loci amplioris arctatam fuisse, arbitramur e re Monastici nostri instituti futurum, atque singulari multarum solatio quae religionem nostrum ambiunt, si nonnullae huius nostrae Congregationis Professae cum aliquot Novitiis et Discipulis alibi constituantur" (Since . . . this our congregation has been confined for some years by a growing number [and] the lack of greater space, we judge of the matter that it would be an unparalleled comfort to our monastic institution and the many women who strive for our religion, if some professed [nuns] of this our congregation with some novices and scholars were established elsewhere).[37] Berkeley may have hoped that Lovell would leave for this filiation, solving in one stroke the house's problems with space as well as the question of Lovell's vocation. After Berkeley's suit was denied, Jesuit priests urged several postulants to found a new monastery, as Lucy Knatchbull later noted: "Some Persons whose judgment I knew no reason to suspect advised divers of us that were Scholars to begin a new Monastery. That which made me hearken to it was a report (not bruited of malice, as I hope) that the Fathers of the Society of Jesus should not be suffered by the Superior of this House, to continue to give us that direction for Spirit which we expected."[38] As these women had not yet professed, they could leave without the archbishop's permission, unlike Percy. Knatchbull, Lovell, and Digby consequently went to Louvain, an ideal location because the English Jesuits had recently formed a novitiate there under the guidance of Gerard. Yet by August the venture had clearly failed, and Baldwin interceded with Berkeley so that Knatchbull and Digby could return to the Brussels convent.[39]

Several anecdotes from 1609 suggest that the nuns who remained at Brussels viewed these events as significant threats to the convent's well-being. An anecdote associated with lay sister Martha (Margaret) Whittaker provides useful insight into the tensions between Berkeley and an unnamed man, identified by the house's nineteenth-century *Chronicles* as Baldwin:

> Being one morning in prayer, she suddenly heard within her: "Go to such a person . . . and tell him to leave off what he is about, for he shall never bring to pass what he desires." Whereupon, going unto him, she told him on the part of God what His Divine Majesty had commanded her. But the person believed her not, & answered that the business would take effect, for that the persons were now about to go forth. . . . Whereunto she answered, "Father, you shall never have them forth." Soon after this, she again understood the following words to be spoken to her in prayer. "Tell that person that he has made disquiet between Superior & Superiors, between children & Superior; and therefore let him make peace with all speed." Whereunto she answered. "Lord why will you send me unto him? I am a simple woman, and he a learned man, he will not believe me." But she being encouraged by God went and told the person what she had been commanded. Upon which he presently laboured to make the peace, which was performed.[40]

This tale evokes the discord caused by the departure of Knatchbull's party, as Baldwin may have seemed to support Lovell rather than Berkeley, her abbess and superior. Accordingly, Baldwin must "make peace" by ending the "disquiet" between Berkeley and the Jesuit fathers ("Superior & Superiors") as well as between Berkeley and either her community or the returning novices ("children & Superior"). Another account suggests that the house had already been saved by divine intervention that February: "A very devout good man fell into so great a disgust agaynst the monastery, and so ill an oppinion agaynst them, as he determined some great mischeefe to the hows." While this man slept, "our Blessed lady, having all the Religious of the monastery under her mantle, warnd him with threats to desist from his ill intentions, adding that her sweete Sonn Jesus & her selfe had taken this monastery under theyr protection."[41] Chastened, the man sought confession from Chambers the next day and renounced his plans. The timing suggests that this man's "disgust" may have arisen from the convent's ongoing difficulties with Lovell and, by extension, her Jesuit supporters.

As a result, Berkeley may have begun to rethink the house's previous dependence upon Jesuit assistance. Faced with a financial crisis in April 1611, Berkeley wrote to Benedictine superiors in Flanders for aid: "Being strangers in (this Country) their condition & circumstances are known to very few; hence they have received as yet but little, or no help, from any: the house they dwell in is very small, but has been purchased by their own fortunes; from which . . . they suffer scarcity & many incommodities."[42] Although the house had already received considerable financial help from the Jesuits and their contacts, Berkeley omits this fact and instead stresses the convent's isolation from other English Catholics. That December, she similarly rewrote the house's history in a letter to the archbishop regarding their proposed statutes. While Berkeley acknowledges that English Jesuits helped establish the house and later reviewed its statutes, she presents the monastery as the fulfillment of the missionary movement begun by Cardinal William Allen, who had attended her clothing in 1580. After mentioning the notable history of the Benedictine order in England, she remarks, "Quae illustrissimae memoriae Illustrissimum et Reverendissimum Cardinalem Alanum . . . ita permoverunt ut . . . in hoc strenue incubuerit, qua ratione cum Catholica religione huius etiam Sacri Ordinis alumnos, et praecipue Moniales impia Haereticorum tyrannide flagitiosissime deletas, et exitio datas patriae suae restitueret" (Which most illustrious memories so moved the Most Illustrious and Most Reverend Cardinal Allen . . . that . . . he strenuously devoted himself to this: by what method he might restore to their country—along with Catholic religion—likewise the nurslings of this sacred order, and chiefly the nuns most shamefully destroyed by the impious tyranny of heretics and cast into exile).[43] Yet Allen had died before Percy arrived in Flanders and consequently played no direct role in the house's foundation. Even though Allen and Persons had a close working relationship, Berkeley downplays the house's identification with Jesuit interests by presenting the labors of Persons and Holt as the realization of Allen's plan.

Even as Berkeley's reconsideration of Jesuit influence threatened to undermine the role of Jesuit priests at the Brussels Benedictines, Mary Percy affirmed that Ignatian spirituality had value within a monastic context through her translation of *The Abridgment of Christian Perfection.* During this period, Percy strongly favored the Jesuit priests associated with the Brussels house, even writing Mutio Vitelleschi, the newly appointed general of the Jesuits, in 1618 to request that English Jesuits continue to advise the community.[44] Percy's translation of the *Abridgment* is an even earlier marker of her commitment to Ignatian piety, for several reasons. First, Percy collaborated with Hoskins on the translation, as Augustine Baker relates: "[The] preface was so Translated into English, by Fa[ther] Antony Hoskins, of the Society of Jesus (as I have bin Informed by One of the Dames of This House, who then was of Brussels) . . . the Residue (I mean, the whole Body of the Book) being of the Translation of the Said Lady Abbesse: whom the Said Father A. Hoskins did moreover somewhat Aid (as I am likewise Informed) in the Translation of the Said Body of the Book; and did Procure, or Help for the Getting of it printed."[45] The text had first appeared in Italian (*Breve compendio,* c. 1588), but Percy and Hoskins worked from an intermediary French version (*Abregé de la perfection chrestienne,* 1598). Second, the translation offers a mixture of mysticism and Ignatian meditation that reflects Percy's own interests. Scholars now agree that Achille Gagliardi, SJ, and his penitent Isabella Berinzaga collaborated on the *Abridgment,* but in 1612 the work's authorship was unknown.[46] While Baker strenuously argued that the *Abridgment* could not have been composed by a Jesuit, readers steeped in Ignatian piety would have recognized the text's indebtedness to the *Spiritual Exercises.* Besides offering Ignatian-style meditations, the *Abridgment* cites two sections of the *Spiritual Exercises*—the "First Principle and Foundation" (no. 23) and the "Introduction to Making a Choice of a Way of Life" (no. 169)—as foundations for mystical progress: "The practice of all this consisteth, first in a totall indifferency in respect of things created, as we have set downe for the foundation of our exercises. Secondly to make election of an estate conformable to Gods wil . . . praying & working continually with the selfe same rules of our exercises."[47] Furthermore, as André Derville has observed, the text is based on Ignatian principles: "Plus d'un passage dépend directement des *Exercices.* L'ensemble est en cohérence avec la doctrine ignatienne de l'indifférence, de l'humilité, de l'*agere contra*" (More than one passage directly depends on the *Exercises.* The whole is in agreement with the Ignatian doctrine of indifference, of humility, of *agere contra*).[48] Percy may also have been drawn to this text due to its emphasis on self-abnegation. In 1609, Gerard remarked of Percy, "Often she asks her director for permission to become a recluse; but he is not in favour of it, and she has submitted to his advice."[49] Percy's translation probably stemmed from her personal interest in using Ignatian methods as a means of pursuing detachment from the world.

Yet in publishing her translation, Percy framed the *Abridgment* as a model of monastic spirituality fit for all religious readers. Drawing on the French source text's preface, Percy crafts a humble authorial persona as an anonymous religious who might seem to speak for the larger English monastic community. D. C. M., the work's unknown French editor, dedicates the *Abridgment* to monks and nuns, observing that their praiseworthy "modesty, & humility" prevented him from dedicating the work to a specific individual (*ACP,* 5). Similarly, Percy's preface addresses "the religious of our nation" (*ACP,* *3r), and she states that the treatise is most appropriate for those who have taken the monastic vows of poverty, chastity, and obedience known as the evangelical counsels: "I doubt not to judg it fitly presented to the reading of all such, as have entred, or resolved to enter the pathes of Perfection, by imitation of Christ our Lord in practise and performance of the Counsells Evangelicall" (*ACP,* *3r, *3v–*4r). Percy, like D. C. M., may only sign her preface with her initials ("P. M."), but she nevertheless indicates that she has undertaken religious vows by including herself among those striving for this "Perfection": "For the obtaining of this [perfection], I beseech his divine Goodnes to assist *us* all with his holy grace, and to replenish your soules with the comfort of his celestiall spirit" (*ACP,* *7v, emphasis mine). Readers might therefore have viewed the translation as the work of an anonymous monastic who followed the methods contained in the *Abridgment.* Percy further suggests the monastic context of her translation by imitating other elements of D. C. M.'s preface. Just as D. C. M. cites Matthew 7:6 as evidence that secular readers could not appreciate the worth of this treatise ("the advertisment which our Saviour giveth us, that we give not holy things unto doggs, nor cast pearles before swine"; *ACP,* 3), Percy states that the *Abridgment* is not fit for "sensuall minds, who cannot discerne the worth of such a pearle, but would rather trample it with their feete" (*ACP,* *3v). Similarly, D. C. M. praises the text by comparing it to the work of Saint Catherine of Siena, and Percy alludes to Catherine's mystic experiences to explain the value of subordinating self-will, a key tenet of the *Abridgment:* "Now it seemeth not to be her will that worketh, but the will of God which worketh in her: as though she had given her owne hart unto Christ: and, as we read of S[aint] Catherine of Siena, had receaved his in exchange" (*ACP,* *6v–7r). Percy refers to John Fen's 1609 translation of Catherine of Siena's life, which recounted this "exchange": "She made a special petition to him, that he would vouchsafe to take awaie her owne hart and will, and geve her an other newe hart and will."[50] As the title page to Fen's translation noted, he was confessor to the English Augustinians of Louvain, so that Percy's allusion evoked the milieu of English monasticism. By dedicating her translation to monks and nuns, identifying herself as an anonymous religious, and placing her work in conversation with other texts originating from the cloister, Percy suggested that the *Abridgment* was representative of English monasticism.

In introducing the main ideas of the *Abridgment,* Percy furthermore claimed that the text would help readers achieve a spiritual union with Christ that is inherently compatible with monastic life. *An Abridgment* guides readers through spiritual stages that eventually lead to deiformity, or complete fusion with God's will. Elaborating upon D. C. M.'s description of the work as a "thresor" (treasure), Percy develops an extended metaphor of minting coins that invokes the monastic virtues of humility, poverty, chastity, and obedience.[51] In the stage of annihilation, the soul "dig[s] & descend[s] into his owne nothing," achieving the humility required by monastic life. The state of disappropriation causes the soul "to cast up and throw from him all the earthly substance which lieth between him & the treasure" (*ACP,* *5r), and Percy connects this phase with the monastic vow of poverty by offering a second definition for this term: "or as it is called in the Ghospel, by Renunciation of all things which he possesseth." Here Percy alludes to Christ's exhortation that the disciples embrace poverty (Luke 14:33), a command obeyed by monks and nuns: "every one of you that doth not renounce al that he possesseth, cannot be my disciple."[52] The next state, indifference, allows the soul "to cleanse" the treasure "from the dust of his private affections, and self-interest" (*ACP,* *5r), and then the stage of conformity "teacheth him first how to purifie the same from the drosse of all self-love" (*ACP,* *5v), leaving only a love for God that marks the soul as a truly chaste spouse of Christ. In the stage of uniformity, refinement through "the touchstone of Christ his example" transforms the soul "so that it then comes to be *Aurum ignitum,* spoken of in the Apocalyps, and one thing, as it were, with the fire it selfe." Percy had already praised monastic imitation of Christ, and her reference to Revelation 3:18 suggests that the treatise offers Christ's life as a "touchstone" that will lead to spiritual rewards: "I counsel thee to bye of me gold fire-tried [aurum ignitum], that thou maiest be made riche."[53] Finally, deiformity results in complete obedience to God as the treasure becomes "pliable to the will of him that worketh it" and ultimately "receave[s] the stampe of the heavenly King, that so it may be currant coyne in his divine Court. . . . This is the worke of grace in the soule, the workman is God himself, and the stampe he imprinteth in it, is his owne Image" (*ACP*, *6r). Since souls achieving this final stage all bear God's "stampe," they become interchangeable tokens of God that collectively represent his treasure, mirroring the communal ideal of convent life. Readers who were aware of Percy's identity might view this metaphor as evidence that the Brussels community remained united despite its recent problems. More broadly, this metaphor suggested that the *Abridgment* offered valuable guidance that might reinforce the collective identity of the cloister. By focusing on the treatise's advocacy for mystical self-annihilation, Percy could avoid alienating readers like Berkeley and Baker, who might be skeptical of the value that Ignatian spirituality held for a monastic community.

While Percy's translation generally offers a close rendering of her French source text, at times she reframes the *Abridgment* so that it is clearly aligned with monastic spirituality. Berinzaga and Gagliardi encourage readers to begin their ascent to union with God through complete self-abasement: "The first principle is, to have a meane & a base esteeme of things created, & above all of himself" (*ACP*, 12). To achieve this humility, they recommend that readers identify themselves with "dust, a sinke [cesspool], an Apostume [pustulent abscess]" (*ACP*, 16). As Derville has noted, this language draws on the First Week of the *Spiritual Exercises* (especially no. 58.4–5), which emphasizes self-examination of sins.[54] Berinzaga and Gagliardi develop this theme much more extensively than Ignatius does, and Percy removes several moments that dwell on self-abasement from the chapter on annihilation—perhaps because she and other nuns at the convent had had difficulties with spiritual desolation.[55] Strikingly, Percy replaces these passages with new material emphasizing monastic spirituality. Berinzaga and Gagliardi instruct the soul to enter into annihilation by "thinking herselfe the greatest sinner in the world, . . . attributing to herselfe all the sinnes that are committed, and that all their tormentes duly might be inflicted upon her" (*ACP*, 16–17). Percy omits the sentence following this passage: "Et cecy suppose une grande cognoissance du peché, comme offencez de Dieu, &c" (*APC*, 174; And this assumes a great knowledge of sin, as offenses of God, etc.). This remark might seem to suggest that the soul should embark on a potentially unhealthy examination of sinfulness. Percy instead alleviates the severity of this passage by inserting a reminder of God's providence: "For there is no sinne but she might have committed it, if God had not preserved her: examples of this may be seene in the lives of S[aint] Francis and S[aint] Catherine of Siena" (*ACP*, 17). An English translation of Francis's life had recently been published, just as Fen had translated Catherine's life, so that this alteration of the text again places the *Abridgment* in conversation with other English-language works promoting monasticism.[56] Readers might already know that Saint Francis lived pleasurably before founding the Franciscan order and that Saint Catherine's parents attempted to prevent her from becoming a Dominican tertiary. As she had done in the preface, Percy alludes to exemplary models of monastic piety to emphasize the worth of this text for English members of religious orders.

An even more striking example of Percy's license with her source text occurs when she radically condenses a section that similarly advises readers to practice an excessive amount of self-degradation. As the 1599 edition is scarce, it may be useful to print the entire passage omitted by Percy:

> Elle doit descendre en la cognoissance de ses pechez, vices, & defauts particuliers, s'abaissant tous les jours par ceste lumiere de la benignité de Dieu qui l'a supporté. Secondement faisant continuel progrez, en tel estime de sa bassesse elle doit venir en la practique d'icelle, laquelle consiste premierement, en la haine de toute loüange honneur & dignité, & quand se presente l'occasion d'icelles les fuir de tout son pouvoir, puis que c'est hors de toute raison qu'à un rien & à une creature si vile & si meschante on donne ou fasse honneur; & l'ame qui vrayement sent sa petitesse, pense luy estre impossible de s'elever par loüange quelconque qui luy soit faicte, & à par soy s'en rit & s'en mocque, & tant plus se confound elle, & s'humilie davantage qu'elle apperçoit, combien elle est eloignee de toute bonté vertu & merite de loüange & honneur. Elle embrasse volontiers toutes occasions de mespris, confusions, affronts, persecutions, infamies, & autres choses semblables, & va au devant d'icelles avec joye & jubilation, & les accepte comme choses dignes de soy, & qu'elle a bien merité, remerciant nostre Seigneur qui l'a traicté comme il convient, & qui plus est s'estimant indigne d'estre ainsi visitée de Dieu, qui daigne exercer envers elle sa justice & sur tout s'esjouit grandement de cecy, à sçavoir de son opprobre & ignominie, pour autant qu'il en provient grande gloire à Dieu, & principalement à sa bonté, laquelle a daigné creér gouverner, racheter, & sauver chose si vile, & a luy tant rebelle. Tiercement de son costé tant qu'elle peut doit elire les choses plus basses & viles. (*APC*, 174–77)
>
> She must descend into the knowledge of her sins, vices, and particular defaults, abasing herself every day by this light of the goodness of God who has supported her. Secondly, making continual

> progress in such esteem of her lowness she must come to the practice of this, which consists first in the hatred of all praise, honor, and dignity, and when the occasion of these things presents itself, to flee them with all her power, since it is beyond all reason that one would give or do honor to a nothing and a creature so vile and evil; and the soul who truly feels her smallness, thinks it is impossible to raise herself by whatever praise which may be done to her, and by herself she laughs at and mocks it, and she confounds herself more and humbles herself further as much as she perceives how far she is estranged from all goodness, virtue, and merit of praise and honor. She voluntarily embraces all occasions of contempts, confusions, affronts, persecutions, infamies, and other similar things, and she goes past them with joy and jubilation, and accepts them as worthy of herself, and what she has well deserved, thanking our Lord who has treated her as it is fitting, and, what is more, esteeming herself unworthy to be thus visited by God, who deigns to exercise toward her his justice, and especially rejoices greatly in this, to know of her opprobrium and ignominy, for as much as great glory comes from these things to God, and principally to his goodness, which has deigned to create, govern, redeem, and save a thing so vile, and so rebellious to him. Thirdly, for her part as much as she can it is necessary to choose the lowest and most vile things. (my translation)

Repeatedly characterizing the soul as "vile," Berinzaga and Gagliardi encourage the soul to dwell upon its own "sins, vices, and particular defaults" in order to abase itself so absolutely that the soul rejects all honor and welcomes scorn. This guidance is impractical in a monastic setting, where certain offices—such as abbess and prioress—not only require a degree of "praise, honor and dignity" but also must be fulfilled by members of the community. Percy shortens this passage so that it advocates renunciation of the world rather than the self: "She ought to descend to the knowledg of these thinges of the world, the better to contemne them: and for the rejecting of them, she must make choice of the vilest and basest of them" (*ACP,* 17). This alteration is reminiscent of Percy's preface, which valorized those who have the "fortitude of mind as to contemne their former worldly estate, for the purchase of this field or state of religious life" (*ACP,* *4v). While the motive for this drastic abridgment appears to have been Percy's distaste for the work's extreme self-abasement, she takes this opportunity to reshape the *Abridgment* so that it supports her prefatory claims about the text's relevance to monasticism.

Besides adding monastic elements to the *Abridgment,* Percy highlights several Ignatian aspects of the text, subtly legitimating the value of Ignatian spirituality within the cloister. As previously noted, Percy's preface asserted that monks and nuns "enter[ed] the pathes of Perfection, by imitation of Christ our Lord" (*ACP,* *4r). The text offers Ignatian-style contemplations that presented Christ as a model for monastic life with the "Ladder of Perfection," a series of exercises keyed to specific stages of the *Abridgment.* In format and intention, these meditations are reminiscent of the *Spiritual Exercises,* in which readers reflect on Christ's life in a methodical sequence that includes preparatory prayer, preludes, points to consider, and colloquies. Similarly, each set of meditations in the "Ladder" begins with a preparatory prayer focused on a moment in Christ's life followed by points for consideration meant to guide the reader's contemplation. As in the *Spiritual Exercises,* the overall effect of these meditations is to inspire readers to imitate Jesus Christ. For example, the preparatory prayer for the stage of conformity cites John 4:34 as a pattern for obeying God's will: "We must consider in these wordes (*Cibus meus est, ut faciam voluntatem Patris mei qui in caelis est*) that is to say, my meat is to doe the will of my father which is in heaven: and in other like speaches the great conformity that our Saviour Jesus had with the will of his eternall father. . . . And of this we may gather how much more we are obliged to do the same in his imitation" (*ACP,* 100). Percy underscores this insight by heightening Christ's willingness to die in the second point of the ensuing meditation: "The contentment in this conformity, did not bring him any asswagement of his sorrowes, but only made that his will sweetly reposed in them, and with so *prompt and ready a mind* [gayeté de coeur], *he willed and desired* them [vouloit]" (*ACP,* 104; *APC,* 302). By translating "vouloit" (he willed) with the doublet "he willed and desired," Percy emphasizes the harmony between the will of Christ and God, and her translation of "prompt and ready a mind" for "gayeté de coeur" (alacrity of heart) further underscores Christ's willingness to obey God. As a result, Percy reinforces the preparatory prayer's injunction that readers should take Christ as an example of conformity. By offering readers set exercises meant to facilitate mystical union with God, the "Ladder" implicitly legitimized Ignatian meditation as a useful means of helping readers to achieve the monastic ideals outlined in Percy's preface.

The *Abridgment* also emphasizes the Ignatian practice of discernment as a method to overcome self-love, which Berinzaga and Gagliardi present as the primary impediment to self-mortification. Within a monastic setting, self-love was highly problematic because it might interfere with the ability to submit to superiors and monastic rules, and Lovell's case might have seemed to suggest that Jesuit priests only encouraged such insubordination. Percy, however, reworks the *Abridgment* so that it insists even more strongly on discernment as a tonic for self-love. The *Spiritual Exercises* instruct exercitants to use discretion in identifying the source of their spiritual movements: "It is characteristic of God and His Angels, when they act upon the soul, to give true happiness and spiritual joy, and to banish all the sadness and disturbances which are caused by the enemy. It is characteristic of the evil one to fight against such happiness and consolation by proposing fallacious reasonings, subtilties [*sic*], and continual deceptions."[57] In keeping with this idea, Berinzaga and Gagliardi offer "Remedies against Selfe-Love" that instruct the soul to determine whether apparent spiritual consolations actually result from self-love: "All thinges, how good and holy soever they be, are not alwayes pleasing to God, but only those that come from him, *and are required by him* [added]. And by this we may know, *that they come from him* [added] when the said things do not move us nor *lift us up unto pride* [haussent & eslevent] in having them" (*ACP*, 142; *APC*, 367). Percy's additions to this passage underscore its point about the necessity of utilizing discernment to avoid self-love. Besides adding qualifying phrases claiming that God only "require[s]" certain consolations and that it is furthermore possible to know whether "they come from him," Percy hints at the possible spiritual danger of forgoing discernment by translating "haussent & eslevent" (raise and elevate) as "lift us up unto pride." Berinzaga and Gagliardi also argue that confessors who are well versed in discernment can provide crucial aid to souls experiencing self-love: "The soule infected herewith must seeke to have a person very much enlightned by God, that hath the discretion of [s]pirits" (*ACP*, 141). Percy reinforces this point by altering Berinzaga and Gagliardi's later advice to confessors: "The spirituall father, who *to take away, and cleere* [oster] the soule from all selfe love, in all that she pretendeth in her actions, and desires must first seeke all the meanes to penetrate into her hart, *that is to gaine her good opinion and estimation, and to be gratefull unto her* [added]; & afterwards he must begin with great sweetnes *to apply his remedies, and so to cure and heale her* [à la penser & mediciner]" (*ACP*, 143; *APC*, 368). Here Percy underscores the confessor's ability to aid mortification by translating "oster" (remove) with the doublet "take away and cleere" as well as by recasting the phrase "à la penser & mediciner" (to take care of her and to give her medicine) in solely medical terms: "to apply his remedies and so to cure and heale her." She also adds an explanatory gloss after "to penetrate into her hart" ("that is to gaine her good opinion and estimation, and to be gratefull unto her"), suggesting the psychological subtlety needed to deal with these troubled souls. If Percy's preface depicted the *Abridgment* as offering a method for enhancing monastic conformity, this emphasis on the role of discretion in eradicating self-love implies that Jesuit confessors are necessary allies in ensuring the spiritual perfection of individual nuns and preserving the concord of monastic institutions. After Lovell's departure, this idea would have been particularly useful in refuting negative views of Jesuit involvement at the Brussels Benedictines.

Ultimately, Percy's translation offered readers a form of monastic spirituality that was based upon Ignatian methods and motifs, legitimating the role of Ignatian practices at the Brussels Benedictines and beyond. The events of 1609 had threatened the unity of the Brussels Benedictines, and Berkeley may very well have viewed Lovell's Jesuit advisers as the instigators of this breach of monastic order. Percy's translation implicitly responded to these concerns by suggesting that Ignatian methods could encourage conformity to God's will and so enhance the nuns' adherence to monastic virtues. Within the immediate setting of Percy's convent, this translation might have encouraged the house's unwavering adherence to Ignatian precepts after Lovell's departure. More generally, Percy's self-presentation as an anonymous monastic translator might have suggested that the work was representative of English monasticism. While readers versed in Ignatian precepts may have received the impression that English monasticism was strongly tied to Ignatian spirituality, the text's understated reliance on the *Spiritual Exercises* allowed it to serve as a model for readers who rejected Ignatian ideas, including Baker.

Percy's translation saw two more editions that emphasized the Ignatian associations of her work even more firmly.[58] In 1612, Etienne Binet, SJ, published another French translation of the *Breve Compendio* that attributed the work to Gagliardi for the first time. John Wilson subsequently republished Percy's translation in 1625, ascribing the work to Hoskins alone: "Written in Italian, by Fa[ther] Achilles Galliardi of the Society of Jesus & translated into English by A. H. of the same Society." Wilson also strengthened the 1625 edition's association with Ignatian piety by adding material from the First Week of the *Spiritual Exercises:* "The Dayly Examen of Our Conscience" (no. 43), "The Particular Examen" (nos. 25–26), and "Foure Additions Very Profitable, for the More Easy & Speedy Rooting out of Any Vice" (nos. 27–31). Another paratext, "Certayne Advertisments Necessary for the Better Making of Our Prayer," offers instructions on adapting aspects of the *Spiritual Exercises,* such as composition of place, for individual prayer.[59] In a second edition dated 1626 but probably published in 1628, Wilson restored Percy's authorship, now ascribing the translation to "The Right Honourable, & Religious Lady, the La[dy] M. P." As Wilson retained the excerpts of the *Spiritual Exercises* added in the 1625 version, this edition implied that Percy, now abbess of the Brussels Benedictines, supported Ignatian spirituality. Ironically, by 1628 Percy was actively engaged in a dispute with pro-Jesuit nuns at her convent who objected to the appointment of an anti-Jesuit ordinary confessor. Percy's *Abridgment* thus continued to suggest the usefulness of Ignatian spirituality within a monastic setting even after she herself had decided that Jesuit confessors were not conducive to the spiritual health of her convent.

A Dame of Cambrai: Potentiana Deacon, François de Sales, and Monastic Order

As a member of Benedictine convents in Brussels and Cambrai, Potentiana Deacon had two distinct models for the way that translation could define a house's spirituality. Deacon professed at the Brussels Benedictines, where she would have gained firsthand knowledge of translations by Mary Percy and her confessors that intervened in public and private debates over Catholicism. Translated spiritual treatises were arguably even more important within the daily life of the Cambrai nuns as Augustine Baker, the Cambrai convent's unofficial spiritual guide, and several of the Cambrai nuns translated texts conducive to the house's focus on contemplative mysticism. Baker, however, resuscitated the medieval tradition in which the learning produced by and for the house remained largely within the cloister. Rather than seeking to influence the wider English Catholic community, most of the Cambrai translators circulated their work in manuscript to assist the house's spiritual development. While these two groups of translators may have disagreed over the place of monastic spirituality within the public sphere, both nonetheless viewed translation itself as an influential means of instilling piety.

The Cambrai nuns' interest in translation stemmed from Baker's view that reading mystical and spiritual works could facilitate contemplative progress.[60] Nevertheless, Baker did not take a prescriptive stance, instead urging the nuns to determine which texts met their particular needs: "Observe your own way, spirit, and call; and of books, take and practise according as you shall find to be proper and answerable to such a way, spirit, and call of yours; and no more or further."[61] Baker assembled a library of diverse texts that would allow the Cambrai nuns the necessary latitude to search for their distinctive calls. His *Catalogue of Such English Bookes as Are in This House, Most Helping toward Contemplation* recommends a variety of contemporary publications, including translations of saints' lives (*The Life of the Glorious Bishop S[aint] Patricke,* 1625), spiritual classics (*The Confessions of S[aint] Augustine,* 1620), and contemporary treatises (Percy's *Abridgment*).[62] As Baker noted in a letter to Robert Cotton requesting manuscript copies of medieval devotional texts, few printed books offered guidance on mystical practices: "Their lives being contemplative the comon bookes of the worlde are not for their purpose, and litle or nothing is in thes daies printed in English that is proper for them."[63] Baker attempted to fill this gap by composing his own treatises, modernizing medieval classics (including *The Cloud of Unknowing*), and translating continental authors such as Louis de Blois. Baker's purpose in translating was primarily utilitarian: to provide the nuns with reading material that offered examples for readers to follow or reject. For example, Gertrude (Helen) More requested that Baker translate part of Constantine Barbanson into English after finding one passage especially inspiring: "O, O, that must be my waie, I pray you . . . lette me have that place translated into English."[64] Baker made no attempt to publish his translations, probably out of a belief that mystical works were not appropriate for general readers: "Not all are fit to read them [mystical treatises]. And it may be questioned whether they be fit at all to be printed and published."[65] Baker thus helped establish an environment in which literary production—including translation—took place largely for the spiritual benefit of the Cambrai nuns themselves rather than secular readers.

Baker's model endured after his departure from the house in 1632, as several Cambrai nuns translated French works into English to share exemplary mystical texts with the rest of the house. Abbess Catherine Gascoigne translated Charlotte de Saint-Jean l'Êvangéliste Le Sergent's *Collection of Some Familiar Answers upon the Conduct of Soules in a Mistick Life* into English (*Recueil de quelques réponses familières, sur la conduit des âmes en la vie mystique,* 1657). While Le Sergent penned a dedicatory preface explaining that she had published the *Recueil* to contest an erroneous and unauthorized edition of her work, Gascoigne omitted this preface: "This booke was dedicated to Madame de Guise Abbesse of the monastery but because there was nothing in the epistle but civility & respect therfore it was not translated."[66] This remark reveals the practical orientation of Gascoigne's translation, which wastes no time on "civility & respect" but rather moves directly to Le Sergent's spiritual instruction. Agnes More, meanwhile, translated part of Jeanne de Cambry's *Building of Divine Love* (*La ruine de l'amour propre et bâtiment de l'amour divin,* 1627). Like Gascoigne, More excises her source text's prefatory materials, including commendatory verses, de Cambry's preface to the reader, and a dedicatory preface to the Infanta Isabella. More also reshapes the text by omitting its first book, which discusses self-mortification. The manuscript's 1691 title page concludes with a description of the final chapters that emphasizes the mystical focus of the resulting translation: "The holy repose of the faithfull soul Spouse of Jesus Christ, wherin by a beatifying Love to her Spouse her Spirit being transformed into God & united to him, nature is annihilated by a divine martyrdom."[67] Both Gascoigne and More circulated their translations within the house rather than seeking a wider audience through print. At most, the Cambrai nuns shared their work with family members or other convents. Catherine Gascoigne and Clementia (Anne) Cary translated Baker's works into French for the convent of St. Lazare in Cambrai.[68] Meanwhile, Barbara Constable dedicated several manuscript translations to her sister and niece, but even she expected that her work would see limited circulation.[69]

Yet the nuns at Cambrai were also well aware of translation's ability to publicize the spiritual methods associated with a particular order or institution. Baker's *Enquiry* defended Percy's authorship of the *Abridgment,* noting that "One of the Dames of This House, who then was of Brussels"—possibly Deacon—had vouched for her role as translator.[70] Furthermore, his *Catalogue* twice mentions Elizabeth Evelinge's *Admirable Life of S[aint] Catherine of Bologna,* which was associated with the Gravelines Poor Clares.[71] Toby Matthew's translation of *A Treatise of Mental Prayer* (1627) by Alfonso Rodriguez, SJ, was also popular among some of the Cambrai nuns. Baker's *Enquiry* devotes considerable energy to demonstrating that this work's focus on Ignatian meditation made it unsuitable for a contemplative order: "[Rodriguez's] Book of Mentall Prayer, hath bin Sent to This House (viz, One from The Benedictines of Brussels, and Another from those of Gant) with Such Singular Commendations, as if there were none, but he. And Some in the House do Extoll it as Much: whereas, indeed, the Book is Even Nothing at all for the Purpose of that Spirit, which should be, and Reign, in This House, and throughout our Whole Order."[72] While Baker does not identify the "Some" who "Extoll" this book, the nuns originally from Brussels, including Deacon, are probable candidates. Matthew's translation tacitly authorized the use of Jesuit practices in English monasteries through its connection to Abbess Lucy Knatchbull of the Ghent Benedictines. Knatchbull probably collaborated with Matthew—her spiritual director and very likely a Jesuit himself—on the publication of his translation. John Wilson, overseer of the Jesuit press at Saint Omer, composed a dedicatory epistle for one version (STC 21148) that identifies Knatchbull as his source for the text: "I should have wronged this Excellent Treatise, had I directed the same, into any other, then your Ladishipps Hands, from whome I first receaved it; and to whome, by the Translatours Intention, and for many other respects, it is singularly due."[73] Another version (STC 21149) features Matthew's dedication of the translation to Knatchbull, which presents the work as evidence that Jesuits are unfairly maligned: "It will appeare to any indifferent honest eye, how unlikely it is, for the Religious men of this Order, to have any thing in them of that spirit, which either Heretikes, or Politikes, or other envious persons lay to their charg."[74] Thanks to these prefaces, Matthew's translation positioned the Ghent house as a haven for women interested in Ignatian piety. The Brussels and Ghent nuns who sent copies of this book to Cambrai may have hoped that Matthew's translation could endorse Ignatian spirituality elsewhere. Deacon was therefore familiar with two powerful, if conflicting, models of the potential influence that translation could have on devotional practices inside and outside the cloister.

In 1632, Potentiana Deacon responded to a controversy over spiritual direction among the Cambrai Benedictines by publishing a translation of François de Sales that publicly associated her house with Ignatian piety. Originally a member of the Brussels Benedictines, in 1623 Deacon was one of three nuns—along with Frances Gawen and Viviana (Mary) Yaxley—sent to assist with the foundation of the Cambrai house. Deacon and Gawen were probably selected due to their conflicts with Abbess Mary Percy. A deep rift had arisen in the Brussels house after the 1622 appointment of Francis Ward as a second ordinary confessor intended to assist Robert Chambers.[75] Percy's relationship with both Chambers and the house's Jesuit confessors had already grown strained by this point, and her apparent favoring of Ward alienated many of the Brussels nuns. While a pro-Jesuit group led by Lucy Knatchbull left for Ghent in 1624, Deacon and Gawen were part of another faction that viewed Percy's preference for Ward as a breach of monastic order. Deacon, for example, petitioned the archbishop of Mechelen more than ten times in 1623 on behalf of Chambers: "Mon humble request est, qu'il plairoit a vostre Seig[neu]rie de vouloir ainsy ordonné que Madame en des affaires de government suivre son advice, a fin que les choses puet [*sic*] estre bien dispose a L'honneur de dieu, et a nostre salut, reputations, et bien de nostre Monastre" (my humble request is that it will please your Lordship to desire it to be so ordained that Madame follows his [Chambers's] advice in matters of governance, so that things can be well arranged for the honor of God and for our health, reputations, and the good of our Monastery).[76] Gawen sent similar complaints, eventually observing that "il seroit mieulx changer madame que de perdre Un pere Confesseur si juste, docte et de bonne conscience" (it would be better to change Madame than to lose a father Confessor so just, learned, and of good conscience).[77] The reasons for Yaxley's transfer are less clear as she had only professed in 1621 and did not petition the archbishop regarding Ward. While Gawen became abbess of the new community, Deacon served simultaneously as cellarer and novice mistress.[78] In this latter position, Deacon attempted to inspire her charges with the spirit of Ignatian devotion characteristic of the Brussels Benedictines. Deacon approved of the arrangement predating Ward's arrival, in which Chambers administered the sacraments while Jesuit priests instructed the house in meditation: "Fa[ther] Cham[bers] . . . ever would the fathers [of the Society] should derect for meditation, and the method for young ones [postulants] to practice it."[79] While Deacon and Gawen were not as strongly in favor of Ignatian piety as the founders of the Ghent house, they nonetheless had been trained according to this system and probably viewed Ignatian prayer as a natural component of monastic spirituality.

The Cambrai postulants, however, found Ignatian piety uncongenial to their spiritual progress, and their requests for additional direction led to the installation of Augustine Baker as the house's unofficial spiritual guide. As previously noted, in contrast with the prescribed exercises common to Ignatian prayer at the time, Baker held that individuals could reach mystical union with God by following their own particular calls to devotion.[80] While Yaxley appears to have adapted to this new spiritual environment, Deacon and Gawen found Baker's teachings irreconcilable with their previous spiritual training.[81] After initially welcoming Baker, Deacon showed a disdain that influenced some of her charges: "The mistress [of novices] did likewise shew much esteem of him at the first; but shortly all [the postulants] fell off again for a time, upon their own and their mistress's new conceived dislike."[82] The results of the house's 1629 election of a new abbess further suggest that Deacon and Gawen had little sympathy for Baker's methods. Rather than reelecting Gawen or choosing Deacon, the convent selected Catherine Gascoigne despite the fact that her young age required a special dispensation from Rome. By this point, the Cambrai nuns clearly preferred an abbess who supported the method that most of them followed. Nevertheless, these two spiritual models appear to have coexisted without outright acrimony during this initial period. According to More, Deacon even sent her to Baker in 1625 in the hope that he might resolve her doubts over her vocation: "My Mystris advised me to go to Father Baker telling me that fowre or five in the howse had found good by him, and that at least it was no harm to try, and it would do me no harme though it did me no good; for he was a very grave man, and one that was much respected in the Congregation."[83]

Only after Francis Hull, OSB, arrived as official confessor in 1629 did these competing spiritual modes become a source of open hostility. Concerned that Baker's influence limited his own rightful authority as the house's appointed confessor, Hull encouraged the nuns to follow an Ignatian method of prayer distinct from Baker's contemplative instructions. As Christina Brent later recalled, "The present Confes[sor] apprehending it to derogate from his Authority, that another should give instructions to some of those under his charge . . . began to speake to some of them as if they were not in a way of obedience, raysing by that occasion scruples & difficullties in them, & they comming to him he sought to direct them in a course of prayer according to his opinion."[84] If Hull hoped to reinforce monastic order, he was not successful. More, for example, rejected the idea that Hull's form of prayer was compatible with Baker's mysticism: "Those instructions . . . do much seeme to be like the Jesuits as I gather by their books, yet I hold them to be nothing so intelligible as theirs, but more confused by reason he would bring these, and Fa[ther] Bakers into one, & make a compleat life for a soul out of both."[85] Besides refusing to follow Hull's method of prayer, Baker's adherents reworked the convent's schedule to find additional time for prayer, a strategy approved by Baker himself, as More acknowledged: "What was allowed by Fa[ther] Baker concerning shifting to get time and meanes for our prayer, was but in case that Superiors did account it but an unprofitable exercise."[86] The "Superior" in question here was obviously Hull, who was opposed to extending the nuns' time for prayer. In 1632, Hull brought Baker before the English Benedictine Congregation on charges of heresy and anti-authoritarianism, alleging that Baker's supporters refused to accept the authority of superiors who did not share Baker's views: "They have this Doctrin amongst them, that so much respect and Obedience is not to be given to Vicarius, Abbesse, or other Superior, that is not a Contemplative person."[87] While the congregation absolved Baker of wrongdoing in 1633, it also attempted to prevent further discord by removing both Baker and Hull from the house.

Since the leaders of the Cambrai convent put their energy toward preserving Baker's writings, little direct evidence remains of the spiritual views of Baker's opponents aside from Hull's complaint. Deacon's translation of de Sales thus offers a rare glimpse of the way that the minority faction within the convent used literature to advance Ignatian practices. Hull claimed that Baker's writings bred factionalism within the convent: "There must be a kinde of spirituall Confederacie, league, or freindship [*sic*] among those of his followers, together with communication of Bookes and Doctrins, different from the rest; which cannot but be perceaved by the others; and consequentlie breed partialitie, disaffections, and murmurs."[88] Deacon and Gawen were probably among these "others," given their apparent disinterest in Baker's methods and their preference for Ignatian piety. After their experiences at Brussels, Deacon and Gawen must have felt a disquieting sense of déjà vu as their abbess seemed to support another priest over the house's appointed confessor. Yet if Baker's adherents had their special books, so did his opponents. Contemporary sources report that Hull wrote meditations and instructions for the Cambrai nuns, and Baker's tangential rebuttal of one such tract in his *Life and Death of Dame Gertrude More* may suggest the popularity of Hull's work.[89] As previously noted, Baker also objected to the enthusiasm that some nuns showed for Matthew's translation of Rodriguez. Deacon's translation of de Sales's *Delicious Entertainments of the Soule* (*Les vrays entretiens spirituels du bien-heureux,* 1629) was yet another expression of this minority viewpoint. Much as Percy had done, Deacon translated a source text that supported her own spiritual methods even as it appealed to members of her house who had no interest in Ignatian spirituality. In publishing her translation in 1632, Deacon ambitiously attempted to influence public views of her convent by suggesting that the Cambrai nuns followed the more active philosophy advocated by Hull rather than the contemplative mysticism of Baker.

Within the immediate context of the Cambrai convent, Deacon's translation of de Sales participated in the tradition of spiritual reading promoted by both Baker and his opponents. When Deacon's translation saw print in 1632, she noted that she had composed the work "for her private imployment & instruction; never intending more then the use of a particular cloister."[90] This statement was not just a display of false modesty; Baker's *Catalogue* (c. 1630–32) indicates that the work was extant "in written hande" before its publication.[91] Given her role as novice mistress, Deacon may have found the text appealing due to its instruction on the fundamentals of convent life, yet her translation also offered an alternative view of Salesian spirituality that was based on Ignatian methods rather than mysticism. Baker recommends that the Cambrai nuns read both the *Delicious Entertainments* and de Sales's

Traité de l'amour de Dieu, in either its French original (1616) or its English translation (*Treatise of the Love of God,* 1630). De Sales addressed this latter work "to soules that are advanced in devotion," particularly the order that he and Jeanne de Chantal had founded: the Sisters of the Visitation of the Blessed Virgin, or Visitandines.[92] This explicitly mystical text presented advanced prayer as a personalized and private discourse with God, a viewpoint congruent with Baker's ideal of contemplation: "Praier, and mysticall Divinite are one same thing," so that "there is nothing saied in it betwixt God and the soule, save onely from heart to heart by a communication incommunicable to all, but themselves."[93] *Delicious Entertainments* had a similar origin, as the Visitandines had transcribed de Sales's conferences, or familiar addresses, from memory. Baker therefore probably viewed this work as a source of additional guidance on mysticism.

Yet Deacon's preface to the printed version of her translation reveals that she was drawn to *Les vrays entretiens* out of her preference for Ignatian piety. Deacon presents the *Delicious Entertainments* as a continuation of de Sales's *Introduction to a Devoute Life:* "If thou like & love not the Introduction to a Devout Life, composed by the same Byshop, I should call thy devotion into question; if thou approove and applaud it (as all truely devout doe) thou shall find that this after-borne fruict is but as it were a supplement, or explication thereof" (*DE,* Ă3r). The *Entertainments* might seem to be a "supplement" to the *Introduction* because de Sales refers to this latter work twice in the *Entertainments.*[94] In the preface to the *Introduction,* however, de Sales states that he composed this treatise specifically for secular readers: "Those that have treated of devotion before me, have allmost all attended onely to the instruction of persons alltogether retired from worldly conversation. . . . But my intention is particularly and principally to instruct such as live in cities and townes, busied with the affaires of their houshold, or forced by their place and calling to folow their princes court; such as by the obligation of their estate, are bound to take a common course of life in outward shew."[95] De Sales had been strongly influenced by Jesuit spiritual directors, and the *Introduction*—translated into English in 1613—offers Ignatian methods of prayer that are appropriate for the active life, including structured meditations and contemplation of biblical mysteries.[96] Unsurprisingly, Baker found the *Introduction* less appropriate for mysticism, recommending that the Cambrai nuns read only selections: "in the 4th parte, the 13th Chapter and thence to the ende of the 4th parte, being concerning desolations."[97] Deacon's presentation of the work as "a supplement" to de Sales's *Introduction* suggests that she was primarily interested in the ways that the active spirituality of the *Introduction* might apply to the cloister. Her claim that "all truely devout" share an enthusiasm for this work may even covertly criticize Baker and his supporters.

In its printed form, Deacon's translation evoked the Ignatian nature of de Sales's piety and, in turn, suggested that the Cambrai convent approved of Jesuit methods. Deacon and her allies cannily sought out Gheerart Pinchon, the Flemish printer who had recently published de Sales's mystical treatise *Of the Love of God.* Yet the title page of *Delicious Entertainments* conveys the work's Ignatian associations through a woodcut of the Jesuit insignia IHS below a cross and above a heart pierced by three nails (see figure 8). This woodcut seems especially significant as it does not recur in any of Pinchon's other English publications, perhaps indicating that Deacon or her collaborators requested this image.[98] The title page implicitly connects the Cambrai nuns with this symbol of Ignatian spirituality by attributing the work to "a Dame of our Ladies of comfort of the order of S[aint] Bennet in Cambray," allowing Deacon to serve as an anonymous representative of her convent. Deacon's dedicatory preface to the "Christian and religious reader," invoking both secular and cloistered audiences, further associates the unknown translator with her house: "If in peruseing this translated treatese of sound doctrine and solide documents, thou meet with some faults . . . know that . . . the translatresse [was] a woman, that had not much skille in the Frenche, but why did shee then undertake it? wilt thou say, truely for her private imployment & instruction; never intending more then the use of a particular cloister, though God and her superiours have otherwise disposed of it; & exposed it to the publierk view of the world" (*DE,* Ă2r). Deacon could have refrained from identifying herself as a member of a specific institution much as Percy had done, but instead she emphasizes the translation's origins to present the work as characteristic of her house's piety. While Deacon's compliance with her superiors' decision to publish the book demonstrates a praiseworthy conformity to monastic obedience, the superiors' interest in the book further strengthens the impression that the spirituality of the *Delicious Entertainments* is characteristic of the convent's practices. Considering that the conflict over Baker's instructions centered on alleged insubordination to Hull, Deacon's claim that the will of God is manifested through her superiors is particularly pointed. These superiors were probably not Gascoigne or Baker—both of whom showed no interest in publishing their own translations—but rather Hull and other members of the English Benedictine Congregation opposed to Baker. The 1632 publication of Deacon's

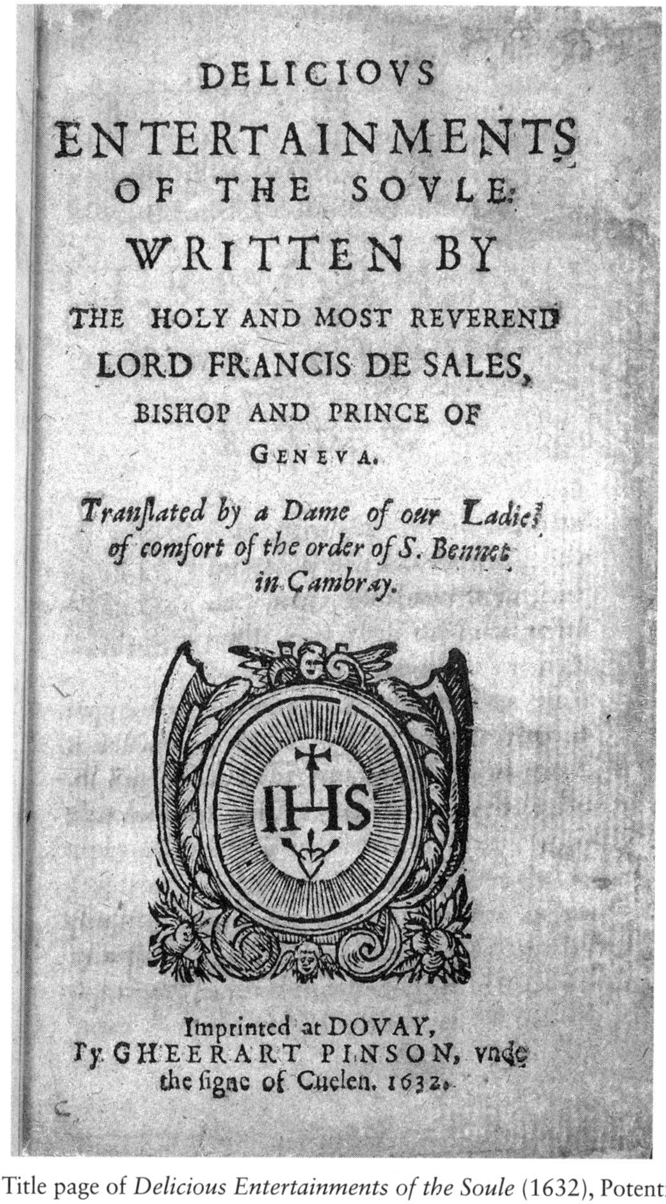

DELICIOVS
ENTERTAINMENTS
OF THE SOVLE:
WRITTEN BY
THE HOLY AND MOST REVEREND
LORD FRANCIS DE SALES,
BISHOP AND PRINCE OF
GENEVA.

Translated by a Dame of our Ladies of comfort of the order of S. Bennet in Cambray.

Imprinted at DOVAY,
By GHEERART PINSON, vnder
the signe of Cuelen. 1632.

Figure 8. Title page of *Delicious Entertainments of the Soule* (1632), Potentiana Deacon's translation of François de Sales. Reproduced by permission of the Folger Shakespeare Library.

translation was therefore a collaborative effort between Deacon and her Benedictine superiors to reshape the convent's spiritual reputation. Even as the English Benedictine Congregation launched an official investigation into the Cambrai convent's spiritual practices, Deacon's translation publicly suggested that the house practiced the active spirituality rejected by Baker and the majority of the Cambrai nuns.

Deacon's preface also attempts to redress any damage to the house's reputation caused by its ongoing discord over spirituality. Deacon presents the *Entertainments* as an authoritative glimpse into cloistered piety that can counteract potential objections to monastic life: "If any illwillers of Catholike religion, & ill-wishers of a religious vocation come to the view of this booke, they may see the lives, Rules, vertues, & customes, of Religious families disciphered without passion or partiality, & admire with what charity, discretion, devotion, & humility they passe over the pilgrimage of this mortall & miserable life" (*DE,* Ă3r–Ă3v). By revealing "the lives, Rules, vertues, & customes, of Religious families . . . without passion or partiality," the *Delicious Entertainments* offers both a defense of and a template for monastic life. Deacon nevertheless admits that sometimes religious institutions fall short of this ideal:

> And if perchaunce some scandals arrive amongst them by the meanes of some wolves or foxes in sheep-skins, I meane by some false brethren & Apostates, it is not to be attributed to the Orders & ordination of holy Church or Religious institution, but to the malice of satan & humane frailtie, for never yett since the Church began, was it free from scandals, and false brethren & Apostats, nor never will it be untill the worlds end; yett cursed are they that voluntarily blow & kindle the fire of faction or division in the house of God, or that adde fewel unto it to continew it, & blessed are the peaceable, humble, and innocent spirits that are prooved & purified ther-in. (*DE,* Ă3v)

This charged evocation of "faction or division in the house of God" likely comments on the rift among the Cambrai nuns. While a few "false brethren" who appear holy—possibly Baker and his adherents—encourage "the fire of faction or division in the house," those nuns who exemplify monastic virtues such as peacefulness and humility achieve true sanctity as they are "prooved & purified ther-in." Deacon self-righteously suggests that Hull's supporters will only reap spiritual advancement from their trials. At the same time, she frames her translation as a source of guidance that could resolve monastic discord: "I dare boldly say, that whosoever will follow really & cordially the spirit of this Author & booke, hee shall live in peace with God, with his neighbour, & with himself" (*DE,* Ă3v–Ă4r). Within the house, Deacon's preface might have served as a condemnation of Baker's faction, yet the *Delicious Entertainments* also suggested that Ignatian methods were a pattern for monastic harmony and devotion at Cambrai and beyond.

Even though Deacon's translation is generally so faithful that she uses English cognates for French terms wherever possible, she does subtly reshape the text to endorse Hull's views on spiritual direction. The Visitandines traditionally sought guidance from Jesuit confessors, and the *Delicious Entertainments* accordingly had an implicitly Ignatian basis that might seem to offer support for Hull and his followers.[99] For example, de Sales encourages even the most advanced souls to use the examination of conscience recommended by the *Spiritual Exercises:* "The spirituall lovers, spouses of the celestiall king, truely doe viewe themselves, from time to time as Doves who are neere the most pure waters: to see if they bee well accommodated to the liking of their Lover, and this is performed in the examens of their Conscience, whereby they cleanse, purifie, and adorne themselves" (*DE,* 192). Baker, however, objected to Ignatian self-examination, and Hull had complained that he advised the Cambrai nuns "to make Riddances of Examins."[100] Deacon's own support for this practice is evident in her slight modification of another passage discussing self-examination: "We ought to accustome our selves, to *examine diligently* [rechercher] the successe of our perfection, according to the ordinarie waies" (*DE,* 120 [*vere* 150]; *Lve,* 344). By translating "rechercher" (to seek diligently) as "examine diligently," Deacon adds an allusion to examination of conscience that strengthens the underlying Ignatianism of her source text. Similarly, Baker disapproved of Ignatian meditation because it stirred intellectual faculties that might impede contemplation. De Sales notes that some souls are "drawne to a certayne sweete simplicitie, which houldeth them in great tranquillitie before God" (*DE,* 290), a method of affective prayer reminiscent of Baker's contemplative ideal. Nevertheless, de Sales also views Ignatian meditation on the mysteries of Christ's life as the foundation of monastic prayer: "Generallie speaking, we ought to provide that all the sisters begin by the methode of prayer, which is the most sure, & which carrieth them to the reformation of life and manners, which is . . . made about the mysteries of the Life and death of our Lord; there wee walke in securitie. Therefore wee ought to apply our selves *sweetlie and simply* [à la bonne foy] about our Maister to learne that which hee would wee should doe, and likewise those that can use their imagination ought to doe it" (*DE,* 290–91; *Lve,* 680). Interestingly, Deacon suggests a parity between affective and Ignatian prayer by translating "à la bonne foy" (in good faith) with the doublet "sweetlie and simply," thus echoing de Sales's description of the "sweete simplicitie" practiced by those suited for contemplation. Not only did the *Delicious Entertainments* sanction the role of Ignatian piety within a monastic context, but Deacon's translation carefully reiterates this idea.

Deacon also underscores an antimystical streak within the *Delicious Entertainments,* especially de Sales's censure of nuns who questioned their confessors' directions—a condemnation with obvious relevance to the dispute at Cambrai. De Sales explicitly refuses to discuss contemplative prayer within the *Entertainments:* "But for other kinds of prayer more elevated, unlesse that God send them absolutelie, I praye you that you undertake them not of your selfe, and without the advise of those who guide you" (*DE,* 292). De Sales addresses the need for spiritual guides in more detail in the third conference on Jesus's flight to Egypt, arguing that the sisters must follow their directors just as Mary and Joseph obeyed Gabriel's command to flee to Egypt without hesitation:

> It is a *strange* [*grand*] case of mans spiritt that will not be brought to adore the secrett mysteries of God, and his most holy will, if it have not some kind of knowlege, wherefore this or wherefore that. I have a better spiritt, (say they, *in praise of themselves* [de soy]) more experience, and the like goodlie reasons, that are proper for nothing else then to produce unquietnesse, inconstant humours; and murmours? . . . *These spirits truely are greatly to be pittied.* [Grand pitié!] Assoone as we give our selves over to search narrowlye into everie thing that we see done; *Alas* [added] what doe we not, for to loose the tranquillitie of our harts? Wee ought not to seeke any other reason, but that God will have it so, and that must suffice; but who *shall, or will assure* me [m'asseurera], that this is the will of God, say they? (*DE,* 44–45; *Lve,* 93)

Deacon's alterations to this passage emphasize the unhappy plight of these presumptuous souls. By translating "grand" (great) as "strange," Deacon suggests that this desire to question spiritual directors is unusual, painting insubordination to superiors as a sign of unorthodoxy. She also shows psychological insight into the delusions of grandeur that prompt this behavior by rendering "de soy" (of themselves) as "in praise of themselves," a change that implies these souls lack proper monastic humility. Deacon stresses their subsequent inability to comply with superiors through her translation of "m'asseurera" (will assure me) as "who shall, or will assure me." Yet she balances this heightened critique by displaying a compassionate concern over the consequences of this behavior. First, Deacon expands upon de Sales's exclamatory phrase "Grand pitié" (Great pity), both intensifying this interjection and specifying its referent: "These spirits truely are greatly to be pittied." Second, she inserts "Alas" before de Sales's comment "what doe we not, for to loose the tranquillitie of our hearts," adding a sense of mourning for the loss of spiritual peace that accompanies such rebellion. By underscoring the pathos of these erroneous souls, Deacon's translation warns readers against falling into this trap and subtly critiques the freedom associated with Baker's approach to spiritual direction.

Deacon's translation also addresses the issues of monastic governance that had prompted the discord between Baker and Hull, as the third conference continues with a condemnation of souls who prefer to indulge in an unsupervised mysticism rather than rely upon spiritual directors. Hull claimed that Baker's adherents believed "they maie follow their Divin Call, and disobey . . . a Superior."[101] De Sales's treatise could be taken as evidence for Hull's contention that obedience to superiors was essential to achieving spiritual progress: "We would peradventure be taught and instructed by God hymselfe, by way of extasies, or ravishments, and visions, and I know not what like *childish fopperies* [niaiseries], that we frame in our spiritts, rather then submitt ourselves, to the *assured* [commune] and most amiable way of *true & holy* [une saincte] submission, to the government of those, whome God hath *placed to direct us* [nous a donné], and the observance and direction aswell of our Rules as of our superiours" (*DE*, 45; *Lve*, 94). If de Sales suggested that such disregard for directors threatened the monastic order intended by the Visitandines' "Rules," Deacon emphasizes the hierarchical relationship between penitents and their directors by rendering "nous a donné" (whom God has given us) as "whome God hath placed to direct us." The addition of the phrase "to direct" presents the traditional confessor-penitent relationship as a divinely appointed institution, counteracting Baker's claim that the nuns could disregard superiors who did not seem to further their progress. Deacon also suggests that "submission" to superiors is the only foolproof means of spiritual advancement by translating "commune" (common) as "assured" and "une saincte" (one holy) with the doublet "true & holy." Furthermore, Deacon's rendering of "niaiseries" (stupidities) as "childish fopperies" neatly captures the implications of childishness and silliness attached to this French term, emphasizing the immaturity of those who hope to rely on mystic revelation alone. Since

Deacon's translation legitimizes the traditional relationship between confessor and penitent as a sign of monastic order, it might seem to endorse Hull's views of confession and to suggest that Cambrai eschewed the mysticism associated with Baker.

Finally, the *Delicious Entertainments* offered a model of monastic order based on obedience, which may explain Hull's interest in publishing the work. Indeed, in his 1632 complaint Hull suggested that obedience could resolve the house's discord: "order must be taken to supresse or moderate this Doctrin of Divin Call, and that of Obedience more published and protected."[102] One of Hull's major concerns was that Baker's ideas might encourage the nuns to "neglect, carelesly or willfullie transgresse, or disesteeme the Rule, Statutes, ordinances and commands."[103] In contrast, de Sales warns against deliberate infringement of monastic rules by comparing those who eat outside of prescribed meals due to a sudden passion with those who do so in order to be disobedient: "*they who sinn through neglect, or disesteeme* [qui mange par mespris] of the Rule, and by disobedience; they *will and intend* [veut] the same disobedience, in such sorte that they doe not the worke, nor would doe it, if they weare not moved to doe it by *the will and pourpose* [la volonté] they have to disobey. The one then disobeyeth, *willing and intending* [voulant] that to the which disobedience is joyned, the other disobeyeth *willing and pourposing* [voulant] the same thing because disobedience is conjoyned ther unto" (*DE,* 3; *Lve,* 5). Deacon transforms this exemplum into a broader critique of monastic disobedience by translating "qui mange par mespris" (who eat by contempt) as "they who sinn through neglect, or disesteeme." Her consistent use of doublets for "veut," "la volonté," and "voulant" (all forms of "will") suggests that the "intent" or "pourpose" of these actions is of paramount importance, obliquely censuring those who deliberately break monastic order—as Baker's adherents seemed to do in their dismissal of Hull. Likewise, de Sales advocates for total compliance with a superior's spiritual instructions even if they are unhelpful: "it is intirelie necessarie, that wee subject our though[t]s to certayne objects; in such sort, that when *our superiour doth give us sett exercises* [on nous marque des exercices], or practice of vertue, wee remayne in those exercises, and submitt our spiritt" (*DE,* 147; *Lve,* 336). Deacon's rendering of "on nous marque des exercices" (we are appointed some exercises) transforms this injunction into authorization for Hull's position, as she omits de Sales's impersonal phrasing in order to specify the source of these "exercises": the "superiour." Furthermore, Deacon gives this guidance a subtly Ignatian orientation by adding in the modifier "sett," which opposes the inherent liberty of Baker's model. Readers aware of the disputes at Cambrai might thus have taken the *Delicious Entertainments* as an implicit critique of Baker's adherents, who resisted Hull's authority and purposely created monastic disobedience.

As these changes suggest, both the manuscript and print versions of Deacon's translation emerged from the ongoing dissension over spiritual practices at Cambrai. Having already experienced a similar controversy at Brussels, Deacon translated a work supporting her belief that monastic order hinged on obedience to appointed confessors. While Deacon's alterations may be subtle, they nevertheless heighten the relevance of de Sales's text to the situation at Cambrai by playing up his emphasis on monastic order, his rejection of unsupervised mysticism, and his endorsement of Ignatian methods. Ironically, Baker himself recommended that his adherents read Deacon's translation, perhaps unaware of its implicit suggestion that the Cambrai nuns should submit to Hull's authority. More important, the 1632 publication of the *Delicious Entertainments* boldly positioned the text as representative of the house's spirituality, suggesting that the Cambrai Benedictines practiced an Ignatian style of devotion similar to other English Benedictine houses. As a result, the *Delicious Entertainments* tried to reframe the convent's reputation among English Catholics by distancing the house from the mysticism espoused by Baker. Deacon may have ultimately failed in her attempt to undercut Baker's influence at Cambrai, but the possible success of Deacon's synecdochic authorship is shown by later critical assumptions that Agnes More translated this work despite its bias against mysticism. While these critics accepted Deacon's contention that the work was emblematic of Cambrai's spirituality, they nevertheless associated her text with the very majority whose influence she hoped to challenge.

Conclusions

The printed translations of Mary Percy and Potentiana Deacon reveal the ways that anonymity could allow a member of a well-defined religious group to stand for the larger spiritual community. Both women used anonymous translation for polemical purposes, attempting to suggest that their source texts' endorsements of Ignatianism represented the mainstream practices of English monasticism. Percy's version of Berinzaga and Gagliardi's mystical treatise offered a model for incorporating hallmarks of Ignatian piety, such as indifference and discernment, into monastic contemplation. In the context of the recent disputes over Jesuit influence among the Brussels Benedictines, Percy's translation argued for the validity of Ignatian spirituality within a monastic setting and furthermore implied that these methods enhanced monastic order. By dedicating the work to other English religious and hinting at her membership within this community, Percy suggested that the Ignatian piety of the *Abridgment of Christian Perfection* was representative of English monasticism writ large. Well aware of Percy's *Abridgment,* Deacon used a similar strategy in response to conflicts over spirituality among the Cambrai Benedictines. She heightened the Ignatian undertones of the *Delicious Entertainments,* urging the Cambrai Benedictines to comply with their appointed superior despite his hostility to their form of prayer. The anonymous publication of Deacon's translation appeared to represent the Cambrai house itself and consequently implied that the convent followed Hull's methods.

The authorial implications of these anonymous works are helpful in rethinking critical assumptions about early modern women's publication strategies. From a feminist vantage point, anonymity might seem to be a form of cooperation with proscriptions on women's public speech and consequently a sign of compliance with patriarchal oppression. Yet, as these examples have shown, anonymity could be a potent form of authorship. Deacon and Percy submerged their individual identities within their religious communities, transforming their publications from the work of one nun into representations of English monasticism. In keeping with their monastic vows, Deacon and Percy demonstrated a praiseworthy modesty that only enhanced the authority of their translations as the product of the cloister. These case studies indicate that anonymity was not always just a means of hiding the translators' identities or of privileging the original authors of their source texts. Rather, anonymity allowed Deacon and Percy to link their religious affiliations with the agendas of their translations. The immediate contexts of their translations further reveal the potency of this synecdochic authorship. Both women collaborated with male confessors—Hull and Hoskins, respectively—to publish works that promoted their shared view of monastic spirituality, actively championing spiritual preferences that were controversial within their houses and disliked by their superiors. Anonymity thus allowed these translators to legitimize their spiritual practices and to offer them as a model of piety to both religious and secular readers. As these attempts to shape public views of English monasticism suggest, anonymity could be a form of authorship that was both subversive and assertive in its own right.

Conclusion

Authority and Authorship in Early Modern England

In 1590, Anne Lock Prowse described her published translation of Jean Taffin's *Of the Markes of the Children of God* as a modest contribution to the larger project of furthering Calvinism: "Everie one in his calling is bound to doo somewhat to the furtherance of the holie building; but because great things by reason of my sex, I may not doo, and that which I may, I ought to doo, I have according to my duetie, brought my poore basket of stones to the strengthning of the walles of that Jerusalem, whereof (by grace) wee are all both Citizens and members."[1] Prowse's contrast between the "great things" done by men and her "poore basket of stones" might seem to support the idea that translation was a denigrated literary activity fit for women. Yet, as this book has demonstrated, female translators and their editors manipulated contemporary gender expectations to develop various forms of literary authority that achieved larger cultural goals. If Prowse gestures at the dictum that women should remain within the private sphere, her "poore basket" nevertheless contributes to ongoing religious controversies over the English church, and she legitimated her views by associating them with Taffin, a prominent continental Calvinist. Indeed, Prowse herself acknowledges that she translated Taffin to rouse English Protestants from their complacency, and she dedicated the book to Anne Russell Dudley, Countess of Warwick and lady-in-waiting to Elizabeth I. Even as Prowse conformed to standards of feminine modesty, her translation of Taffin served as an authoritative means of petitioning the courtly elite to support the agendas of "hotter" Protestants.

As the case studies discussed in the previous chapters suggest, faithful translators like Prowse—whether female or male—often held cultural power precisely because of the authorial multiplicity inherent in translation. Religious translations had a number of functional and practical habitus during the early modern period, allowing translators to advance their doctrinal views by drawing on the authority of their source texts. Translators who circulated their work in print could shape public views of their private lives by associating translation with their leisure time. In these cases, the original author often took precedence over the translator, who denied that the work had a public purpose. If this evocation of privacy was useful for Thomas More and John More, then Margaret Roper and Mary Basset could eschew any appearance of claiming a public voice. Sometimes the translator's reputation equaled or eclipsed that of the original author, as when Edward Seymour, Duke of Somerset, translated Calvin to restore his own reputation and to support the Edwardian Reformation. Translators with a high social rank could popularize theological doctrines and devotional practices, allowing the translations of aristocratic women such as the Tudor princesses to serve a political function. Meanwhile, translators might associate themselves with authoritative source texts to cultivate their own political influence. Male and female courtiers ranging from Anthony Cooke to Elizabeth Tudor presented patrons with unique manuscript copies of translations that offered counsel on religious policy. The limited circulation of these works helped female translators circumvent restrictions on women's public speech and political careers, while male translators supplemented their official roles within the Tudor government. Finally, some translators cloaked their identities to associate their larger religious communities with particular source texts, attempting to influence public opinion about specific groups or religious orders. Faithful translators thus made use of a rich variety of authorial positions tailored to serve vital cultural functions. Further work now remains to be done on the forms of authorship developed by translators of religious texts, particularly by nonaristocratic translators such as merchant women.

Throughout, this book has argued that women were not simply relegated to the role of translators because translation itself was deemed secondary and therefore suitable for women. Nevertheless, translation clearly appealed to women because of the limitations imposed by contemporary gender stereotypes. Since women generally did not occupy official positions in the government, they had less scope to develop a public voice or participate in politics. Elite women, for example, translated religious works for political ends more frequently than did male aristocrats and gentlemen, who already had the ability to influence Tudor policy through governmental service. When elite men circulated religious translations—as in the cases of Thomas More and Edward Seymour—they often did so to accomplish specific purposes outside of their official capacities. Female translators differed from their male counterparts in other ways. Women generally did not translate source texts beyond their confessional identities, meaning that they had little reason to develop the freer translation strategies used by men such as Thomas Rogers. Women may have translated more conservatively than some of their male counterparts, but many men display a similar deference while translating the Bible or source texts written by authors of their own faith. Furthermore, female translators often dedicated their work to other women, creating a special sense of religious community, whether Catholic (Mary Basset and Mary Tudor), Protestant (Elizabeth Tudor and Katherine Parr), or interconfessional (Mary Tudor and Katherine Parr). It may be significant that many female translators of this period knew other translators, meaning that their work responded to models established within families or monastic communities. Female translators frequently participated in closely knit, identifiable religious networks that normalized their productions.

As cultural views about female authorship changed over the course of Elizabeth's reign, the number of women's translations dwindled, particularly of religious works. The comparatively large body of translations produced by Elizabeth I and Mary Sidney Herbert may appear to refute any such decline, but most female translators of the late Elizabethan era and early Stuart period had been educated decades earlier. Elizabeth Cooke Hoby Russell, for instance, published a translation of John Ponet's *Way of Reconciliation* in 1605, but she had translated the work before 1572. Retha Warnicke has argued that Elizabeth's court did not foster a cadre of highly educated women, and the Stuart court was similarly inhospitable to women's learning.[2] Consequently, it became less fashionable for aristocratic women to translate even though Elizabeth and others of her generation continued to do so. By this time, women had already developed alternative means of disseminating their religious beliefs. Katherine Parr emphasized study of "goddes wordes" in her spiritual memoir *The Lamentacion of a Synner* (1547), demonstrating how biblical knowledge could authorize women's original compositions.[3] Subsequent publications such as Thomas Bentley's *Monument of Matrones* (1582) provided alert readers with models of other genres appropriate for women, such as prayers, meditations, religious poetry, and mothers' advice tracts. Translation certainly remained a valid option, but its importance lessened as women ranging from Eleanor Davies Douglas to Mary Wroth penned secular and religious works. After the civil wars, women concentrated on translating creative works rather than religious texts, as in the cases of Aphra Behn, Lucy Hutchinson, and Katherine

Philips.[4] In doing so, they developed further models of authorship; Margaret Ferguson, for example, has noted that Behn productively clouded "distinctions between translation, imitation, and original creation."[5] English nuns such as Catherine Holland continued to translate spiritual works from French into English, but many of their works remained within the cloister.[6]

Although translation of religious texts became less characteristic of women's literary pursuits over the course of the early modern period, the figure of the faithful translator retained its cultural power. If in 1526 Richard Hyrde had felt the need to defend Margaret Roper's learning by depicting translation as an appropriately feminine activity, a century later Edward Denny castigated Mary Wroth for writing an original work (*Urania*, 1621) rather than translating. Believing that an episode in Wroth's *Urania* lampooned his family, Denny scathingly urged Wroth to abandon "lascivious tales and amorous toyes" and instead to "followe the rare, and pious example of your vertuous and learned Aunt [Mary Sidney Herbert], who translated so many godly books and especially the holly psalmes of David, that no doubt now shee sings in the quier of Heaven those devine meditations which shee so sweetly tuned heer belowe, and which being left to us heer on earth will begett hir dayly more and more glory in heaven as others by them shalbe enlightened, who as so many trophies shall appeare to her further exaltation in gods favour."[7] Denny's response depends on the rhetorical ploys associated with earlier female translators, which had cast translation as not just an acceptable enterprise for "vertuous and learned" women but also as an acceptable form of public service that could "enlighten" others. Denny's critique thus reveals how influential the paradigm of the female translator became, especially as a model of women's pious learning.

Female translators have been peripheral to studies of early modern women writers and early modern literature in general. Nonetheless, translation raises questions of authorship that are germane to our understanding of the relationship between intertextuality and literary authority during this period. Male and female authors used a variety of intertextual strategies while composing secular and religious literature, appropriating the work and ideas of past authors through techniques such as translation, paraphrase, and imitation. Allusion and citation allowed writers to deploy intertextuality through heteroglossia, a device that Mikhail Bakhtin first identified in novels but that also operates in other literary genres: "Heteroglossia . . . is *another's speech in another's language*, serving to express authorial intentions but in a refracted way.

Such speech constitutes a special type of *double-voiced discourse.* It serves two speakers at the same time and expresses simultaneously two different intentions."[8] Scholars have already focused on intertextuality to identify early modern writers' sources, to consider their politics, and to trace the development of the English literary canon.[9] Recently, Susan Felch has noted that women's paraphrases and scriptural collages involved a heteroglossia requiring significant authorial dexterity and originality.[10] If borrowing from biblical, classical, and continental models allowed writers to compensate for the perceived poverty of English literature, intertextuality could also be an aggressive means of asserting literary authority. The title page to George Gascoigne's *Hundreth Sundrie Flowres* (1573), for example, states that the work was "Gathered partely (by translation) in the fyne outlandish Gardins of Euripides, Ovid, Petrarke, Ariosto, and others," allowing Gascoigne to position himself within the company of elite classical and continental poets.[11] Since *Hundreth Sundrie Flowres* was Gascoigne's first publication, this commingling of translation, imitation, and original composition helped to establish his literary aspirations and may have even attracted readers. Gascoigne offers a particularly interesting example of ways that intertextuality could create a sense of literary authority, but many works of this period exhibit some form of polyvocality.

Just as female translators capitalized on their knowledge of foreign languages to advance their political goals, other writers displayed their learning and rhetorical skill through commonplaces and allusions. Sententiae create isolated moments of heteroglossia, subordinating the source text to the aims of the writer while also incorporating its authority. If William Cecil's letters judiciously use sententiae to develop political authority, Thomas Wyatt integrates sententiae into his poetry, deploying the phrase *circa regna tonat* (it thunders about thrones) from Seneca's *Hippolytus* in "Who Lyst His Welth and Eas Retayne" to underscore the dangers of the Henrician court.[12] Women with humanist educations—including Cecil's sister-in-law Elizabeth Cooke Hoby Russell—similarly cited classical writers for rhetorical effect.[13] The Bible was perhaps the single most popular source of sententiae for women writers, permitting them to demonstrate a praiseworthy knowledge of scripture that could justify their theological positions.[14] Katherine Parr promoted Lutheranism by referring repeatedly to Paul's epistles in her *Lamentacion:* "As Saynt Paule sayeth, no man can say the lorde Jesus, but by the holy ghost. The spirit helpeth our infirmities, and maketh continuall intercession for us, with suche soroful groninges, as can not be expressed."[15] Marginalia accompanying this passage helpfully identify Parr's incorporation of

Romans 8:26 and 1 Corinthians 12:3, passages supporting justification by faith. Meanwhile, Catholic women such as Barbara Constable interlaced quotations from biblical, patristic, medieval, and contemporary religious authorities within their works.[16]

Modes such as paraphrase and imitation allowed authors to experiment with intertextuality in a more sustained manner. Besides associating the writer with well-known works much as translation did, these activities invited readers to appreciate the author's clever adaptations and extensions of his or her source(s). Thomas Wyatt and Henry Howard, Earl of Surrey, made good use of this effect in their imitations, adaptations, and paraphrases of Petrarch and the Bible. Other writers paid homage to their literary models more freely, as when Edmund Spenser invoked Virgil and adapted Ovid in the *Faerie Queene,* or Milton reworked Genesis and imitated classical epic in *Paradise Lost.* Women likewise turned to precedents as a means of establishing literary authority. Elizabeth Grymeston modified verse from the commonplace book *Englands Parnassus* (1600) and other publications so that they matched the crypto-Catholic tenor of her *Miscelanea, Meditations, Memoratives* (1606).[17] The Bible provided a ready source of material for women writers, such as Aemilia Lanyer, in her loose adaptation of Christ's Passion (*Salve Deus Rex Judaeorum,* 1611). Sometimes women writers acknowledged the polyvocality inherent in their work to carve out a public position as an author. Isabella Whitney emphasized her creativity in versifying sententiae from Hugh Plat's *Floures of Philosophie* (1572): "[I] did step into an others garden for these Flowers: which I beseech you . . . to accepte: and though they be of an others growing, yet considering they be of my owne gathering and makeing up: respect my labour and regard my good wil."[18] Whitney's distinction between "growing," "gathering," and "makeing" casts her versification as a genuine literary "labour."

The potential benefits of heteroglossia and intertexuality were so great that some writers downplayed their own originality. Gascoigne's revised *Posies of George Gascoigne* (1575) presented his original narrative "The Adventures of Master F. J." from *Hundreth Sundrie Flowres* as a translation from Italian: "The pleasant Fable of Ferdinando Jeronomi and Leonora de Valasco, translated out of the Italian riding tales of Bartello."[19] By recasting "Master F. J." as a translation, Gascoigne distanced himself from the salacious content of the story even as he appealed to contemporary interest in Italian literature.[20] Women may not have indulged in such outright misrepresentation, but at times they did overstate their reliance on their sources. Anne Dowriche explains that her

French Historie (1589) resulted from a process of "collecting & framing," observing that "the same Storie in effect is alreadie translated into English prose."[21] This reference to accounts such as Jean de Serres's *The Three Partes of Commentaries . . . of the Civill Warres of Fraunce* (1574) permitted Dowriche to deny responsibility for the work's content and to place herself within ongoing conversations about the civil wars in France. Nevertheless, Dowriche's text is largely her own, thanks to her decisions to write a poetic narrative, add two new narrators, and incorporate a host of biblical allusions. As Elaine Beilin has noted, Dowriche "grossly underplays her ambitious and largely successful undertaking to transpose historical narrative into a form that would both teach and delight her coreligionists."[22]

Finally, the paratexts by male editors that accompanied the work of some female translators created a sense of religious community that implicitly legitimated the translations themselves. Early modern publications frequently intermingled the compositions of various writers, often imitating the literary coteries of manuscript circulation. Verse miscellanies—whether in manuscript or print—incorporated multiple authors by their very nature, legitimating minor authors by associating them with more famous writers. The title page to *Tottel's Miscellany* emphasizes Surrey's poetry even though Wyatt's verse formed the bulk of the book, drawing attention to Surrey's nobility and avoiding the negative associations of the Wyatt name after the unsuccessful rebellion led by Wyatt's son: *Songes and Sonettes, Written by the Right Honorable Lorde Henry Haward Late Earle of Surrey, and Other* (1557). A second edition accentuated Surrey's prominence by facing the title page with a woodcut featuring his image.[23] Later poets attempted to mimic the coteries involved in manuscript circulation and printed miscellanies. Isabella Whitney included a series of poetic exchanges in *The Copy of a Letter* (1567), and she addressed poems to relatives in *A Sweet Nosgay* (1573).[24] Commendatory verse also allowed the construction of literary communities through print, one well-known instance being Ben Jonson's prefatory poem for Shakespeare's First Folio.[25] Similarly, Jonson and others wrote prefatory poems for Alice Sutcliffe's *Meditations of Man's Mortalitie* (1634), placing her work within a domestic context.

Women's religious translations have significant implications for our understanding of the early modern period and its authorial practices. Translation offered male and female writers an extreme form of polyvocality, but it was not the only means of using intertextuality to create literary authority. The time is ripe for scholars to examine heteroglossia and intertextuality on their own terms, seeing polyvocality as a means of developing authorial credibility rather than simply as a form of literary appropriation. A turn to intertextuality allows us to ask new questions about the ways that early modern authors worked with preexisting texts and narratives. What profit did Shakespeare or his company derive when he wrote plays based on popular texts, such as Thomas North's translation of Plutarch, or well-known myths, such as the story of Venus and Adonis? When Wyatt revised Petrarch and Elizabeth Cary reworked Josephus, how did they challenge or benefit from the prestige of their sources? Ultimately, how were English writers—whether as translators, imitators, or original authors—positioned in relationship to authors from other cultures? As this book's consideration of women's religious translations has attempted to demonstrate, association with other authors can place writers in a position of strength rather than weakness. In fact, translation and other so-called derivative forms of authorship were at times attractive to early modern writers precisely because of their polyvocality. When women translated religious works, they were not simply participating in a politicized activity that was vital to the English Reformation—they were also cultivating an intertextuality essential to developing literary authority in early modern England.

NOTES

Introduction

1. John Florio, "Dedicatory Preface," in Michel de Montaigne, *The Essayes or Morall, Politike, and Millitarie Discourses,* trans. John Florio (1603; STC 18041), A2r (hereafter cited in text as "DP," *Essayes*).

2. F. O. Matthiessen, *Translation: An Elizabethan Art* (Cambridge, Mass.: Harvard University Press, 1931), 3.

3. Neil Rhodes, "Status Anxiety and English Renaissance Translation," in *Renaissance Paratexts,* ed. Helen Smith and Louise Wilson (Cambridge: Cambridge University Press, 2011), 107.

4. Lawrence Venuti, *The Translator's Invisibility: A History of Translation* (New York: Routledge, 1995).

5. *Oxford English Dictionary,* s.v. "female, III.7b," accessed November 24, 2012, http://www.oed.com/view/Entry/69157.

6. Jonathan Goldberg, *Desiring Women Writing: English Renaissance Examples* (Stanford, Calif.: Stanford University Press, 1997), 78.

7. Mary Ellen Lamb, "The Cooke Sisters: Attitudes Toward Learned Women in the Renaissance," in *Silent but for the Word: Tudor Women as Patrons, Translators, and Writers of Religious Works,* ed. Margaret P. Hannay (Kent, Ohio: Kent State University Press, 1985), 116.

8. Ibid., 124.

9. Massimiliano Morini, *Tudor Translation in Theory and Practice* (Aldershot, UK: Ashgate, 2006), 24.

10. See, for example, Patricia Demers, *Women's Writing in English: Early Modern England* (Toronto: University of Toronto Press, 2005), 64; Louise Schleiner, *Tudor and Stuart Women Writers* (Bloomington: Indiana University Press, 1994), 30–51; Tina Krontiris, *Oppositional Voices: Women as Writers and Translators of Literature in the English Renaissance* (New York: Routledge, 1992), 20–21; and Elaine V. Beilin, *Redeeming Eve: Women Writers of the English Renaissance* (Princeton, N.J.: Princeton University Press, 1987), 61.

11. Sherry Simon, *Gender in Translation: Cultural Identity and the Politics of Transmission* (New York: Routledge, 1996), 1; Lori Chamberlain, "Gender and the Metaphorics of Translation," *Signs* 13, no. 3 (1988): 454–72.

12. Michel Foucault, "What Is an Author?" in *The Foucault Reader,* ed. Paul Rabinow (New York: Pantheon Books, 1984), 118–19. Also see Roland Barthes, "The Death of the Author," in *Image Music Text,* trans. Stephen Heath (New York: Hill and Wang, 1977), 142–48.

13. See Maria Tymoczko, *Enlarging Translation, Empowering Translators* (Manchester, UK: St. Jerome Publishing, 2007); André Lefevere, *Translation,*

Rewriting, and the Manipulation of Literary Fame (New York: Routledge, 1992); Barbara Godard, "Theorizing Feminist Discourse/Translation," in *Translation, History, and Culture,* ed. Susan Bassnett and André Lefevere (London: Pinter, 1990), 87–109; Susan Bassnett and André Lefevere, *Constructing Cultures: Essays on Literary Translation,* Topics in Translation 11 (Clevedon, UK: Multilingual Matters, 1998); and Jacques Derrida, *The Ear of the Other: Otobiography, Transference, Translation,* ed. Christie V. McDonald, trans. Peggy Kamuf (New York: Schocken Books, 1985).

14. Paul Trolander and Zeynep Tenger, *Sociable Criticism in England 1625–1725* (Newark: University of Delaware Press, 2007); Margaret J. M. Ezell, *Social Authorship and the Advent of Print* (Baltimore: Johns Hopkins University Press, 1999); Roger Chartier, *The Order of Books: Readers, Authors, and Libraries in Europe between the Fourteenth and Eighteenth Centuries,* trans. Lydia G. Cochrane (Stanford, Calif.: Stanford University Press, 1994).

15. Arthur F. Marotti, *Manuscript, Print, and the English Renaissance Lyric* (Ithaca, N.Y.: Cornell University Press, 1995); Harold Love, *Scribal Publication in Seventeenth-Century England* (Oxford: Clarendon, 1993).

16. Stephen B. Dobranski, *Milton, Authorship, and the Book Trade* (Cambridge: Cambridge University Press, 1999); Wendy Wall, *The Imprint of Gender: Authorship and Publication in the English Renaissance* (Ithaca, N.Y.: Cornell University Press, 1993).

17. William W. E. Slights, *Managing Readers: Printed Marginalia in English Renaissance Books* (Ann Arbor: University of Michigan Press, 2001); Kevin Dunn, *Pretexts of Authority: The Rhetoric of Authorship in the Renaissance Preface* (Stanford, Calif.: Stanford University Press, 1994); Evelyn B. Tribble, *Margins and Marginality: The Printed Page in Early Modern England* (Charlottesville: University of Virginia Press, 1993).

18. Grace Ioppolo, *Dramatists and Their Manuscripts in the Age of Shakespeare, Jonson, Middleton and Heywood: Authorship, Authority and the Playhouse* (New York: Routledge, 2006); Nora Johnson, *The Actor as Playwright in Early Modern Drama* (Cambridge: Cambridge University Press, 2003); Jeffrey Masten, *Textual Intercourse: Collaboration, Authorship, and Sexualities in Renaissance Drama* (Cambridge: Cambridge University Press, 1997).

19. William H. Sherman, *Used Books: Marking Readers in Renaissance England* (Philadelphia: University of Pennsylvania Press, 2008); Stephen B. Dobranski, *Readers and Authorship in Early Modern England* (Cambridge: Cambridge University Press, 2005).

20. Deborah Uman, *Women as Translators in Early Modern England* (Newark: University of Delaware Press, 2012); Goldberg, *Desiring Women Writing,* 75–90; Suzanne Trill, "Sixteenth-Century Women's Writing: Mary Sidney's *Psalmes* and the 'Femininity' of Translation," in *Writing and the English Renaissance,* ed. William Zunder and Suzanne Trill (New York: Longman, 1996), 140–58.

21. Danielle Clarke, *The Politics of Early Modern Women's Writing* (New York: Longman, 2001), 13.

22. Peter Burke, "Cultures of Translation in Early Modern Europe," in *Cultural Translation in Early Modern Europe,* ed. Peter Burke and R. Po-chia Hsia (Cambridge: Cambridge University Press, 2007), 34. For a consideration of the differences and similarities between medieval and early modern translations, see Morini, *Tudor Translation,* 3–34.

23. For example, see Brenda Hosington, "Translation in the Service of Politics and Religion: A Family Tradition for Thomas More, Margaret Roper, and Mary Clarke Basset," in *Between Scylla and Charybdis: Learned Letter Writers, Politics, and Religion,* ed. Jeanine de Landstheer and Hank Nellen (Leiden: Brill, 2010), 93–108; Jessica L. Malay, "Jane Seager's Sibylline Poems: Maidenly Negotiations Through Elizabethan Gift Exchange," *English Literary Renaissance* 36, no. 2 (2006): 173–93; Victor Skretkowicz, "Mary Sidney Herbert's *Antonius,* English Philhellenism, and the Protestant Cause," *Women's Writing* 6, no. 1 (1999): 7–25.

24. Micheline White, "Renaissance Englishwomen and Religious Translation: The Case of Anne Lock's *Of the Markes of the Children of God* (1590)," *English Literary Renaissance* 29, no. 2 (1999): 400.

25. For literary translations, see Paul Davis, *Translation and the Poet's Life: The Ethics of Translating in English Culture, 1646–1726* (Oxford: Oxford University Press, 2008); Thomas Greene, *The Light in Troy: Imitation and Discovery in Renaissance Poetry* (New Haven, Conn.: Yale University Press, 1982); Matthiessen, *Translation;* C. H. Conley, *The First English Translators of the Classics* (New Haven, Conn.: Yale University Press, 1927). To note just a few works on the English Bible, see Gordon Campbell, *Bible: The Story of the King James Version, 1611–2011* (Oxford: Oxford University Press, 2010); Hannibal Hamlin and Norman W. Jones, eds., *The King James Bible After 400 Years: Literary, Linguistic, and Cultural Influences* (Cambridge: Cambridge University Press, 2010); David Daniell, *The Bible in English: Its History and Influence* (New Haven, Conn.: Yale University Press, 2003).

26. Preliminary overviews of religious translation include Louis Kelly, "Translation and Religious Belief," in *The Oxford History of Literary Translation in England,* vol. 2, *1550–1660,* ed. Gordon Braden, Robert Cummings, and Stuart Gillespie (Oxford: Oxford University Press, 2010), 24–31; Alison Shell, "Spiritual and Devotional Prose," in Braden, Cummings, and Gillespie, *Oxford History of Literary Translation,* 418–30; and H. S. Bennett, *English Books & Readers 1475–1557* (Cambridge: Cambridge University Press, 1952), 152–77, *English Books & Readers 1558–1603* (Cambridge: Cambridge University Press, 1965), 87–111, and *English Books & Readers 1603 to 1640* (Cambridge: Cambridge University Press, 1970), 67–77.

27. Brenda M. Hosington, "Translation as a Currency of Cultural Exchange in Early Modern England" (keynote address, Centre for Early Modern Exchanges, University College London, September 16, 2011); Renaissance Cultural Crossroads website of the Centre for the Study of the Renaissance at University of Warwick, accessed February 18, 2013, http://www.hrionline.ac.uk/rcc/index.php.

28. Brenda M. Hosington, "Lady Margaret Beaufort's Translations as Mirrors of Practical Piety," in *English Women, Religion, and Textual Production, 1500–1625,* ed. Micheline White (Aldershot, UK: Ashgate, 2011), 186 n3.

29. Deborah Uman and Bistué Belén, "Translation as Collaborative Authorship: Margaret Tyler's *The Mirrour of Princely Deedes and Knighthood,*" *Comparative Literature Studies* 44, no. 3 (2007): 298–323.

30. André Lefevere, "Why Waste Our Time on Rewrites? The Trouble with Interpretation and the Role of Rewriting in an Alternative Paradigm," in *The Manipulation of Literature: Studies in Literary Translation,* ed. Theo Hermans (New York: St. Martin's, 1985), 236.

31. Uman, *Women as Translators,* 3.

32. Harold Love, *Attributing Authorship: An Introduction* (Cambridge: Cambridge University Press, 2002), 43.

33. For useful overviews of this turn, see Michaela Wolf, "Introduction: The Emergence of a Sociology of Translation," in *Constructing a Sociology of Translation,* ed. Michaela Wolf and Alexandra Fukari (Amsterdam: John Benjamins, 2007), 1–36; Anthony Pym, "Introduction: On the Social and Cultural in Translation Studies," in *Sociocultural Aspects of Translating and Interpreting,* ed. Anthony Pym, Miriam Shlesinger, and Zuzana Jettmarova (Amsterdam: John Benjamins, 2006), 1–25; Theo Hermans, *Translation in Systems: Descriptive and System-Oriented Approaches Explained* (Manchester, UK: St Jerome, 1999), 131–36.

34. Jean-Marc Gouanvic, "Outline of a Sociology of Translation Informed by the Ideas of Pierre Bourdieu," trans. Laura Schultz, *MonTI* 2 (2010): 119–29; Moira Inghilleri, "The Sociology of Bourdieu and the Construction of the 'Object' in Translation and Interpreting Studies," *Translator* 11, no. 2 (2005): 125–45; Jean-Marc Gouanvic, "A Bourdieusian Theory of Translation, or the Coincidence of Practical Instances: Field, 'Habitus,' Capital, and 'Illusio,'" *Translator* 11, no. 2 (2005): 147–66; Daniel Simeoni, "The Pivotal Status of the Translator's Habitus," *Target* 10, no. 1 (1998): 1–40.

35. Pierre Bourdieu, *The Logic of Practice,* trans. Richard Nice (Stanford, Calif.: Stanford University Press, 1990), 53, 55.

36. Pierre Bourdieu, *The Field of Cultural Production: Essays on Art and Literature,* ed. Randal Johnson (New York: Columbia University Press, 1993), 163.

37. Bourdieu, *Field of Cultural Production,* 37.

38. Michaela Wolf, "The Female State of the Art: Women in the 'Translation Field,'" in Pym, *Sociocultural Aspects of Translating,* 136.

39. For an overview of the relationship between profit, print, and translation, see Brenda M. Hosington, "Commerce, Printing, and Patronage," in Braden, Cummings, and Gillespie, *Oxford History of Literary Translation,* 47–57.

40. Arthur Golding, preface to *A Postill or Exposition of the Gospels,* by Niels Hemmingsen, trans. Arthur Golding (1569; STC 13062), A3r.

41. John Calvin, *Psalmes of David and Others* (1571; STC 4395); Augustin Marlorat, *A Catholike Exposition upon the Revelation of Sainct John* (1574; STC 17408); John Calvin, *Sermons of M. John Calvine upon the Epistle of*

Saincte Paule to the Galathians (1574; STC 4449); John Calvin, *Sermons of M. John Calvin upon . . . Deuteronomie* (1583; STC 4442); *Sermons of Maister John Calvin upon the Booke of Job* (1584; STC 4447.5).

42. William Caxton, preface to *Legenda aurea,* by Jacobus de Voragine, trans. William Caxton (1483; STC 24873), no sig.

43. British Library Royal MS 17 A xli; Guillaume du Bartas, *Bartas: His Devine Weekes and Workes,* trans. Josuah Sylvester (1605; STC 21649).

44. The latest publications of the mid-Tudor theologians are Philipp Melanchthon et al., *Whether It Be Mortall Sinne to Transgresse Civil Lawes* (1570; STC 10391.5); Philipp Melanchthon, *A Godly and Learned Assertion in Defence of the True Church*, trans. Richard Robinson (1580; STC 17790); Peter Martyr Vermigli, *The Common Places of the Most Famous and Renowmed Divine Doctor Peter Martyr* (1583; STC 24669); Heinrich Bullinger, *Fiftie Godlie and Learned Sermons* (1587; STC 4058).

45. E.g., Gaspar Loarte, *The Exercise of a Christian Life*, trans. Stephen Brinkley (1579; STC 16641.5); Roberto Bellarmino, *An Ample Declaration of the Christian Doctrine,* trans. Richard Hadock (1604; STC 1835).

46. Preface to Martin Luther, *Here After Ensueth a Propre Treatyse of Good Workes* (1535; STC 16988), A2r.

47. J. B., preface to *Father Cotton a Jesuite, the Kings Confessour, His Two and Thirtie Demands,* by Pierre du Moulin, trans. J. B. (1614; STC 5857), A2r–A2v.

48. Eusebius Pamphilus, preface to *A Faythful Admonycion of a Certen Trewe Pastor,* by Martin Luther, trans. Eusebius Pamphilus (Strasbourg, 1554; STC 16980), A2v–A3r. For Cromwell's role in this publication, see Edward Ronald Riegler, "Printing, Protestantism, and Politics: Thomas Cromwell and Religious Reform" (Ph.D. diss., University of California, Los Angeles, 1978), 62–65.

49. Richard Hopkins, preface to *Of Prayer and Meditation,* by Luis de Granada, trans. Richard Hopkins (Paris, 1582; STC 16907), A6v.

50. Gilbert Burnet, *History of the Reformation of the Church of England,* vol. 4, ed. C. Pocock (Oxford, 1865), 417–18.

51. *Calendar of the Manuscripts of the Most Hon. the Marquis of Salisbury,* vol. 17, *1605*, ed. M. S. Giuseppi (London: His Majesty's Stationery Office, 1938), 613, no. 1256.

52. Flora Ross Amos, *Early Theories of Translation* (New York: Columbia University Press, 1920), 118.

53. See Louis Kelly, "Pedagogical Uses of Translation," in Braden, Cummings, and Gillespie, *Oxford History of Literary Translation,* 12–16.

54. Nicholas Orme, *Medieval Schools from Roman Britain to Renaissance England* (New Haven, Conn.: Yale University Press, 2006), 111–18.

55. Roger Ascham, *The Scholemaster* (1570; STC 832), 1v.

56. See, for example, G. D. L. M. N., preface to *The French Alphabeth* (1592; STC 6545.5), 5v–6r.

57. See, for example, Thomas Elyot, *The Boke Named the Governour* (1537; STC 7636), 32r.

58. Juan Luis Vives, *Vives: On Education, A Translation of the De Tradendis Disciplinis*, ed. Foster Watson (1913; repr., Totowa, N.J.: Rowman and Littlefield, 1971), 51, 52.

59. Thomas Drant, preface to *A Medicinable Morall,* by Horace, trans. Thomas Drant (1566; STC 13805), A3v.

60. Myles Smith, preface to *The Holy Bible Conteyning the Old Testament, and the New* (1611; STC 2216), A6v.

61. For a discussion of the impetus for accuracy in early Bible translations, see David Norton, *A History of the English Bible as Literature* (Cambridge: Cambridge University Press, 2000).

62. Preface to *The New Testament of Jesus Christ* (Rheims, 1582; STC 2884), B2r–B2v.

63. For these neologisms, see A. C. Partridge, *English Biblical Translation* (London: André Deutsch, 1973), 97–103.

64. Preface to *The Bible and Holy Scriptures* (Geneva, 1560; STC 2093), ***4r.

65. Dedicatory preface to *The Holy Bible*, A2v; Smith, preface to *The Holy Bible*, A6v.

66. Myles Coverdale, preface to *Biblia the Byble* (STC 2063), †4r.

67. Thomas Norton, preface to *The Institution of Christian Religion,* by John Calvin, trans. Thomas Norton (1562; STC 4416), A1r.

68. Richard Harrison and Reynald Wolf, preface to *The Institution of Christian Religion,* by John Calvin, trans. Thomas Norton (1561; STC 4415), A1v.

69. Lawrence Venuti, *The Scandals of Translation: Towards an Ethics of Difference* (New York: Routledge, 1998), 44.

70. William Tyndale, preface to *The Pentateuch*, trans. William Tyndale (Antwerp, 1530; STC 2350), A3v.

71. *A Waying and Considering of the Interim*, trans. John Rogers (1548; STC 17799); *A Newe Worck Concernyng Both Partes of the Sacrament* (1548; STC 17796); *The Epistle of the Famous and Great Clerke Philip Melancton* (Antwerp, 1547; STC 17789).

72. Leonard Cox, preface to *The Paraphrase of Erasmus Roterdame upon the Epistle of Saint Paule unto His Discyple Titus,* by Desiderius Erasmus, trans. Leonard Cox (1534; STC 10503), A6r–A6v.

73. Francis Meres, preface to *The Sinners Guyde,* by Luis de Granada, trans. Francis Meres (1598; STC 16918), A3r.

74. *A Pretious Booke of Heavenlie Meditations* (1581; STC 944); *A Right Christian Treatise* (1581; STC 950).

75. Thomas Rogers, preface to *Of the Imitation of Christ,* by Thomas à Kempis, trans. Thomas Rogers (1580; STC 23973), no sig. Edward Hake, following Sébastien Castellion's version, excised the fourth book in his 1567 translation: *The Imitation or Following of Christ,* trans. Edward Hake (1567; STC 23969).

76. Thomas Rogers, preface to *Soliloquium animae,* by Thomas à Kempis, trans. Thomas Rogers (1592; STC 23995), A3v.

77. Nicholas Breton, *An Olde Mans Lesson* (1605; STC 3674), E4r–E4v.

78. See, for example, Jane Stevenson, *Women Latin Poets: Language, Gender, & Authority from Antiquity to the Eighteenth Century* (Oxford: Oxford University Press, 2005), 258.

79. *Oxford English Dictionary*, s.v. "cunning, 1a, 5a," accessed November 24, 2012, http://www.oed.com/view/Entry/45866.

80. William Camden, *Annals or the Historie of the Most Renowned and Victorious Princesse Elizabeth,* trans. R. N. (1635; STC 4501), 422.

81. Nicolas Caussin, *The Holy Court in Five Tomes,* trans. T. H. (1650; Wing C1547), 302.

82. British Library Royal MS 17 B xviii, 2r.

83. Francis Bell, preface to *A Short Relation, of the Life, Virtues, and Miracles, of S. Elizabeth,* by François Paludanus, trans. Catherine Greenbury (Brussels, 1628; STC 19167), A2v.

84. Matthew Parker, preface to *An Apologie or Answere in Defence of the Churche of Englande,* by John Jewel, trans. Anne Bacon (1564; STC 14591), no sig.

85. Elizabeth Cary, preface to *The Reply of the Most Illustrious Cardinall of Perron,* by Jacques Davy Du Perron, trans. Elizabeth Cary (Douai, 1630; STC 6385), ā2v.

86. Micheline White, "The Dedication and Prayers from Anne Gawdy Jenkinson's Translation of Guillaume Du Vair's *Meditations upon The Lamentations of Ieremy,*" *English Literary Renaissance* 37, no. 1 (2007): 34–46.

87. Steven W. May, introduction to *Selected Works,* by Elizabeth I, ed. Steven W. May (New York: Washington Square Press, 2004), xxxv.

88. Anne Lock, preface to *Sermons of John Calvin,* by John Calvin, trans. Anne Lock (1560; STC 4450), A8r.

89. British Library Harley MS 1860, 3v–4r.

90. Lock, preface to *Sermons of John Calvin*, A3r.

91. Jean Taffin, *Of the Markes of the Children of God*, trans. Anne Lock Prowse (1590; STC 23652).

92. François Hendricq, *The History of the Angelicall Virgin Glorious S. Clare,* trans. Elizabeth Evelinge (Douai, 1635; STC 24924), č4r, 17–72; Frans Korsten, "Introductory Note," in *Elizabeth Evelinge I,* ed. Frans Korsten (Aldershot, UK: Ashgate, 2002), xii–xiii.

Chapter One

1. John Archer Gee, "Margaret Roper's English Version of Erasmus' *Precatio Dominica* and the Apprenticeship behind Early Tudor Translation," *Review of English Studies* 13, no. 51 (1937): 259.

2. Richard Hyrde, "Dedicatory Preface," in Desiderius Erasmus, *A Devout Treatise upon the Pater Noster,* trans. Margaret Roper (1526) in *Early Tudor Translators: Margaret Beaufort, Margaret More Roper, and Mary Basset,* ed. Lee Cullen Khanna (Aldershot, UK: Ashgate, 2001), A4r (hereafter cited in text as "DP," *DT*).

3. John Wilkinson, preface to *The Ethiques of Aristotle,* by Aristotle, trans. John Wilkinson (1547; STC 754), A2r–A2v.

4. Gillian Wright, "Translating at Leisure: Gentlemen and Gentlewomen," in Braden, Cummings, and Gillespie, *Oxford History of Literary Translation*, 63.

5. Burke, "Cultures of Translation," 12.

6. For a useful discussion of privacy in early modern England, see Lena Cowen Orlin, *Locating Privacy in Tudor London* (Oxford: Oxford University Press, 2007).

7. See, for example, John Guy, *A Daughter's Love: Thomas More and His Dearest Meg* (New York: Houghton Mifflin Harcourt, 2009); Marion Wynne-Davies, *Women Writers and Familial Discourse in the English Renaissance* (Houndmills, UK: Palgrave Macmillan, 2007), 12–21; Mary Ellen Lamb, "Margaret Roper, the Humanist Political Project, and the Problem of Agency," in *Opening the Borders: Inclusivity in Early Modern Studies; Essays in Honor of James V. Mirollo,* ed. Peter C. Herman (Newark: University of Delaware Press, 1999), 83–108; Peter Iver Kaufman, "Absolute Margaret: Margaret More Roper and 'Well Learned' Men," *Sixteenth Century Journal* 20, no. 3 (1989): 453–54; Jonathan V. Crewe, "The '*Encomium Morae*' of William Roper," *English Literary History* 55, no. 2 (1988): 287–307; and Rita Verbrugge, "Margaret More Roper's Personal Expression in the *Devout Treatise upon the Pater Noster*," in Hannay, *Silent but for the Word,* 30–42.

8. Margo Todd has argued that male humanist writers conducted a "literary campaign against idleness": *Christian Humanism and the Puritan Social Order* (Cambridge: Cambridge University Press, 1987), 123. Useful discussions of early modern leisure include Virginia Krause, *Idle Pursuits: Literature and Oisiveté in the French Renaissance* (Newark: University of Delaware Press, 2003); Lawrence Stone, *The Crisis of the Aristocracy 1558–1641* (Oxford: Oxford University Press, 1965); and Robert Matz, *Defending Literature in Early Modern England: Renaissance Literary Theory in Social Context* (Cambridge: Cambridge University Press, 2000).

9. Thomas Elyot, *The Boke Named the Governour* (1531; STC 7635), 95r.

10. Thomas Elyot, preface to *The Education or Bringinge up of Children*, by Plutarch, trans. Thomas Elyot (1532; STC 20057), A2r.

11. Thomas Phaer, preface to *The Seven First Bookes of the Eneidos of Virgill,* by Virgil, trans. Thomas Phaer (1558; STC 24799), A2r.

12. Jürgen Habermas, *The Structural Transformation of the Public Sphere: An Inquiry into a Category of Bourgeois Society,* trans. Thomas Burger (Cambridge, Mass.: MIT, 1989), 6. For the early modern public sphere, see Bronwen Wilson and Paul Yachnin, eds., *Making Publics in Early Modern Europe: People, Things, Forms of Knowledge* (New York: Routledge, 2009); and David Zaret, *Origins of Democratic Culture: Printing, Petitions, and the Public Sphere in Early Modern England* (Princeton, N.J.: Princeton University Press, 2000).

13. Habermas, *Structural Transformation,* 7, his emphasis.

14. Caxton, preface to *Legenda aurea,* no sig.

15. Thomas Hoby, preface to *The Courtyer*, by Baldassare Castiglione, trans. Thomas Hoby (1561; STC 4778), B1v; Thomas Hoby, preface to *The Gratulation of the Mooste Famous Clerke M. Martin Bucer,* by Martin Bucer, trans. Thomas Hoby (1549; STC 3963), A2v.

16. Nicholas Udall, "Dedicatory Preface," in Desiderius Erasmus, "The Paraphrase of Erasmus upon the Gospell of Sainct John," in *The First Tome or Volume of the Paraphrases* in *Elizabeth and Mary Tudor,* ed. Anne Lake Prescott (Aldershot, UK: Ashgate, 2001), 2v.

17. G. B., preface to *Fouretene Sermons,* by Bernardino Ochino, trans. Anne Cooke (1551?; STC 18767), A2v.

18. William Rastell, preface to *Of the Sorowe, Werinesse, Feare, and Prayer of Christ,* by Thomas More, trans. Mary Clarke Basset, in Khanna, *Early Tudor Translators,* 1350 (hereafter cited in text as *OS*).

19. British Library Harley MS 1860, 1r.

20. John Bale, conclusion to *A Godly Medytacyon of the Christen Sowle,* by Marguerite de Navarre, trans. Elizabeth Tudor, in Prescott, *Elizabeth and Mary Tudor*, 40r.

21. Elizabeth I, *Elizabeth I: Translations, 1544–1589,* ed. Janel Mueller and Joshua Scodel (Chicago: University of Chicago Press, 2009), 42.

22. For a consideration of translation within the More family, see Hosington, "Translation in Politics and Religion," 93–108. For Roper's education, see Elizabeth McCutcheon, "The Education of Thomas More's Daughters: Concepts and Praxis," in *East Meets West*, ed. Roger L. Hadlich and J. D. Ellsworth (Honolulu: University of Hawaii Press, 1988), 193–207.

23. For More's ideas on translation, see Brenda M. Hosington, "Thomas More's Views on Language and Translation and Their Place in the Classical and Humanist Tradition," *Moreana* 40, no. 153–54 (2003): 69–98.

24. Thomas More, *The Complete Works of St. Thomas More*, vol. 3, part 1, *Translations of Lucian,* ed. Craig R. Thompson (New Haven, Conn.: Yale University Press, 1974), 5.

25. Desiderius Erasmus, *Collected Works of Erasmus*, vol. 2, *Correspondence of Erasmus,* trans. R. A. B. Mynors and D. F. S. Thomson (Toronto: University of Toronto Press, 1975), 107–8.

26. Thomas Stapleton, *The Life of Sir Thomas More,* trans. Philip E. Hallett, ed. E. E. Reynolds (Bronx, N.Y.: Fordham University Press, 1966), 92.

27. Thomas More, *Selected Letters,* ed. Elizabeth Frances Rogers (New Haven, Conn.: Yale University Press, 1961), 151.

28. Stapleton, *Life of More,* 92.

29. More, *Selected Letters,* 100, his emphasis.

30. Anthony G. S. Edwards, "Introduction to *Life of Pico,*" in Thomas More, *The Complete Works of St. Thomas More,* vol. 1, *English Poems, Life of Pico, The Last Things*, ed. Anthony S. G. Edwards, Katherine Gardiner Rodgers, and Clarence H. Miller (New Haven, Conn.: Yale University Press, 1997), xxxviii–xxxix.

31. More, *Complete Works,* 1:51.

32. Ibid., 1:xlv–xlvii; Stanford E. Lehmberg, "Sir Thomas More's Life of Pico della Mirandola," *Studies in the Renaissance* 3 (1956): 61–74. Gerard B. Wegemer furthermore notes that More interpolates injunctions to take up a public career: *Young Thomas More and the Arts of Liberty* (Cambridge: Cambridge University Press, 2011), 84–85.

33. Richard Hyrde, preface to *The Instruction of a Christen Woman,* by Juan Luis Vives, trans. Richard Hyrde (1529; STC 24856), A3r.

34. John More, preface to *The Legacye or Embassate of the Great Emperour of Inde Prester John,* by Damião de Góis, trans. John More (1533; STC 11966), 3v.

35. Ibid., 12v–15r.

36. Friedrich Nausea, *A Sermon of the Sacrament of the Aulter,* trans. John More (1533; STC 18414), C4v, E1r–E1v.

37. For Erasmus and Luther, see Roland H. Bainton, *Erasmus of Christendom* (New York: Charles Scribner's Sons, 1969), 151–200.

38. As Erasmus himself quoted the Franciscans on his relationship with Luther, "I laid the egg, and Luther hatched it." Desiderius Erasmus, *Collected Works of Erasmus,* vol. 10, *Correspondence of Erasmus,* trans. R. A. B. Mynors and Alexander Dalzell (Toronto: University of Toronto Press, 1992), 464.

39. Carl R. Trueman, *Luther's Legacy: Salvation and the English Reformers, 1525–1556* (Oxford: Clarendon, 1994); James Edward McGoldrick, *Luther's English Connection: The Reformation Thought of Robert Barnes and William Tyndale* (Milwaukee: Northwestern Publishing House, 1979). For the relationship between Erasmus's *Paraphrases* and later religious reform in England, see Gregory D. Dodds, *Exploiting Erasmus: The Erasmian Legacy and Religious Change in Early Modern England* (Toronto: University of Toronto Press, 2009).

40. Erasmus, *Collected Works,* 10:285. Interestingly, Eugenio M. Olivares-Merino notes that Vives's acquaintance with Roper occurred during this period and that Vives probably encouraged Roper to publish her translation: "A Month with the Mores: The Meeting of Juan Luis Vives and Margaret More Roper," *English Studies* 88, no.4 (2007): 397. If so, Vives may have been motivated for both political and scholarly reasons.

41. Erasmus, *Collected Works,* 10:417.

42. Desiderius Erasmus, *Collected Works of Erasmus,* vol. 12, *Correspondence of Erasmus,* ed. Charles G. Nauert Jr., trans. Alexander Dalzell (Toronto: University of Toronto Press, 2003), 165.

43. Ibid., 12:167.

44. Ibid., 12:171.

45. Ibid., 12:403.

46. James Kelsey McConica, *English Humanists and Reformation Politics under Henry VIII and Edward VI* (Oxford: Clarendon, 1965), 71–72. The *Precatio dominica* also had a dubious reputation in France, as Jonathan Goldberg notes (*Desiring Women Writing,* 109).

47. Gentian Hervet also emphasizes the scholarly supremacy of Erasmus in the dedicatory epistle of his translation: "He is the man/to whom in lernynge no lyvyng man may hym selfe compare." Gentian Hervet, preface to *A Sermon of the Excedynge Great Mercy of God,* by Desiderius Erasmus, trans. Gentian Hervet (1526; STC 10474), A2v.

48. John Fisher, *A Sermon Had at Paulis* (1526; STC 10892), E1r.

49. Bainton discusses *De immensa* (*Erasmus of Christendom*, 184). For the *Precatio*, see Hilmar Pabel, *Conversing with God: Prayer in Erasmus' Pastoral Writings* (Toronto: University of Toronto Press, 1997), 109–54.

50. Erasmus, *Collected Works,* 10:205.

51. Desiderius Erasmus, *Collected Works of Erasmus,* vol. 9, *Correspondence of Erasmus,* trans. R. A. B. Mynors (Toronto: University of Toronto Press, 1989), 440.

52. Erasmus, *Sermon of the Excedynge Great Mercy of God,* M1r.

53. Pabel, *Conversing with God,* 123.

54. A. W. Reed, *Early Tudor Drama: Medwall, the Rastells, Heywood, and the More Circle* (London: Methuen, 1926), 165–66.

55. Ibid., 170.

56. McConica, *English Humanists,* 73–74.

57. This woodcut probably indicates that the 1526 printing was the second, licensed version of this text, as Verbrugge has observed ("Roper's Personal Expression," 37).

58. Reed, *Early Tudor Drama,* 164.

59. Thomas More, *The Confutacyon of Tyndales Answere* (1532; STC 18079), cxxvii–cxxviii.

60. John A. Guy, *The Public Career of Sir Thomas More* (New Haven, Conn.: Yale University Press, 1980), 21. Richard Marius notes that More's polemical writings during this period originated in his official duties: *Thomas More: A Biography* (New York: Alfred A. Knopf, 1984), 276–91, 325–26.

61. For the official nature of this text, see John M. Headley, introduction to *The Complete Works of St. Thomas More,* vol. 5, pt. 2, *Responsio ad Lutherum,* by Thomas More, ed. John M. Headley (New Haven, Conn.: Yale University Press, 1969), 775–803.

62. Lisa Jardine, *Erasmus, Man of Letters: The Construction of Charisma in Print* (Princeton, N.J.: Princeton University Press, 1993), 73–79.

63. Lamb, "Margaret Roper," 84–85.

64. Sarah Gwyneth Ross, *The Birth of Feminism: Woman as Intellect in Renaissance Italy and England* (Cambridge, Mass.: Harvard University Press, 2009), 66–79; Lisa Jardine, "Cultural Confusion and Shakespeare's Learned Heroines: 'These Are Old Paradoxes,'" *Shakespeare Quarterly* 38, no. 1 (1987): 1–18; Beilin, *Redeeming Eve,* 3–28. For the link between masculinity and Latin, see Walter J. Ong, "Latin Language Study as a Renaissance Puberty Rite," *Studies in Philology* 56, no. 2 (1959): 103–24.

65. Erasmus, *Collected Works,* 10:134.

66. Martin Luther, *The Babylonian Captivity of the Church,* trans. A. T. W. Steinhäuser, in *Three Treatises* (1948; repr., Philadelphia: Fortress, 1986), 156.

67. Roper, *Devout Treatise*, D4v (as previously established, hereafter cited in text as *DT*); Desiderius Erasmus, *Precatio dominica,* trans. Margaret More Roper, in *Opera omnia,* vol. 5, ed. Joannis Clericus (1703–1706; London: Gregg Press, 1962), 1224A (hereafter cited in text as *Pd*). I have added italics throughout to mark alterations of the source text.

68. This particular translation appears to be a deliberate choice on Roper's part, for she does not always translate "voluntas" as "mynde & pleasure." For example, later on she renders this word with its more common meaning of "will" (*DT*, E1r).

69. Patricia Demers has also noted that Roper's translation "reinforce[s] the scriptural foundations of Erasmus's commentary," but she does not place this emphasis within the anti-Lutheran campaign (*Women's Writing in English*, 72).

70. More, *Selected Letters*, 100.

71. Stapleton, *Life of More*, 91–92.

72. For Greek scholarship at the university level as well as Cheke's and Ascham's translations, see J. W. Binns, *Intellectual Culture in Elizabethan and Jacobean England: The Latin Writings of the Age* (Melksham, UK: Francis Cairns, 1990), 216–18, 222–24, 227.

73. John Christopherson, preface to *Philonis Judaei scriptoris eloquentissimi libri quattuor jam primum de Graeco in Latinum conversi*, by Philo, trans. John Christopherson (Antwerp, 1555), C1r, my translation. Unless otherwise noted, all translations from Latin are mine.

74. Ibid., B4r.

75. See ibid., C1v. For Christopherson and Eusebius, see Binns, *Intellectual Culture*, 218–22.

76. John Christopherson, preface to *Historiae ecclesiasticae scriptores graeci*, by Eusebius, trans. John Christopherson (Cologne, 1581), †††1v.

77. Bodleian Library, MS Bodl. 439.

78. British Library Royal MS 13 B x, 4v–5r.

79. Ibid., 12r.

80. British Library Harley MS 1860, 4v.

81. For discussions of the political significance of Basset's Eusebius, see Hosington, "Translation in Politics and Religion"; Jaime Goodrich, "The Dedicatory Preface to Mary Roper Clarke Basset's Translation of Eusebius' *Ecclesiastical History*," *English Literary Renaissance* 40, no. 3 (2010): 301–28; and Eugenio M. Olivares-Merino, "Some Notes about Mary Roper Clar(c)ke Basset and her Translation of Eusebius," *Moreana* 46, nos. 177–78 (2009): 146–80.

82. British Library Harley MS 1860, 6v-7r.

83. John Guy, *Thomas More* (London: Arnold, 2000), 166–85; and Maria Dowling, *Fisher of Men: A Life of John Fisher, 1469–1535* (New York: St. Martin's, 1999), 159–76.

84. Thomas Wilson, *The Arte of Rhetorique* (1553; STC 25799), 79v.

85. John Fisher, *A Sermon Very Notable, Fruicteful, and Godlie, Made at Paules Crosse, in London* (1554; STC 10896), A1r.

86. John Foxe, *Actes and Monuments* (1563; STC 11222), 1499. For other contemporary sources on Cole's sermon, see Diarmaid MacCulloch, *Thomas Cranmer: A Life* (New Haven, Conn.: Yale University Press, 1996), 600–601.

87. Miles Huggarde, *The Displaying of the Protestantes & Sondry Their Practises* (1556; STC 13558), 69r.

88. James Cancellar, *The Pathe of Obedience* (1556; STC 4565), B7r.

89. For Huggarde and Bonner, see Eamon Duffy, *Fires of Faith: Catholic England Under Mary Tudor* (New Haven, Conn.: Yale University Press, 2009), 175.

90. Guy, *Thomas More,* 8; Duffy, *Fires of Faith,* 179–86.

91. William Rastell, preface to *The Workes of Sir Thomas More,* by Thomas More (1557; STC 18076), ¶2r-2v.

92. Ibid., ¶2v. Nicholas Harpsfield concludes his *Life* with a similar description of More's "devout intercession." Nicholas Harpsfield, *The Life and Death of Sir Thomas Moore,* ed. Elsie Vaughan Hitchcock (London: Early English Text Society, 1932), 217–18.

93. William Thynne's *The Workes of Geffray Chaucer* was printed in folio format in 1532 (STC 5068), 1542 (STC 5070), and 1550 (STC 5071).

94. Rastell, preface to *Workes,* ¶3v.

95. Rastell also includes two untranslated Latin pieces: Latin verses to a pageant written by More in his youth and "A Devout Prayer in Latin, Collected out of the Psalmes of David" (More, *Workes,* C4r, 1406–16). I follow the Yale edition's view that *De tristitia* is a separate work: *The Yale Edition of the Complete Works of St. Thomas More,* vol. 14, pt. 2, *De tristitia Christi,* ed. Clarence Miller (New Haven, Conn.: Yale University Press, 1976), 740–43 (hereafter cited in text as *YE*).

96. More, *Workes,* 1421. For a modern translation, see More, *Selected Letters,* 182.

97. For a useful introduction to this work, see Katherine Gardiner Rodgers, "The Lessons of Gethsemane: *De tristitia Christi,*" in *The Cambridge Companion to Thomas More,* ed. George M. Logan (Cambridge: Cambridge University Press, 2011), 239–62.

98. Here "nece" is used in the archaic sense of "granddaughter": *Oxford English Dictionary,* s.v. "niece, I.1.c," accessed November 24, 2012, http://www.oed.com/view/Entry/126872.

99. Rastell, preface to *Workes,* ¶2v.

100. *Le premier divorce de Henry VIII et la schisme d'Angleterre: Fragment d'une chronique anonyme en Latin,* ed. Charles Bémont (Paris: Édouard Champion, 1917), 68. The title page of the More's *Workes* does mention the financial contributions of three men: "Printed at London at the costes and charges of John Cawood, John Waly, and Richarde Tottell."

101. As questions prepared for the interrogation of Geoffrey Pole indicate, Henrician authorities showed a special interest in Roper's preservation and circulation of More's writings: National Archives, Kew, State Papers 1/138, 10r–23v.

102. More, *De tristitia Christi,* 307 (in *YE,* hereafter cited in text as *DtC* to distinguish Latin quotations from English ones in that edition).

103. See, for example, More, *Selected Letters,* 149. Ross has characterized this marginal note as evidence that Basset viewed translation "a form of intellectual bravura" (*Birth of Feminism,* 165).

104. I have added italics throughout to mark alterations of the source text.

105. A repeated marginal note in More's *History of Richard III* comes the closest to Basset's in function and tone: "This that is here betwene thys mark ± & this mark * was not written by M[aster] More in this history written by him in englishe, but is translated out of this history which he wrote in laten" (*Workes*, 52, 66–67). Yet even these notes do not contain the insistent editorial "I" of Basset's marginalia.

Chapter Two

1. Udall, "Dedicatory Preface," in Prescott, *Elizabeth and Mary Tudor,* 2r.

2. John Bale, conclusion to *A Godly Medytacyon of the Christen Sowle,* by Marguerite de Navarre, trans. Elizabeth Tudor, in Prescott, *Elizabeth and Mary Tudor,* 40v.

3. James Cancellar, preface to *A Godly Meditation of the Soule,* by Marguerite de Navarre, trans. Elizabeth Tudor (1580; STC 17321), A3r. For Cancellar's conservatism, see Maureen Quilligan, *Incest and Agency in Elizabeth's England* (Philadelphia: University of Pennsylvania Press, 2005), 56–65.

4. Thomas Bentley, *The Monument of Matrones* (1582; STC 1892), B1r.

5. *Catechismus . . . A Short Instruction into Christian Religion* (1548; STC 5993), [?]3r.

6. Ibid., A1r. For discussion of the text's translation and aims, see Diarmaid MacCulloch, *Thomas Cranmer: A Life* (New Haven, Conn.: Yale University Press, 1996), 386–92.

7. D. G. Selwyn, introduction to *A Catechism Set Forth by Thomas Cranmer* (Abingdon, UK: Sutton Courtenay Press, 1978), 60–64.

8. Carl I. Hovland, Irving L. Janis, and Harold H. Kelley, *Communication and Persuasion: Psychological Studies of Opinion Change* (New Haven, Conn.: Yale University Press, 1953), 13.

9. Ibid., 21.

10. For the role of translation in the mid-Tudor period, see Edward J. Baskerville, *A Chronological Bibliography of Propaganda and Polemic Published in English between 1553 and 1558* (Philadelphia: American Philosophical Society, 1979), 9; W. K. Jordan, *Edward VI: Young King, The Protectorship of the Duke of Somerset* (Cambridge, Mass.: Harvard University Press, 1968), 141–42.

11. A. S., preface to *Oppositions of the Word of God,* by Pierre du Moulin, trans. A. S. (1610; STC 7333), A3r.

12. Edward Seymour, preface to *An Epistle Both of Godly Consolacion and Also of Advertisement,* by John Calvin, trans. Edward Seymour (1550; STC 4407), A2r.

13. Augustine, *Two Bokes of the Noble Docter . . . Augustine* (Emden, 1556; STC 921); Cyprian, *Certaine Workes of Blessed Cipriane the Martyr* (Emden, 1556; STC 6152).

14. Preface to *The Mirroure of Golde for the Synfull Soule,* trans. Margaret Beaufort (1506; STC 6894.5), A2r.

15. Philippe de Mornay, *A Discourse of Life and Death,* trans. Mary Sidney Herbert (1592; STC 18138).

16. John Ponet, *A Way of Reconciliation,* trans. Elizabeth Russell (1605; STC 21456). For Russell's self-fashioning, see Elizabeth Cooke Hoby Russell, *Our English Sappho: The Writings of Elizabeth Cooke Hoby Russell,* ed. Patricia Phillippy (Toronto: Centre for Reformation and Renaissance Studies, 2011), 319–20.

17. John Field, preface to *A Notable and Comfortable Exposition of M. John Knoxes,* by John Knox (1583; STC 15068), no sig.

18. White, "Renaissance Englishwomen and Religious Translation," 375–400.

19. Micheline White, "A Biographical Sketch of Dorcas Martin: Elizabethan Translator, Stationer, and Godly Matron," *Sixteenth Century Journal* 30, no. 3 (1999): 775–92.

20. Aysha Pollnitz has already situated Mary's translation within the context of translations by Margaret Beaufort and Katherine Parr: "Religion and Translation at the Court of Henry VIII: Princess Mary, Katherine Parr and the *Paraphrases* of Erasmus," in *Mary Tudor: Old and New Perspectives,* ed. Susan Doran and Thomas S. Freeman (Houndmills, UK: Palgrave Macmillan, 2011), 129–32.

21. British Library Cotton MS Vitellius C i, 24v. Mary's schooling has attracted growing scholarly interest: Andrew W. Taylor, "'*Ad omne virtutum genus*'? Mary between Piety, Pedagogy, and Praise in Early Tudor Humanism," in Doran and Freeman, *Mary Tudor*, 103–22; Aysha Pollnitz, "Christian Women or Sovereign Queens? The Schooling of Mary and Elizabeth," in *Tudor Queenship: The Reigns of Mary and Elizabeth,* ed. Alice Hunt and Anna Whitelock (New York: Palgrave Macmillan, 2010), 127–42; Timothy G. Elston, "Transformation or Continuity? Sixteenth-Century Education and the Legacy of Catherine of Aragon, Mary I, and Juan Luis Vives," in *High and Mighty Queens of Early Modern England: Realities and Representations,* ed. Carole Levin, Debra Barrett-Graves, and Jo Eldridge Carney (New York: Palgrave Macmillan, 2003), 11–26; and Kathi Vosevich, "The Education of a Prince(ss): Tutoring the Tudors," in *Women, Writing, and the Reproduction of Culture in Tudor and Stuart Britain,* ed. Mary E. Burke, Jane Donawerth, Linda L. Dove, and Karen Nelson (Syracuse, N.Y.: Syracuse University Press, 2000), 61–76.

22. Juan Luis Vives, "Plan of Girls' Studies," in *Vives and the Renascence Education of Women,* ed. Foster Watson (New York: Longmans, 1912), 144.

23. Giles Du Wés, *An Introductorie for to Lerne to Rede, to Pronounce, and to Speake Frenche* (1533; STC 7377), DD2r–EE1r.

24. British Library Arundel MS 151, 195r.

25. *Letters and Papers, Foreign and Domestic, Henry VIII*, vol. 16, *1540–1541,* ed. James Gairdner and R. H. Brodie (1898; Institute for Historical Research), no. 1253, accessed March 2, 2013, http://www.british-history.ac.uk/report.aspx?compid=76261.

26. Beaufort's influence on religious publications has been traced by Lotte Hellinga in *William Caxton and Early Printing in England* (London: British Library, 2010), 156–68. For considerations of Beaufort's translations, see

Hosington, "Beaufort's Translations," 185–203; Demers, *Women's Writing in English,* 65–69; and Rebecca L. Krug, *Reading Families: Women's Literate Practice in Late Medieval England* (Ithaca, N.Y.: Cornell University Press, 2002), 106–11.

27. Hervet, preface to *A Sermon of the Excedynge Great Mercy of God,* A2r.

28. Jaime Goodrich, "Mary Tudor, Lord Morley, and St. Thomas Aquinas: The Politics of Pious Translation at the Henrician Court," *ANQ* 24, nos.1–2 (2011): 11–20.

29. Janel Mueller, introduction to *Prayers or Meditations,* in *Complete Works & Correspondence,* by Katherine Parr (Chicago: University of Chicago Press, 2011), 369–86; Andrew Hiscock, "'A supernal liuely fayth': Katherine Parr and the Authoring of Devotion," *Women's Writing* 9, no. 2 (2002): 177–98; Janel Mueller, "Devotion as Difference: Intertextuality in Queen Katherine Parr's 'Prayer or Meditations' (1545)," *Huntington Library Quarterly* 53, no. 3 (1990): 171–97.

30. MacCulloch, *Thomas Cranmer,* 329–30.

31. Pollnitz, "Religion and Translation," 131–32.

32. Vives, "Plan of Girls' Studies," 147; British Library Royal MS 17 A xlvi. For Morley's gifts to Mary, see James P. Carley, "The Writings of Henry Parker, Lord Morley: A Bibliographical Survey," in *"Triumphs of English": Henry Parker, Lord Morley, Translator to the Tudor Court,* ed. Marie Axton and James P. Carley (London: British Library, 2000), 27–68.

33. On the English *Paraphrases,* see Gregory D. Dodds, *Exploiting Erasmus: The Erasmian Legacy and Religious Change in Early Modern England* (Toronto: University of Toronto Press, 2009); John Craig, "Forming a Protestant Consciousness? Erasmus' *Paraphrases* in English Parishes, 1547–1666," in *Holy Scripture Speaks: The Production and Reception of Erasmus' "Paraphrases on the New Testament,"* ed. Hilmar M. Pabel and Mark Vessey (Toronto: University of Toronto, 2002), 313–59; John N. Wall, "Godly and Fruitful Lessons: The English Bible, Erasmus' Paraphrases, and the Book of Homilies," in *The Godly Kingdom of Tudor England: Great Books of the English Reformation,* ed. John E. Booty (Wilton, Conn.: Morehouse-Barlow, 1981), 47–135; and E. J. Devereux, "The Publication of the English *Paraphrases of Erasmus,*" *Bulletin of the John Rylands Library* 51 (1968–1969): 348–67. For Katherine Parr's role in the *Paraphrases,* see Susan E. James, *Kateryn Parr: The Making of a Queen* (Aldershot, UK: Ashgate, 1999), 227–34.

34. *Injunccions Geven by the Moste Excellent Prince, Edward the Sixte* (1547; STC 10089), A4v–B1r, B4r.

35. *Certayne Sermons or Homelies Appoynted by the Kynges Majestie* (1547; STC 13640), A4r.

36. *Articles to be Inquired of in Visitacions to Bee Had within the Diocesse of Cantorbury* (1548; STC 10148), A3r–3v, A4v.

37. For their ties to the Edwardian regime, see John N. King, "Freedom of the Press, Protestant Propaganda, and Protector Somerset," *Huntington Library Quarterly* 40, no. 1 (1976): 7–8.

38. Katherine Parr, *The Lamentacion of a Sinner* (London, 1547; STC 4827), no sig.

39. For Katherine's declining influence and reputation during her final months, see Parr, *Complete Works,* 25, 29. For the reformist nature of her *Prayers* and *Lamentation*, see Parr, *Complete Works,* 372–84, 425–42; Hiscock, "'A Supernal Liuely Fayth,'" 177–97; Frank Howson, "Queen Kateryn Parr's *Lamentacion of a Synner* and the Formularies," *Cahiers Elisabéthains* 57 (2000): 1–30; and William P. Haugaard, "Katherine Parr: The Religious Convictions of a Renaissance Queene," *Renaissance Quarterly* 22, no. 4 (1969): 346–59.

40. Stephen Gardiner, *The Letters of Stephen Gardiner,* ed. James Arthur Muller (New York: Macmillan, 1933), 396.

41. Parr, *Complete Works,* 88. Mueller dates this letter either to September 1545 or 1547, preferring 1545, but Parr's letter requests that Mary give her a finished version of the translation so "that it may be given to the press in its time," which suggests the later date.

42. Pollnitz, "Religion and Translation," 123–37.

43. George Joye, *A Present Consolation for the Sufferers of Persecucion for Ryghtwysenes* (Antwerp, 1544; STC 14828), B1r; John Bale, *The Image of Bothe Churches* (Antwerp, 1545; STC 1296.5), 138v.

44. William Turner, *The Rescuynge of the Romishe Fox* (Bonn, 1545; STC 24355), L5r–L5v, M2r; George Joye, *The Refutation of the Byshop of Winchesters Derke Declaration of His False Articles* (1546; STC 14828.5), 52r–52v, 88v–89r.

45. Gardiner, *Letters*, 383.

46. Craig, "Forming a Protestant Consciousness?" 313–59. Also see Christopher Haigh, *English Reformations: Religion, Politics, and Society Under the Tudors* (Oxford: Oxford University Press, 1993), 170; Jordan, *Edward VI,* 165, 185–86, 220, 324, 342. Erika Rummel has discussed Noël Béda's earlier critiques of the *Paraphrases*: "Why Noël Béda Did Not Like Erasmus' *Paraphrases*," in Pabel and Vessey, *Holy Scripture Speaks,* 265–78.

47. Nicholas Udall, "Dedicatory Preface to Katherine Parr," in Desiderius Erasmus, *The First Tome or Volume of the Paraphrases* (1548; STC 2854.4), 16v–17r.

48. Devereux, "Publication of the *Paraphrases*," 363.

49. The haste in printing noted by Devereux may explain why Parr's arms are reversed: ibid., 356–57.

50. Nicholas Udall, "Dedicatory Preface to Edward VI," in Erasmus, *Paraphrases*, 6r (hereafter cited in text as "DPE").

51. For further discussion of how Udall repositions Erasmus, see Dodds, *Exploiting Erasmus*, 9, 18–22, and James Kelsey McConica, *English Humanists and Reformation Politics Under Henry VIII and Edward VI* (Oxford: Oxford University Press, 1965), 242.

52. Udall, "Dedicatory Preface," 2r (hereafter cited in text as "DP," *Para*).

53. McConica also dates Mallett's work to after the *Injunctions* (*English Humanists*, 241–42).

54. John N. King, "Patronage and Piety: The Influence of Catherine Parr," in Hannay, *Silent But for the Word,* 48. Pollnitz disagrees with this idea, claiming that Mary enthusiastically participated in a tradition of learned courtly women ("Religion and Translation," 124, 128–32).

55. D. M. Loades, *Mary Tudor: A Life* (Oxford: Basil Blackwell, 1989), 146, 152.

56. David Loades, "Introduction: The Personal Religion of Mary I," in *The Church of Mary Tudor,* ed. Eamon Duffy and David Loades (Aldershot, UK: Ashgate, 2006), 15.

57. For a consideration of doublets within this translation, see Pollnitz, "Religion and Translation," 132–36.

58. Erasmus, "Sainct John," in *The First Tome or Volume of the Paraphrases,* 3v (hereafter cited in text as "SJ"); Desiderius Erasmus, *Paraphrasis in Evangelium secundum Ioannem* (Basel, 1534), 5 (hereafter cited in text as *PE*). I have added italics throughout to mark alterations of the source text. All translations of Latin or French are mine.

59. See, for example, Loades, "Personal Religion," 11.

60. Desiderius Erasmus, *Collected Works of Erasmus,* vol. 46, *Paraphrase on John,* trans. Jane E. Phillips (Toronto: University of Toronto Press, 1991), 249–50 n. 7.

61. For Mary and papal primacy, see Loades, "Personal Religion," 12–13, 18.

62. *Oxford English Dictionary,* s.v. "vicar, 1b," accessed November 24, 2012, http://www.oed.com/view/Entry/223087.

63. *Oxford English Dictionary,* s.v. "repentance, 3a," accessed November 24, 2012, http://www.oed.com/view/Entry/162745; William Tyndale, *An Answere unto Sir Thomas Mores Dialoge* (1531; STC 24437), 12r. For More's attack, see *The Complete Works of St. Thomas More,* vol. 6, part 1, *A Dialogue Concerning Heresies,* ed. Thomas C. Lawler, Germain Marc'hadour, and Richard C. Marius (New Haven, Conn.: Yale University Press, 1981), 284–90.

64. Glyn Redworth, "A Study in the Formulation of Policy: The Genesis and Evolution of the Act of Six Articles," *Journal of Ecclesiastical History* 37, no. 1 (1986): 42–67.

65. Loades, *Mary Tudor,* 119; Loades, "Personal Religion," 14–17, 28–29.

66. *Oxford Dictionary of National Biography,* s.v. "Francis Mallett" by C. S. Knighton, accessed November 24, 2012, http://www.oxforddnb.com/view/article/17891.

67. Gardiner, *Letters,* 385.

68. Haigh, *English Reformations,* 173.

69. Scholars disagree on whether Mary or her bishops banned the *Paraphrases.* Nicholas Harpsfield oversaw the removal of the *Paraphrases* from Canterbury parishes, but Craig has found no evidence of nationwide action: Craig, "Forming a Protestant Consciousness?" 327–28; Philip Hughes, *The Reformation in England,* vol. 2, *Religio depopulata* (New York: Macmillan, 1954), 243.

70. For Elizabeth's education, see Pollnitz, "Christian Women or Sovereign Queens?" 127–42; Vosevich, "Education of a Prince(ss)," 61–76; and T. W. Baldwin, *William Shakespere's Small Latine & Lesse Greeke,* vol. 1 (Urbana: University of Illinois, 1944), 257–84. Linda Shenk provides a helpful consideration of the ways that Elizabeth used this education as queen: *Learned Queen: The Image of Elizabeth I in Politics and Poetry* (New York: Palgrave Macmillan, 2010).

71. *Oxford Dictionary of National Biography,* s.v. "Jean Belmaine," by Gordon Kipling, accessed November 24, 2012, http://www.oxforddnb.com/view/article/2041.

72. David Loades, *Elizabeth I* (London: Hambledon and London, 2003), 49.

73. Ascham, *Scholemaster,* 35r.

74. For a skeptical take on Ascham's claims, see Baldwin, *Small Latine,* 1:258–59.

75. Roger Ascham, *Letters of Roger Ascham*, ed. Alvin Vos, trans. Maurice Hatch and Alvin Vos (New York: Peter Lang, 1989), 167.

76. The translation sent to Seton is now at Cambridge: MS L 3. For Ascham's letters regarding these translations, see Ascham, *Letters of Roger Ascham*, 34–38.

77. British Library Royal MS 20 A xiv, 1r–1v.

78. McConica, *English Humanists,* 231.

79. For a similar consideration of the differences between the texts intended for Henry and Katherine, see Susan Frye, *Pens and Needles: Women's Textualities in Early Modern England* (Philadelphia: University of Pennsylvania, 2010), 32–33.

80. Elizabeth I, *Translations, 1544–1589*, 40.

81. David Scott Kastan, "'Holy Wurdes' and 'Slypper Wit': John Bale's *King Johan* and the Poetics of Propaganda," in *Rethinking the Henrician Era: Essays on Early Tudor Texts and Contexts,* ed. Peter C. Herman (Urbana: University of Illinois Press, 1994), 267–82; Jesse W. Harris, *John Bale: A Study in the Minor Literature of the Reformation* (Urbana: University of Illinois Press, 1940), 27–28.

82. Useful treatments of Bale's polemical writings include Peter Happé, *John Bale* (Amherst: University of Massachusetts, 1996), 26–56; and Leslie P. Fairfield, *John Bale: Mythmaker for the English Reformation* (West Lafayette, Ind.: Purdue University Press, 1976).

83. Happé, *John Bale*, 13, 30–33.

84. *Acts of the Privy Council of England,* vol. 1, *1542–1547* (London: Her Majesty's Stationary Office, 1890), 409.

85. *A Proclamation . . . to Avoide and Abolish Suche Englishe Bookes as Conteine Pernicious and Detestable Errours* (1546; STC 7809).

86. *Acts of the Privy Council,* 1:509; Harris, *John Bale,* 34. Harris estimates that Bale's books made up at least a third of those destroyed at this bonfire.

87. Gardiner, *Letters,* 277.

88. Ibid., 293.

89. For this campaign, see John N. King, "Freedom of the Press, Protestant Propaganda, and Protector Somerset," *Huntington Library Quarterly* 40, no.1 (1976): 1–9.

90. Honor McCusker provides a useful overview of these publications: *John Bale: Dramatist and Antiquary* (Bryn Mawr, Penn.: Bryn Mawr College, 1942).

91. John Bale, *Illustrium majoris Britanniae scriptorum* (Wesel, 1548; STC 1295), A4v.

92. Ibid., A3v.

93. Ibid., A4v.

94. Ibid., A4r.

95. Marguerite de Navarre, *A Godly Medytacyon of the Christen Sowle*, in Prescott, *Elizabeth and Mary Tudor,* 41r (hereafter cited in text as *M*). King has proposed that Bale received the text from his later patron Mary Fitzroy, Duchess of Richmond ("Patronage and Piety," 51). Scholarly consensus, however, favors Katherine Parr as the likely source: Marc Shell, preface to *Elizabeth's Glass,* by Elizabeth I, edited by Marc Shell (Lincoln, Neb.: University of Nebraska Press, 1993), 3; Quilligan, *Incest and Agency,* 51.

96. McConica, *English Humanists,* 224. For connections between Bale's editions of Askew and Elizabeth, see Quilligan, *Incest and Agency,* 51–54; and Jennifer Summit, *Lost Property: The Woman Writer and English Literary History, 1380–1589* (Chicago: University of Chicago Press, 2000), 138–51.

97. John Foxe, *Actes and Monuments,* vol. 1 (1583; STC 11225), 1238–39.

98. Parr, *Complete Works,* 425–26.

99. For Elizabeth's early translations, see Roger Ellis, "The Juvenile Translations of Elizabeth Tudor," *Translation and Literature* 18, no. 2 (2009): 157–80. Marguerite's text did stir up religious controversy in France: Anne Lake Prescott, "The Pearl of the Valois and Elizabeth I: Marguerite de Navarre's *Miroir* and Tudor England," in Hannay, *Silent but for the Word,* 62–63; Marguerite de Navarre, *Le miroir de l'âme pécheresse,* ed. Renja Salminen (Helsinki: Suomalainen Tiedeakatemia, 1979), 21–30. Susan Snyder makes an argument for its reformist orientation: "Guilty Sisters: Marguerite de Navarre, Elizabeth of England, and the *Miroir de l'âme pécheresse,*" *Renaissance Quarterly* 50, no. 2 (1997): 443–58.

100. Quilligan, *Incest and Agency,* 54.

101. Elizabeth I, *Translations, 1544–1589,* 29–31.

102. Navarre, *Le miroir de l'âme pecheresse,* 176, l. 291 (hereafter cited in text as *Ma*); Elizabeth I, *Translations, 1544–1589,* 62 (presentation copy in which hereafter cited in text as *G*); Navarre, *Godly Medytacyon,* 16r (as previously established, cited in text as *M*). I have added italics throughout to mark alterations of the source text.

103. For a discussion of the differences between the presentation copy and Bale's edition, see Elizabeth I, *Translations, 1544–1589,* 34–38. For Bale's possible editing of Askew, see Thomas S. Freeman and Sarah Elizabeth Wall, "Racking the Body, Shaping the Text: The Account of Anne Askew in Foxe's 'Book of Martyrs,'" *Renaissance Quarterly* 54, no. 4 (2001): 1169–70.

104. For psychological readings of the translation, see Quilligan, *Incest and Agency*, 33–75; Georgia E. Brown, "Translation and the Definition of Sovereignty: The Case of Elizabeth Tudor," in *Travels and Translations in the Sixteenth Century: Selected Papers from the Second International Conference of the Tudor Symposium (2000)*, ed. Mike Pincombe (Aldershot, UK: Ashgate, 2004), 88–103; Shell, preface to *Elizabeth's Glass*, 3–73; Prescott, "Pearl of the Valois," 61–76.

105. Mueller and Scodel speculate that Elizabeth omitted Marguerite's name due to her reformist reputation: Elizabeth I, *Translations, 1544–1589*, 29.

106. Salminen, introduction to *Miroir*, 83–84.

107. Ibid., 77–78.

108. Ibid., 71–82.

109. E.g., "of little account": *Oxford English Dictionary*, s.v. "simple, II.7a," accessed November 24, 2012, http://www.oed.com./view/Entry/179955.

110. For a consideration of these reprints, see Quilligan, *Incest and Agency*, 51–75.

Chapter Three

1. Critics have traditionally attributed the embroidered bindings to Elizabeth: Frye, *Pens and Needles*, 31–41; Lisa M. Klein, "Your Humble Handmaid: Elizabethan Gifts of Needlework," *Renaissance Quarterly* 50, no. 2 (1997): 459–93; and Margaret H. Swain, "A New Year's Gift from the Princess Elizabeth," *Connoisseur* 183 (1973): 258–66.

2. British Library, Royal MS 7 D x.

3. Klein, "Humble Handmaid," 477.

4. For Elizabeth's education, see Pollnitz, "Christian Women or Sovereign Queens?," 127–42; Vosevich, "Education of a Prince(ss)," 61–76; and Baldwin, *Small Latine*, 260, 263, 266–67. For the connotations of Elizabeth's italic, see Frances Teague, "Princess Elizabeth's Hand in *The Glass of the Sinful Soul*," *English Manuscript Studies 1100–1700*, 9 (2000): 40.

5. Elizabeth I, *Translations: 1544–1589*, 137.

6. Ibid., 217.

7. See, for example, Margaret P. Hannay, "'Wisdome the Wordes'; Psalm Translation and Elizabethan Women's Spirituality," *Religion & Literature* 23, no. 3 (1991): 65.

8. Discussions of gift exchange in early modern England and France include: Natalie Zemon Davis, *The Gift in Sixteenth-Century France* (Madison: University of Wisconsin Press, 2000); Patricia Fumerton, *Cultural Aesthetics: Renaissance Literature and the Practice of Social Ornament* (Chicago: University of Chicago, 1991), 29–66; and Barbara J. Harris, "Women and Politics in Early Tudor England," *The Historical Journal* 33, no. 2 (1990): 259–81.

9. British Library Royal MS 5 E xvii, 2r–2v.

10. Pierre Bourdieu and Jean-Claude Passeron, *Reproduction in Education, Society, and Culture* (1970), trans. Richard Nice (London: Sage, 1977), 30. Also see Pierre Bourdieu, "The Forms of Capital," trans. Richard Nice, in *Handbook of Theory and Research for the Sociology of Education*, ed. John

G. Richardson (New York: Greenwood Press, 1986), 241–58. For a helpful consideration of the link between education and capital, see Richard Halpern, *The Poetics of Primitive Accumulation: English Renaissance Culture and the Genealogy of Capital* (Ithaca, N.Y.: Cornell University Press, 1991).

11. Bourdieu, "Forms of Capital," 247.

12. National Archives, State Papers, 6/12, 15r, 16r.

13. Henry Parker, Lord Morley, "Preface to His Translation of Paolo Giovio," in *Forty-Six Lives*, trans. Henry Parker, Lord Morley, ed. Herbert G. Wright (1943; repr., New York: Oxford University Press for the Early English Text Society, 1970), 161.

14. British Library Royal MS 15 A iii, 4r, 1v–2r, my translation. Unless otherwise noted, all translations of Latin and French are mine.

15. Prescott, "Pearl of the Valois," 64.

16. Janel Mueller and Joshua Scodel, introduction to *John Calvin's Institution,* in Elizabeth I, *Translations: 1544–1589,* 204–5.

17. Elizabeth I, *Translations: 1544–1589,* 219.

18. Ibid., 303.

19. For the development of the figure of the pious woman within England, see Kimberly Anne Coles, *Religion, Reform, and Women's Writing in Early Modern England* (Cambridge: Cambridge University Press, 2008).

20. Jessica L. Malay, "Jane Seager's Sibylline Poems: Maidenly Negotiations Through Elizabethan Gift Exchange," *English Literary Renaissance* 36, no. 2 (2006): 189.

21. British Library Harley MS 1860, 6r.

22. British Library Royal MS 17 B xviii, 2r–2v.

23. For discussions of Sidney Herbert's poetic development, see Krontiris, *Oppositional Voices;* Gary F. Waller, "The Countess of Pembroke and Gendered Reading," in *The Renaissance Englishwoman in Print: Counterbalancing the Canon,* ed. Anne M. Haselkorn and Betty S. Travitsky (Amherst: University of Massachusetts, 1990), 327–35; and G. F. Waller, *Mary Sidney, Countess of Pembroke: A Critical Study of her Writings and Literary Milieu* (Salzburg: Institut für anglistik und amerikanistik, 1979).

24. For Sidney's political career, see Alan Stewart, *Philip Sidney* (New York: Thomas Dunne Books, 2001), and James M. Osborn, *Young Philip Sidney 1572–1577* (New Haven, Conn.: Yale University Press for the Elizabethan Club, 1972). Other useful sources include Robert E. Stillman, *Philip Sidney and the Poetics of Renaissance Cosmopolitanism* (Aldershot, UK: Ashgate, 2008); Edward Berry, "Hubert Languet and the 'Making' of Philip Sidney," *Studies in Philology* 85, no. 3 (1988): 305–20; and Jan A. Van Dorsten, "Sidney and Languet," *Huntington Library Quarterly* 29, no. 3 (1966): 215–22.

25. For Sidney's Du Bartas, see Philip Sidney, *The Poems of Sir Philip Sidney*, ed. William A. Ringler Jr. (Oxford: Clarendon, 1962), 339.

26. Alan Sinfield, "Sidney and Du Bartas," *Comparative Literature* 27, no. 1 (1975): 8–20.

27. Philippe de Mornay, *De veritate religionis Christianae* (Antwerp, 1583), *1v.

28. Alan Sinfield, "Sidney, De Plessis-Mornay and the Pagans," *Philological Quarterly* 58 (1979): 26–39.

29. For the definitive introduction to Sidney's psalms and their sources, see Sidney, *Poems*, 500–509.

30. Mary Sidney Herbert, *Collected Works*, vol. 2, *The Psalmes of David*, ed. Margaret P. Hannay, Noel J. Kinnamon, and Michael G. Brennan (1998; repr., Oxford: Clarendon, 2003), 3–6; John N. King, *English Reformation Literature: The Tudor Origins of the Protestant Tradition* (Princeton, N.J.: Princeton University Press, 1982); W. Stanford Reid, "The Battle Hymns of the Lord: Calvinist Psalmody of the Sixteenth Century," *Sixteenth Century Essays and Studies* 2 (1971): 36–54.

31. James Simpson, "Martyrdom in the Literal Sense: Surrey's Psalm Paraphrases," *Medieval and Early Modern English Studies* 12, no. 1 (2004): 133–65; Elizabeth Heale, *Wyatt, Surrey and Early Tudor Poetry* (London: Longman, 1998), 154–90; Alexandra Halasz, "Wyatt's David," *Texas Studies in Literature and Language* 30, no. 3 (1988): 320–44; Stephen Greenblatt, *Renaissance Self-Fashioning: From More to Shakespeare* (Chicago: University of Chicago Press, 1980), 115–56.

32. Ruth Hughey, ed., *The Arundel Harington Manuscript of Tudor Poetry*, 2 vols. (Columbus: Ohio State University Press, 1960), 2:433–35. Also see Margaret P. Hannay, *Philip's Phoenix: Mary Sidney, Countess of Pembroke* (Oxford: Oxford University Press, 1990), 98.

33. Hughey, *Arundel Harington Manuscript*, 1:338, 340–41.

34. Also see Margaret P. Hannay, "'Princes You as Men Must Dy': Genevan Advice to Monarchs in the *Psalmes* of Mary Sidney," *English Literary Renaissance* 19, no. 1 (1989): 22–41, esp. 28–30; and *Philip's Phoenix*, 86–88.

35. Philippe de Mornay, *A Woorke Concerning the Trewnesse of God*, trans. Arthur Golding (1587; STC 18149), *3v. Scholars disagree over whether Sidney translated any part of the text published by Golding: Philippe de Mornay, *A Woorke Concerning the Trewnesse of the Christian Religion*, ed. F. J. Sypher (Delmar, N.Y.: Scholars' Facsimiles & Reprints, 1976), ix–xv; Philip Sidney, *The Miscellaneous Prose of Sir Philip Sidney*, ed. Katherine Duncan-Jones and Jan Van Dorsten (Oxford: Clarendon, 1973), 155–57; Philip Sidney, *The Prose Works of Sir Philip Sidney*, vol. 3, *The Defence of Poesie, Political Discourses, Correspondence, Translation*, ed. Albert Feuillerat (1912; repr., Cambridge: Cambridge University Press, 1963), viii–ix.

36. Mornay, *Woorke Concerning the Trewnesse*, *4r.

37. National Archives, State Papers 12/195, 51r–51v. I follow the transcription proposed by H. R. Woudhuysen, *Sir Philip Sidney and the Circulation of Manuscripts 1558–1640* (Oxford: Clarendon, 1996), 416.

38. For the earlier critical tradition, see Diane Bornstein, "The Style of the Countess of Pembroke's Translation of Philippe de Mornay's *Discours de la vie et de la mort*," in Hannay, *Silent but for the Word*, 126–34; Waller, *Mary Sidney, Countess of Pembroke*, 107–51.

39. Hannay, *Philip's Phoenix*, 61–62.

40. Danielle Clarke, "The Politics of Translation and Gender in the Countess of Pembroke's *Antonie*," *Translation and Literature* 6, no. 2 (1997): 149–66; Victor Skretkowicz, "Mary Sidney Herbert's *Antonius*, English Philhellenism and the Protestant Cause," *Women's Writing* 6, no. 1 (1999): 7–25.

41. Hannay, Kinnamon, and Brennan place the dating between 1593 and 1599, noting that a first draft was completed by 1594 at the latest: Sidney Herbert, *Psalmes of David,* 340. For the Psalter's political significance, see Katherine Larson, "From Inward Conversation to Public Praise: Mary Sidney Herbert's *Psalmes*," *Sidney Journal* 24, no. 1 (2006): 21–43; Clarke, *Early Modern Women's Writing,* 138–47; Hannay, "Genevan Advice," 22–41; and Hannay, "'Doo what men may sing': Mary Sidney and the Tradition of Admonitory Dedication," in Hannay, *Silent but for the Word,* 249–65.

42. For this crisis, see R. B. Wernham, *The Return of the Armadas: The Last Years of the Elizabethan War against Spain, 1595–1603* (Oxford: Oxford University Press, 1994), 211–62.

43. Robert Devereux, *An Apologie of the Earle of Essex* (1600; STC 6787.7), C3r.

44. Wernham, *Return of the Armadas,* 241–42.

45. *Calendar of the Manuscripts of the Most Hon. the Marquis of Salisbury,* vol. 8, *1598,* ed. R. A. Roberts (London: Her Majesty's Stationery Office, 1899), 25.

46. Ibid., 29.

47. *Calendar of the Manuscripts of the Most Hon. the Marquis of Salisbury,* vol. 23, *1562–1605,* ed. G. Dyfnallt Owen (London: Her Majesty's Stationery Office, 1973), 20.

48. *Calendar of the Manuscripts of the Most Hon. the Marquis of Salisbury,* vol. 9, *1599,* ed. R. A. Roberts (London: Her Majesty's Stationery Office, 1902), 142.

49. Ibid., 188.

50. For a discussion of the physical characteristics that led Ringler to this identification, see Sidney Herbert, *Psalmes of David,* 310–13. I am very grateful to the present Viscount De L'Isle, MBE, DL, for kindly allowing me to examine and cite MS A.

51. Ringler, among others, suggests that John Aubrey's reference to a manuscript bound in crimson velvet was MS A: Sidney, *Poems,* 547.

52. "Even now that care," Mary Sidney Herbert, *Collected Works,* vol. 1, *Poems, Translations, and Correspondence,* ed. Margaret P. Hannay, Noel J. Kinnamon, and Michael G. Brennan (1998; repr., Oxford: Clarendon, 2008), 103, line 53 (hereafter cited in text and notes as *PTC*). For a useful discussion of early modern views about the appropriateness of psalms to kings and queens as well as Sidney Herbert's possible reference to a rendering of Psalm 13 that accompanied John Bale's publication of Elizabeth's translation of Marguerite de Navarre, see *PTC,* 92–100.

53. I am very grateful to David Vaisey, literary executor for Dr. Bent Juel-Jensen, for kindly allowing me to examine MS J.

54. J. C. A. Rathmell's pioneering edition of the complete Sidney Psalter defines the collection as "poems (for they are more than translations)": *The Psalms of Sir Philip Sidney and the Countess of Pembroke* (New York: New York University Press, 1963), xi. Also see Patricia Demers, "'Warpe' and 'Webb' in the Sidney Psalms: The 'Coupled Worke' of the Countess of Pembroke and Sir Philip Sidney," in *Literary Couplings: Writing Couples, Collaborators, and the Construction of Authorship,* ed. Marjorie Stone and Judith Thompson (Madison: University of Wisconsin Press, 2006), 45; Margaret P. Hannay, "Re-Revealing the Psalms: The Countess of Pembroke and Her Early Modern Readers," *Sidney Journal* 23, nos. 1–2 (2005): 22–24; and Sidney Herbert, *PTC,* 99. For a discussion of the common metaphor of translation as clothing, see Morini, *Tudor Translation,* 36–42.

55. For Sidney Herbert's knowledge of Hebrew, see Sidney Herbert, *Psalmes of David,* 16–19; and Theodore L. Steinberg, "The Sidneys and the Psalms," *Studies in Philology* 92, no. 1 (1995): 1–17.

56. Hannibal Hamlin, *Psalm Culture and Early Modern English Literature* (Cambridge: Cambridge University Press, 2004), 6–13.

57. Robert Crowley, *The Psalter of David Newely Translated into Englysh Metre* (1549; STC 2725); Francis Bacon, *The Translation of Certain Psalmes into English Verse* (1625; STC 1174); *The Psalmes of King David Translated by King James* (Oxford, 1631; STC 2732).

58. *Oxford English Dictionary,* s.v. "metaphrase, 1," accessed November 24, 2012, http://www.oed.com/view/Entry/117340; MSS C (Bodleian Library, MS Rawl. poet. 24) and F (Trinity College, Cambridge, MS O.1.51) use the term "translated" while MSS G (Trinity College, Cambridge, MS R.3.16) and M (Huntington Library, MS HM 117) employ "metaphrased." For the psalms' titles, see Sidney Herbert, *Psalmes of David,* 308–36.

59. John Donne, *The Divine Poems,* ed. Helen Gardner (1952; repr., Oxford: Clarendon, 2000), 35, line 53; John Harington, *The Epigrams of Sir John Harington,* ed. Gerard Kilroy (Farnham, UK: Ashgate, 2009), 227.

60. Hannay has noted that contemporary identifications of David as Elizabeth and his enemies as Catholics made more pointed parallels superfluous ("Genevan Advice," 30).

61. Hannay, *Philip's Phoenix,* 89–90.

62. Noel Kinnamon, "The Sidney Psalms: The Penshurst and Tixall Manuscripts," *English Manuscript Studies, 1100–1700* 2 (1990): 140–43.

63. Two additional psalms lack final ruling and gilding (Psalms 132 and 144), but MS A's versions of Psalms 132 and 144 are present in the first round of revisions preserved in the δ tradition. Perhaps the foul copy of these psalms was too complex for Davies to transcribe with confidence: Sidney, *Poems,* 503, 547.

64. For identification of this hand, see Sidney Herbert, *Psalmes of David,* 312, 341, 347.

65. This reconstruction is based on the extremely helpful information in ibid., 309–10, 337–57. MS F is currently at Trinity College, Cambridge (MS O.1.51) and contains copies of Psalms 27–150 from MS A.

66. The δ tradition consists of MSS C, D, E, F (Psalms 1–26), G, H, I, L, N, K, O, P, and Q. In general the δ tradition preserves preliminary versions of Psalms 1 and 23 and omits the conclusion to Psalm 22; for more details, see Sidney, *Poems*, 502. K, F, and I offer Sidney's version of Psalm 26, while the rest of the δ tradition supplies an intermediary revision that differs from the finalized rendition in A, J, and B. Sidney Herbert must have revised Psalm 16 in χ, a lost working copy, as it is omitted in K, F, and I but not the remainder of the δ tradition.

67. MS B is housed in the Bodleian Library: MS Rawl. poet. 25.

68. Sidney, *Poems,* 289n, 300–301n, 306n.

69. Sidney, *Poems,* 270n, 503.

70. Sidney Herbert, *Psalmes of David,* 358.

71. See, for example, G. F. Waller, "The Text and Manuscript Variants of the Countess of Pembroke's Psalms," *Review of English Studies* 26, no. 101 (1975):1–18. For discussions of Sidney Herbert's revisions, see Sidney Herbert, *Psalmes of David,* 358–61; and Beth Wynne Fisken, "Mary Sidney's *Psalmes*: Education and Wisdom," in Hannay, *Silent but for the Word,* 166–83.

72. Sidney, *Poems,* 270, lines 13–22.

73. Clement Marot and Théodore de Bèze, *Les CL pseaumes de David* (Orleans, 1566), 6v; *The Booke of Common Prayer* (1566; STC 16297), A2r; Théodore de Bèze, *Psalmorum Davidis et aliorum prophetarum* (London, 1580; STC 2032), 2.

74. Sidney, *Poems*, 270n. Sidney Herbert's revisions of Sidney's psalms were not included in *Psalmes of David*, but may be found in footnotes to Sidney, *Poems*. I cite both these footnotes and MS A itself, which does not contain Psalm 1.

75. *Bible and Holy Scriptures*, 235r.

76. Sidney, *Poems*, 270, lines 1–2.

77. Sidney, *Poems*, 305, lines 13–15.

78. Sidney, *Poems*, 306, lines 31–39.

79. Bèze, *Psalmorum Davidis,* 89.

80. MS A, 20v. For the version in MS B, see Sidney, *Poems,* 306n.

81. Théodore de Bèze, *The Psalmes of David,* trans. Anthony Gilby (1580; STC 2033), 49.

82. Bèze, *Psalmes,* 47–48.

83. Bèze, *Psalmorum Davidis,* 88. For commentary on the political applications of this proverb, see Desiderius Erasmus, *Collected Works of Erasmus,* vol. 31, *Adages Ii1 to Iv100,* trans. Margaret Mann Phillips, ed. R. A. B. Mynors (Toronto: University of Toronto Press, 1982), 133–36.

84. *Oxford English Dictionary,* s.v. "stain, 3a, 5a," accessed November 24, 2012, http://www.oed.com/view/Entry/188732.

85. Margaret P. Hannay, "'House-confinéd maids': The Presentation of Woman's Role in the *Psalmes* of the Countess of Pembroke," *English Literary Renaissance* 24, no. 1 (1994): 48–49.

86. Sidney, *Poems,* 301, lines 19–27.

87. *Bible and Holy Scriptures,* 239v; Bèze, *Psalmes,* 42.

88. MS A, 18r; Sidney, *Poems,* 301n.

89. Bèze, *Psalmes*, 42; Bèze, *Psalmorum Davidis,* 78.

90. Shenk, *Learned Queen;* Linda Shenk, "Turning Learned Authority into Royal Supremacy: Elizabeth I's Learned Persona and Her University Orations," in *Elizabeth I: Always Her Free Own Woman,* ed. Carole Levin, Jo Eldridge Carney, and Debra Barret-Graves (Aldershot, UK: Ashgate, 2003), 78–96; Lysbeth Benkert, "Translation as Image-Making: Elizabeth I's Translation of Boethius's *Consolation of Philosophy,*" *Early Modern Literary Studies* 6, no. 3 (January 2001): 2.1–20, http://purl.oclc.org/emls/06-3/benkboet.htm; Mary Thomas Crane, "'Video et Taceo': Elizabeth I and the Rhetoric of Counsel," *SEL* 28, no. 1 (1988), 1–15. T. W. Baldwin presents a more pessimistic view of Elizabeth's learning (*Small Latine,* 1:280–83).

91. Carole Levin, *The Heart and Stomach of a King: Elizabeth I and the Politics of Sex and Power* (Philadelphia: University of Pennsylvania Press, 1994), 121–48; Susan Frye, *Elizabeth I: The Competition for Representation* (Oxford: Oxford University Press, 1993), 1–16; Marie Axton, *The Queen's Two Bodies: Drama and the Elizabethan Succession* (London: Royal Historical Society, 1977), 11–25.

92. Edmund Plowden, *The Commentaries, or Reports of Edmund Plowden, of the Middle-Temple, Esq.* (1779; ESTC T183788), 221.

93. Elizabeth I, *Collected Works,* ed. Leah S. Marcus, Janel Mueller, and Mary Beth Rose (Chicago: University of Chicago Press, 2000), 326.

94. Levin, *Heart and Stomach,* 146–47.

95. Ascham, *Scholemaster,* B2r.

96. Fumerton usefully analyzes Elizabeth's manipulation of privacy (*Cultural Aesthetics,* 67–110).

97. Baldwin, *Small Latine,* 1:284.

98. Shenk notes a similar dynamic in Elizabeth's early university orations, in which Elizabeth places herself as a student rather than a counselor ("Learned Authority," 81).

99. Janel Mueller and Joshua Scodel, introduction to *Elizabeth's Sententiae* in Elizabeth I, *Translations: 1544–1589,* 332.

100. Elizabeth I, *Collected Works*, 87, 88. As Shenk points out, this may not be a correct attribution ("Learned Authority," 83).

101. Elizabeth I, *The Letters of Queen Elizabeth I,* ed. G. B. Harrison (1935; repr., New York: Funk and Wagnalls, 1968), 159.

102. Frye, *Elizabeth I, 5.*

103. Janet M. Green, "Queen Elizabeth I's Latin Reply to the Polish Ambassador," *Sixteenth Century Journal* 31, no. 4 (2000): 987–1008.

104. Janel Mueller and Joshua Scodel, introduction to *Cicero's Pro Marcello*, in Elizabeth I, *Translations: 1592–1598,* ed. Janel Mueller and Joshua Scodel (Chicago: University of Chicago Press, 2009), 3; Leah S. Marcus, "Queen Elizabeth I as Public and Private Poet: Notes toward a New Edition," in *Reading Monarch's Writing: The Poetry of Henry VIII, Mary Stuart, Elizabeth I, and James VI/I,* ed. Peter C. Herman (Tempe: Arizona Center for Medieval and Renaissance Studies, 2002), 142.

105. Henry Savile, preface to *The Ende of Nero and Beginning of Galba: Fower Bookes of the Histories of Cornelius Tacitus,* by Tacitus, trans. Henry Savile (1591; STC 23642), ¶2r-¶2v.

106. Windebank's fair copies of the Plutarch and part of the Boethius survive, respectively, in British Library Royal MS 17 A xliv and National Archives, State Papers 12/289, 100r–102v.

107. Robert Devereux to Francis Bacon, 24 August 1593, in *The Letters and the Life of Francis Bacon,* vol. 1, ed. James Spedding (London: Longman, Green, Longman, and Roberts, 1861), 254–55.

108. Marcus, "Public and Private Poet," 143.

109. For an alternate take on Elizabeth's motivation, see Quan Manh Ha, introduction to *The Consolation of Queen Elizabeth I: The Queen's Translation of Boethius' "De Consolatione Philosophiae,"* ed. Noel Harold Kaylor Jr. and Philip Edward Phillips (Tempe: Arizona Center for Medieval and Renaissance Studies, 2009), 16–20.

110. Anthony Grafton, "Epilogue: Boethius in the Renaissance," in *Boethius: His Life, Thought and Influence,* ed. Margaret Gibson (Oxford: Basil Blackwell, 1981), 411–15.

111. William Camden, *Annals or the Historie of the Most Renowned and Victorious Princesse Elizabeth,* trans. R. N. (1635; STC 4501), 422.

112. National Archives, State Papers 12/289, 7r-9v. For a transcription of these calculations, see Kaylor and Phillips, *Consolation of Queen Elizabeth,* 41, 149–54.

113. While Shenk does note that Elizabeth should not be associated with the character of Boethius alone, she does not see Lady Philosophy as self-referential but rather as a mouthpiece for positions parallel to Elizabeth's stance regarding Henry: Shenk, *Learned Queen,* 142.

114. For Henry's conversion and its politics, see R. B. Wernham, *After the Armada: Elizabethan England and the Struggle for Western Europe 1588–1595* (Oxford: Clarendon, 1984), 488–513. For useful summaries of primary documents, see *List and Analysis of State Papers Foreign Series, Elizabeth I,* vol. 5, *July 1593–December 1594,* ed. Richard Bruce Wernham (London: Her Majesty's Stationary Office, 1989).

115. Wernham, *After the Armada,* 491–94. Indeed, in October 1592 Elizabeth and Burghley had respectively warned Henry and the Duc de Bouillon against the possibility: Wernham, *After the Armada*, 492. For Burghley's letter, see Conyers Read, *Lord Burghley and Queen Elizabeth* (New York: Alfred A. Knopf, 1960), 481–82.

116. National Archives, State Papers 78/31, 223r.

117. National Archives, State Papers, 78/32, 287v.

118. Wernham, *After the Armada,* 506.

119. Elizabeth I, *Autograph Compositions and Foreign Language Originals,* ed. Janel Mueller and Leah S. Marcus (Chicago: University of Chicago Press, 2003), 165. For the translation, see Elizabeth I, *Collected Works,* 370–71.

120. National Archives, State Papers, 78/31, 310r; italics in my translation denote Elizabeth's use of Latin.

121. National Archives, State Papers, 78/32, 74r.

122. National Archives, State Papers, 78/32, 205r.

123. Elizabeth I, *Translations: 1592–1598,* 80 (hereafter cited in text as *T*); Boethius, *The Consolation of Philosophy* in *The Theological Tractates* (Cambridge, Mass.: Harvard University Press, 1973), book 1, meter 2.24–26 (hereafter cited in text as *CP*). I have added italics throughout to mark alterations of the source text. The following analysis of Elizabeth's translation choices is deeply indebted to Mueller and Scodel's extensive annotations to their edition of this translation (*T*).

124. Elizabeth continues this trend by translating "angeret" (tormented) as "greevid" (*T,* 186). As Mueller and Scodel point out, Elizabeth's edition of Boethius utilized "angeret" rather than the "confudit" of modern editions (*T,* 186n57; *CP,* book 3, prose 3.17). When Lady Philosophy begins to question Boethius, Elizabeth omits another reference to his inability to respond to her addresses: "I should like to think that you were ashamed, but I can see that you are quite stupefied" (*CP,* book 1, prose 2.9–8, translation in *CP*).

125. Elizabeth translates "magistra" as "pedagogue" a second time (*T,* 93; *CP,* book 1, prose 4.76).

126. Elizabeth I, *Autograph Compositions,* 165. For the translation, see Elizabeth I, *Collected Works,* 370–71.

127. National Archives, State Papers, 71/31, 248v. As Shenk notes, Burghley wrote these instructions, but his minutes of July 10 reveal that Wilkes's instructions are a revision of Burghley's earlier memoranda and were probably approved by the queen: Shenk, *Learned Queen,* 153.

128. Janel Mueller and Joshua Scodel, introduction to *Boethius' De consolatione philosophiae* (*T,* 51–52, 270n58).

Chapter Four

1. *The Rule of the Most Blissed Father Saint Benedict* (Ghent, 1632; STC 1860), 55.

2. Archives Départementales du Nord Lille, MS 20 H 1, 30.

3. For the practical emphasis of seventeenth-century Ignatian prayer, see Joseph De Guibert, *The Jesuits: Their Spiritual Doctrine and Practice,* trans. William J. Young (Chicago: Institute of Jesuit Sources with Loyola, 1964), 282.

4. See, for example, Toby Matthew, *The Life of Lady Lucy Knatchbull* (London: Sheed and Ward, 1931), 43.

5. Augustine Baker, *The Life and Death of Dame Gertrude More,* ed. Ben Wekking (Salzburg: Institut für Anglistik und Amerikanistik, 2002), 66.

6. Ibid., 91.

7. A. F. Allison and D. M. Rogers, *A Catalogue of Catholic Books in English Printed Abroad or Secretly in England, 1558–1640* (Bognor Regis, UK: Arundel Press, 1956), 63, no. 337.

8. Augustine Baker, *Catalogue of Such English Bookes as Are in This House, Most Helping toward Contemplation,* Beinecke Library, Osborn MS b 268, 245.

9. Frans Blom and Jos Blom, "Introductory Note," in *Pudentiana Deacon,* ed. Frans Blom and Jos Blom (Aldershot, UK: Ashgate, 2002), x–xi. Deacon was given the name of Pudentiana, but she always signed her name with the alternative spelling Potentiana; I have followed Deacon's preferred spelling throughout this chapter. The house's nineteenth-century MS *Annals* identify her baptismal name as Elizabeth: Downside Abbey Archives, Haslemere MS 1876, 45.

10. Janet Wright Starner and Barbara Howard Traister, eds. *Anonymity in Early Modern England: What's in a Name?* (Farnham, UK: Ashgate, 2011); Marcy L. North, *The Anonymous Renaissance: Cultures of Discretion in Tudor England* (Chicago: University of Chicago Press, 2003).

11. Preface to *The Bible and Holy Scriptures,* ***2r.

12. John Calvin, *Letters of John Calvin,* vol. 4, ed. Jules Bonnet, trans. Marcus Robert Gilchrist (Philadelphia: Presbyterian Board of Education, 1858), 46.

13. Gayatri Chakravorty Spivak, "Scattered Speculations on the Subaltern and the Popular," *Postcolonial Studies* 8, no. 4 (2005): 480.

14. Ibid., 481.

15. Preface to *The Holie Bible,* †2r. For Catholic translation in Europe, see Carlos M. N. Eire, "Early Modern Catholic Piety in Translation," in Burke and Hsia, *Cultural Translation in Early Modern Europe,* 83–100.

16. Antonio de Molina, *Spiritual Exercises,* trans. Abraham Ellis (Mechelen, 1621; STC 17998); Bartolomeo Campi, *The Seaven Trumpets of Brother Bartholomew Saluthius,* trans. George Porret (Saint Omer, 1626; STC 4469).

17. Robert Bellarmino, *The Art of Dying Well* (Saint Omer, 1621; STC 1838.5); Vincenzo Bruno, *An Abridgment of the Meditations of the Life . . . of Jesus Christ* (Saint Omer, 1614; STC 3941); Ignatius of Loyola, *A Manuall of Devout Meditations* (Saint Omer, 1618; STC 16877); Teresa of Avila, *The Lyf of the Mother Teresa of Jesus* (Mechelen, 1611; STC 23948.5).

18. Albertus Magnus, *The Paradise of the Soule* (Saint Omer, 1617; STC 269); Antonio de Molina, *A Treatise of Mental Prayer* (Saint Omer, 1617; STC 18000); Luca Pinelli, *The Mirrour of Religious Perfection* (Saint Omer, 1618; STC 19938); Francisco de Borja, *The Practise of Christian Workes* (Saint Omer, 1620; STC 11315).

19. Lock, preface to Calvin, *Sermons of John Calvin,* A3v.

20. Cary, preface to *Reply of the Most Illustrious Cardinall of Perron,* ã2v, ã2r.

21. Jaime Goodrich, "'Ensigne-Bearers of Saint Clare': Elizabeth Evelinge's Translations and the Restoration of English Franciscanism," in White, *English Women,* 83–100.

22. Elizabeth Evelinge, preface to *History of the Angelicall Virgin Glorious S. Clare,* ã3v.

23. John Gerard, *The Autobiography of an Elizabethan,* trans. Philip Caraman (London: Longmans, Green, 1951), 39–40.

24. John Gerard, preface to *The Spiritual Conflict,* by Lorenzo Scupoli, trans. John Gerard (1598; STC 22126.3), 3v.

25. This secret press may have been run by Jesuits, as it published works by Henry Garnet, Robert Persons, and Robert Southwell. See the information on press number twelve in A. F. Allison and D. M. Rogers, *The Contemporary Printed Literature of the English Counter-Reformation Between 1558 and 1640,* vol. 2, *Works in English* (Aldershot, UK: Scolar Press, 1994), 225.

26. *Chronicles of the First Monastery Founded for Benedictine Nuns* (Bergholt, UK: Saint Mary's Abbey, 1898), 24.

27. Jerome, Count of Portia, preface to *The Virgin Maries Life,* by Luca Pinelli, trans. Richard Gibbons (Douai, 1604; STC 19940), †2r.

28. Anthony Hoskins, preface to *The Apologies of the Most Christian Kings of France and Navar, Henry IIII and Lewis XIII,* trans. Anthony Hoskins (Saint Omer, 1611; STC 13122.5), 3. For these allegations, see Eric Nelson, *The Jesuits and the Monarchy: Catholic Reform and Political Authority in France (1590–1615)* (Aldershot, UK: Ashgate, 2005), 147–208.

29. Anthony Hoskins, preface to *A Briefe and Cleare Declaration of Sundry Pointes*, by Leonardus Lessius, trans. Anthony Hoskins (Saint Omer, 1611; STC 13840), 4. Allison and Rogers identify the source text as Lessius's *Defensio potestatis summi pontificis* (*Contemporary Printed Literature*, no. 447).

30. Anthony Hoskins, preface to *The Following of Christ,* by Thomas à Kempis, trans. Anthony Hoskins (Saint Omer, 1613; STC 23987), *4r.

31. Robert Chambers, preface to *Miracles Lately Wrought by the Intercession of the Glorious Virgin Marie, at Mont-Aigu,* by Philippe Numan, trans. Robert Chambers (Antwerp, 1606; STC 18746), C6v.

32. For Holt's role, see M. J. Rumsey, ed., "Abbess Neville's Annals of Five Communities of English Benedictine Nuns in Flanders 1598–1687," in *Miscellanea V* (London: Catholic Record Society 6, 1909), 2. For an overview of the convent's history, see Paul Arblaster, "The Monastery of Our Lady of the Assumption in Brussels (1599–1794)," *English Benedictine History* 25 (1999): 1–36, accessed March 9, 2013, http://www.monlib.org.uk/papers/ebch/1999arblaster.pdf.

33. Rumsey, "Neville's Annals," 5; *Annals,* Downside Abbey Archives, Haslemere MS 1876, 28.

34. This prohibition did not prevent Jesuits from actively assisting convents: De Guibert, *Jesuits*, 308–9.

35. National Archives, State Papers, 77/9.1, 113v.

36. National Archives, State Papers, 77/9.2, 33r–33v.

37. Joanna Berkeley to Mathias Hovius, 31 March 1609, Archdiocesan Archives of Mechelen-Brussels (hereafter AAM), Engelse benedictinessen Brussel/2, my translation. Unless otherwise noted, all translations from Latin and French are my own.

38. Matthew, *Life of Knatchbull,* 30.

39. Ibid., 32. By August 2, 1609, Edmondes reported that Lovell had returned to set up a house in Brussels: National Archives, State Papers, 77/9.2, 64v.

40. *Annals,* 52–53. For a redacted version, see *Chronicles,* 67.

41. Rumsey, "Neville's Annals," 5.

42. *Annals,* 63. I have retained parenthetical glosses inserted by the nineteenth-century composer of the *Annals* for the sake of clarity. For published excerpts of this letter and a discussion of the building projects, see *Chronicles*, 62, 72–73.

43. Joanna Berkeley to Mathias Hovius, 13 December 1611, AAM, Engelse benedictinessen Brussel/12.4.

44. Mary Percy to Mutio Vitelleschi, 4 May 1618, AAM, Fonds Amatus Coriache, Reg 15, 182r–182v.

45. Augustine Baker, *An Enquiry about the Author of the Treatise of the Abridgement and Ladder of Perfection,* Downside Abbey Library, MS 26561, 8–9. While Jos Blom and Frans Blom contend that Hoskins translated "To the Reader," it is more likely that he translated D. C. M.'s preface since "To the Reader" has no analogue in the French text and refers directly to Percy's preface: "Introductory Note," in *Catherine Greenbury and Mary Percy,* ed. Jos Blom and Frans Blom (Aldershot, UK: Ashgate, 2006), xviii. For further discussion of Hoskins's role in this translation, see Jaime Goodrich, "Translating Lady Mary Percy: Authorship and Authority among the Brussels Benedictines," in *The English Convents in Exile, 1600–1800: Communities, Culture and Identity,* ed. Caroline Bowden and James Kelly (Farnham, UK: Ashgate, 2013), 109–22.

46. See Marcel Viller, "La abregé de la perfection de la dame milanaise," *Revue d'ascetique et de mystique* 12 (1931): 44–89; André Derville, introduction to *Commentaire des exercices spirituels d'Ignace de Loyola (1590), suivi de abrégé de la perfection chrétienne (1588),* by Achille Gagliardi (Paris: Desclée de Brouwer, 1996), 19.

47. Isabella Berinzaga and Achille Gagliardi, *An Abridgment of Christian Perfection*, trans. Mary Percy, in *Greenbury and Percy,* 21–22 (hereafter cited in text as *ACP*). The "First Principle and Foundation" states, "we must make ourselves indifferent to all created things," while the "Introduction to Making a Choice of a Way of Life" instructs exercitants that their "first aim should be to seek to serve God": Ignatius of Loyola, *The Spiritual Exercises of St. Ignatius,* trans. Louis J. Puhl (Chicago: Loyola Press, 1951), 12, 71.

48. Derville, introduction to *Commentaire,* 22.

49. Gerard, *Autobiography of an Elizabethan,* 40.

50. *The Life of the Blessed Virgin, Saint Catharine of Siena,* trans. John Fen (Douai, 1609; STC 4830), 183.

51. *Abregé de la perfection chrestienne* (Arras, 1599), 154 (hereafter cited in text as *APC*). As Blom and Blom note, the 1598 edition of the *Abregé* is no longer extant ("Introductory Note," *Greenbury and Percy,* xviii).

52. *The New Testament of Jesus Christ,* trans. Gregory Martin (Rheims: John Fogny, 1582; STC 2884), 182.

53. Ibid., 705–6.

54. Gagliardi, *Commentaire,* 218 n.1.

55. In a 1621 letter to Boonen that describes her ongoing problems with the house's confessor Robert Chambers, Percy mentions her own spiritual trials: "Je scais bien, qu'en temps de desolation, c'est un homme le plus discomfortable,

que se puisse trouver" (I know well that in times of distress, he is the most comfortless man that can be found): Mary Percy to Jacobus Boonen, 8 September 1621, AAM, Engelse benedictinessen Brussel/12.2. Hoskins's experiences with Knatchbull's despair after her profession suggest that he was also well aware of the debilitating results of desolation: Matthew, *Life of Knatchbull,* 35.

56. Bonaventure, *The Life of the Holie Father S. Francis,* trans. A. Browne (Douai, 1610; STC 3271).

57. Ignatius of Loyola, *Spiritual Exercises*, 147, no. 329.1. For Ignatian discretion, see Francesca Bugliani Knox, *The Eye of the Eagle: John Donne and the Legacy of Ignatius Loyola* (New York: Peter Lang, 2011); and Charles J. Healey, *The Ignatian Way: Key Aspects of Jesuit Spirituality* (New York: Paulist Press, 2009).

58. For the bibliographical history of Percy's work, see A. F. Allison, "New Light on the Early History of the *Breve Compendio*: The Background to the English Translation of 1612," *Biographical Studies* 4 (1957): 7–8.

59. Achille Gagliardi and Isabella Berinzaga, *Abridgment of Christian Perfection,* trans. Mary Percy (Saint Omer, 1625; STC 11539), 208–14.

60. See Heather Wolfe, "Reading Bells and Loose Papers: Reading and Writing Practices of the English Benedictine Nuns of Cambrai and Paris," in *Early Modern Women's Manuscript Writing: Selected Papers from the Trinity/Trent Colloquium,* ed. Victoria E. Burke and Jonathan Gibson (Aldershot, UK: Ashgate, 2004), 135–56.

61. Augustine Baker, *The Cloud of Unknowing and Other Treatises*, ed. Justin McCann (1924; repr., Westminster, Md.: Newman Press, 1952), 154.

62. Baker, *Catalogue of English Bookes*, 237–57.

63. British Library Cotton MS, Julius C III, 12r.

64. Baker, *Life and Death,* 38.

65. Baker, *Cloud of Unknowing,* 152.

66. *A Collection of Some Familiar Answers*, Downside Abbey Library, MS 68812, n. p.

67. Jeanne de Cambry, *The Building of Divine Love,* trans. Agnes More, Archives Départementales du Nord Lille, MS 20 H 18, 1. For a modernized edition, see Jeanne de Cambry, *The Building of Divine Love as Translated by Dame Agnes More,* ed. Dorothy L. Latz (Salzburg: Institut für Anglistik und Amerikanistik, 1992).

68. Archives Départementales du Nord Lille, MS 20 H 10, 905; Dorothy L. Latz, *"Glow-Worm Light": Writings of Seventeenth-Century English Recusant Women from Original Manuscripts* (Salzburg: Institut für Anglistik und Amerikanistik, 1989), 65–66; and Joseph S. Hansom, ed., "The English Benedictine Nuns of Our Blessed Lady of Good Hope in Paris," in *Miscellanea VII* (London: Catholic Record Society 9, 1911), 340. Excerpts of these translations may be included in Antoine Civoré's *Les secrets de la science des saints* (1651). Baker's works also reached English Carmelite and Poor Clare convents: Justin McCann and Hugh Connolly, eds, *Memorials of Father Augustine Baker* (London: Catholic Record Society 33, 1933), 139; Durham University, Special Collections, PCD MS 66.

69. See Heather Wolfe, "Dame Barbara Constable: Catholic Antiquarian, Advisor, and Closet Missionary," in *Catholic Culture in Early Modern England*, ed. Ronald Corthell et al. (Notre Dame, Ind.: University of Notre Dame Press, 2007), 158–88.

70. Baker, *Enquiry*, 8.

71. Baker, *Catalogue of English Bookes*, 250, 254.

72. Baker, *Enquiry*, 58.

73. Toby Matthew, preface to *A Treatise of Mentall Prayer with Another of the Presence of God*, by Alfonso Rodriguez, trans. Toby Matthew (Saint Omer, 1627; STC 21148), *2r–*2v.

74. Toby Matthew, preface to *Two Treatises: Of Mentall Prayer and Of the Presence of God*, by Alfonso Rodriguez, trans. Toby Matthew (Saint Omer, 1627; STC 21149), *3v.

75. For this conflict, see Claire Walker, "Securing Souls or Telling Tales? The Politics of Cloistered Life in an English Convent," in *Female Monasticism in Early Modern Europe: An Interdisciplinary View*, ed. Cordula van Wyhe (Aldershot, UK: Ashgate, 2008), 227–44.

76. Potentiana Deacon to Jacobus Boonen, circa 1622, AAM, Engelse benedictinessen Brussel/12.2.

77. Frances Gawen to Jacobus Boonen, circa 1622, AAM, Engelse benedictinessen Brussel/12.4.

78. House tradition identifies Yaxley as the first novice mistress, perhaps due to her stint in 1650 as novice mistress at Cambrai and then Brussels: *In a Great Tradition: Tribute to Dame Laurentia McLachlan, Abbess of Stanbrook by the Benedictines of Stanbrook* (New York: Harper and Brothers, 1956), 9; Rumsey, "Neville's Annals," 9. Deacon's obituary, however, states that she acted as "the cellarier which office, as also Mistress of the novices shee laudably performed for divers years together after the beginning of this monastery": Joseph Gillow, ed., "Records of the English Benedictine Nuns at Cambrai (now Stanbrook), 1620–1793," in *Miscellanea VIII* (London: Catholic Record Society 13, 1913), 78.

79. Potentiana Deacon to Jacobus Boonen, 26 August 1623, AAM, Engelse benedictinessen Brussel/12.2.

80. Helpful introductions to Baker's method include Claire Walker, *Gender and Politics in Early Modern Europe: English Convents in France and the Low Countries* (Houndmills, UK: Palgrave Macmillan, 2003), 143–47; James Gaffney, *Augustine Baker's Inner Light: A Study in English Recusant Spirituality* (Scranton, Penn.: University of Scranton Press, 1989); and Anthony Low, *Augustine Baker* (New York: Twayne, 1970), 53–74. Baker's own most thorough explanation of his method occurs in his biography of Dame Gertrude More: Baker, *Life and Death*, 61–85.

81. When Yaxley requested to be transferred to Brussels on doctor's orders in 1650, she emphasized her happiness at Cambrai: "I have found much content & comfort . . . in the progress & advancement of this Convent": *Annals*, 12. Yaxley's return to Brussels was part of an ill-fated attempt to place the house under the jurisdiction of the English Benedictine

Congregation, which caused pro-Jesuit nuns at Brussels to complain about her partisanship on behalf of the Benedictine monks: Aurea James et al. to Jacobus Boonen, 26 September 1650, AAM, Engelse benedictinessen Brussel/12.3.

82. Serenus Cressy, "Life of Father Baker," in *The Life of Father Augustine Baker, OSB (1575–1641),* ed. Dom Justin McCann (London: Burns, Oates and Washbourne, 1933), 107.

83. Gertrude More, "The Devout Souls Advertisement to the Reader," in *The Spiritual Exercises of the Most Vertuous and Religious D. Gertrude More* (Paris, 1658; Wing M2632), 91.

84. Archives Départementales du Nord Lille, MS 20 H 10, 903; Latz, "*Glow-Worm Light,*" 62.

85. More, "Devout Souls Advertisement," 30–31.

86. Ibid., 10.

87. Augustine Baker, "Selections from Augustine Baker's *Vindication,*" in Baker, *Life and Death,* 373.

88. Ibid, 366.

89. Baker, *Life and Death,* 265–70.

90. Potentiana Deacon, preface to *Delicious Entertainments of the Soule* (1632), by François de Sales, trans. Potentiana Deacon, in *Pudentiana Deacon,* Ă2v (hereafter cited in text and notes as *DE*).

91. Baker, *Catalogue of English Bookes,* 245. The latest printed book in Baker's *Catalogue* is the 1630 translation of de Sales, and the *Catalogue* predates Baker's 1632 departure.

92. François de Sales, *A Treatise of the Love of God,* trans. Miles Carr (Douai, 1630; STC 11323), C1r.

93. Ibid., 320.

94. De Sales refers to material on humility (*Introduction* 3.5) and purgation of the soul (*Introduction* 1.5 and 1.22): *DE,* 72, 137; François de Sales, *The Spiritual Conferences of St. Francis de Sales* (Westminster, Md.: Newman Press, 1962), 80, 156.

95. François de Sales, *An Introduction to a Devoute Life,* trans. John Yaxley (Douai, 1613; STC 11316.5), 13.

96. See, for example, ibid., 64–67, 138–40. For de Sales and the Jesuits, see F. Charmot, *Ignatius Loyola and Francis de Sales: Two Masters—One Spirituality,* trans. M. Renelle (St. Louis: B. Herder Book Co., 1966), 239–47.

97. Baker, *Catalogue of English Bookes,* 246.

98. Prior to 1630, Pinchon's English publications had no overt connection with the Jesuit order: STC 14914 and 20594. After this point, Pinchon regularly uses a woodcut border with the Jesuit insignia: STC 4833, 19910.5, 17130, and 11323. This woodcut appears several times in Deacon's *Delicious Entertainments,* perhaps mimicking a similar woodcut border in her French source text: *DE,* Ă2r and 1; François de Sales, *Les vrays entretiens spirituels du bien-heureux* (Lyon, 1629), 1 (hereafter cited in text as *Lve*).

99. Wendy M. Wright, *Bond of Perfection: Jeanne de Chantal & François de Sales* (New York: Paulist Press, 1985), 134.

100. Baker, "Baker's *Vindication*," 374. Also see Baker, *Life and Death*, 104–15.
101. Ibid., 373.
102. Ibid., 377.
103. Ibid., 373.

Conclusion

1. Taffin, *Of the Markes*, A3v–A4r.
2. Retha Warnicke, "Women and Humanism in England," in *Renaissance Humanism: Foundations, Forms, and Legacy*, vol. 2, *Humanism Beyond Italy*, ed. Albert Rabil Jr. (Philadelphia: University of Pennsylvania Press, 1988), 39–54.
3. Parr, *Lamentacion*, F3r.
4. Hugh de Quehen, ed., *Lucy Hutchinson's Translation of Lucretius: "De Rerum Natura"* (Ann Arbor: University of Michigan Press, 1996); Pierre Corneille, *Pompey: A Tragedy*, trans. Katherine Philips (1663; Wing C6317); Paul Tallemant, *A Voyage to the Island of Love*, trans. Aphra Behn (1684; Wing B1757). On Behn's translations, see Uman, *Women as Translators*, 103–37; Elizabeth Spearing, "Aphra Behn: The Politics of Translation," in *Aphra Behn Studies*, ed. Janet M. Todd (Cambridge: Cambridge University Press, 1996), 154–77.
5. Margaret W. Ferguson, *Dido's Daughters: Literacy, Gender, and Empire in Early Modern England and France* (Chicago: University of Chicago Press, 2003), 8.
6. *A Method to Converse with God*, trans. Catherine Holland, British Library Harley MS 3184.
7. Mary Wroth, *The Poems of Lady Mary Wroth*, ed. Josephine A. Roberts (Baton Rouge: Louisiana State University Press, 1983), 239.
8. M. M. Bakhtin, *The Dialogic Imagination*, ed. Michael Holquist, trans. Caryl Emerson and Michael Holquist (Austin: University of Texas Press, 1981), 324, his emphasis.
9. Syrithe Pugh, *Classical Intertextuality and Politics in Herrick, Fanshawe, and Milton* (Farnham, UK: Ashgate, 2010); Michael J. Redmond, *Shakespeare, Politics, and Italy: Intertextuality on the Jacobean Stage* (Farnham, UK: Ashgate, 2009); Greene, *The Light in Troy*.
10. Susan M. Felch, "'Halff a Scrypture Woman': Heteroglossia and Female Authorial Agency in Prayers by Lady Elizabeth Tyrwhit, Anne Lock, and Anne Wheathill," in White, *English Women*, 147–66.
11. George Gascoigne, *A Hundreth Sundrie Flowres* (1573; STC 11635).
12. For sententiae, see Mary Thomas Crane, *Framing Authority: Sayings, Self, and Society in Sixteenth Century England* (Princeton, N.J.: Princeton University Press, 1993); and "'Video et Taceo': Elizabeth I and the Rhetoric of Counsel," *Studies in English Literature* 28, no. 1 (1988): 1–15.
13. See, for example, Russell, *English Sappho*, 208.

14. For a recent treatment of women's use of biblical allusions, see Michele Osherow, *Biblical Women's Voices in Early Modern England* (Farnham, UK: Ashgate, 2009).

15. Parr, *Lamentacion,* B1v.

16. For example, Barbara Constable, *Considerations for Preests,* Downside Abbey Library, MS 82145.

17. Edith Snook, *Women, Reading, and the Cultural Politics of Early Modern England* (Aldershot, UK: Ashgate, 2005), 83–114.

18. Isabella Whitney, preface to *A Sweet Nosgay* (1573; STC 25440), A4v.

19. George Gascoigne, *The Posies* (1575; STC 11637), 193.

20. Amina Alyal, "Italian Weeds and English Bodies: Translating 'The Adventures of Master F. J.,'" in Pincombe, *Travels and Translations*, 104–19.

21. Anne Dowriche, preface to *The French Historie* (1589; STC 7159), A3v, A4r.

22. Beilin, *Redeeming Eve,* 102.

23. *Songes and Sonettes* (1557; STC 13861).

24. See Laurie Ellinghausen, "Literary Property and the Single Woman in Isabella Whitney's *A Sweet Nosgay,*" *Studies in English Literature* 45, no. 1 (2005): 1–22; and Clarke, *Early Modern Women's Writing,* 194–95.

25. For a useful discussion of prefatory poems, see Franklin B. Williams Jr., "Commendatory Verses: The Rise of the Art of Puffing," *Studies in Bibliography* 19 (1966): 1–14.

SELECTED BIBLIOGRAPHY

The selected bibliography of primary sources contains the translations that serve as major case studies in this book. The selected bibliography of secondary sources includes both the most frequently cited sources as well as sources with special critical significance as regards early modern translation and Translation Studies in general.

Manuscript Primary Sources

Bodleian Library. MS Cherry 36, Elizabeth's translation of Marguerite de Navarre.

National Archives, Kew. State Papers 12/289, Elizabeth's translations of Boethius, Horace, and Plutarch.

Viscount De L'Isle. Sidney Psalter (known as MS A).

Dr. B. E. Juel-Jensen Estate. Sidney Psalter (known as MS J).

Printed Primary Sources

Blom, Jos, and Frans Blom, eds. *Catherine Greenbury and Mary Percy.* The Early Modern Englishwoman: A Facsimile Library of Essential Works, ser. 1, pt. 2, vol. 2. Aldershot, UK: Ashgate, 2006.

———. *Pudentiana Deacon.* The Early Modern Englishwoman: A Facsimile Library of Essential Works, ser. 1, pt. 3, vol. 4. Aldershot, UK: Ashgate, 2002.

Elizabeth I. *The Consolation of Queen Elizabeth I: The Queen's Translation of Boethius' 'De Consolatione Philosophiae.'* Edited by Noel Harold Kaylor Jr. and Philip Edward Phillips. Tempe, Ariz.: Arizona Center for Medieval and Renaissance Studies, 2009.

———. *Elizabeth I: Translations, 1544–1589.* Edited by Janel Mueller and Joshua Scodel. Chicago: University of Chicago Press, 2009.

———. *Elizabeth I: Translations, 1592–1598.* Edited by Janel Mueller and Joshua Scodel. Chicago: University of Chicago Press, 2009.

———. *Elizabeth's Glass.* Edited by Marc Shell. Lincoln, Neb.: University of Nebraska Press, 1993.

Herbert, Mary Sidney. *The Collected Works of Mary Sidney Herbert, Countess of Pembroke.* Edited by Margaret P. Hannay, Noel J. Kinnamon, and Michael G. Brennan. Oxford: Clarendon, 1998.

Khanna, Lee Cullen, ed. *Early Tudor Translators: Margaret Beaufort, Margaret More Roper, and Mary Basset.* The Early Modern Englishwoman: A Facsimile Library of Essential Works, ser. 1, pt. 2, vol. 4. Aldershot, UK: Ashgate, 2001.

Prescott, Anne Lake, ed. *Elizabeth and Mary Tudor.* The Early Modern Englishwoman: A Facsimile Library of Essential Works, ser. 1, pt. 2, vol. 5. Aldershot, UK: Ashgate, 2001.

Sidney, Philip. *The Poems of Sir Philip Sidney.* Edited by William A. Ringler Jr. Oxford: Clarendon, 1962.

Secondary Sources

Allison, A. F. "New Light on the Early History of the *Breve Compendio:* The Background to the English Translation of 1612." *Biographical Studies* 4 (1957): 4–17.

Amos, Flora Ross. *Early Theories of Translation.* New York: Columbia University Press, 1920.

Beilin, Elaine V. *Redeeming Eve: Women Writers of the English Renaissance.* Princeton, N.J.: Princeton University Press, 1987.

Bourdieu, Pierre. *The Field of Cultural Production: Essays on Art and Literature.* Edited by Randal Johnson. New York: Columbia University Press, 1993.

———. *The Logic of Practice.* Translated by Richard Nice. Stanford, Calif.: Stanford University Press, 1990.

Bourdieu, Pierre, and Jean-Claude Passeron. *Reproduction in Education, Society, and Culture.* Translated by Richard Nice. London: Sage, 1977.

Braden, Gordon, Robert Cummings, and Stuart Gillespie, eds. *The Oxford History of Literary Translation in English.* Vol. 2, *1550–1660.* Oxford: Oxford University Press, 2010.

Burke, Peter. "Cultures of Translation in Early Modern Europe." In *Cultural Translation in Early Modern Europe,* edited by Peter Burke and R. Po-chia Hsia, 7–38. Cambridge: Cambridge University Press, 2007.

Chamberlain, Lori. "Gender and the Metaphorics of Translation." *Signs* 13, no. 3 (1988): 454–72.

Clarke, Danielle. *The Politics of Early Modern Women's Writing.* New York: Longman, 2001.

Demers, Patricia. *Women's Writing in English: Early Modern England.* Toronto: University of Toronto Press, 2005.

Ellis, Roger. "The Juvenile Translations of Elizabeth Tudor." *Translation and Literature* 18, no. 2 (2009): 157–80.

Felch, Susan M. "'Halff a Scrypture Woman': Heteroglossia and Female Authorial Agency in Prayers by Lady Elizabeth Tyrwhit, Anne Lock, and Anne Wheathill." In White, *English Women,* 147–66.

Frye, Susan. *Pens and Needles: Women's Textualities in Early Modern England.* Philadelphia: University of Pennsylvania, 2010.

Gee, John Archer. "Margaret Roper's English Version of Erasmus' *Precatio Dominica* and the Apprenticeship Behind Early Tudor Translation." *Review of English Studies* 13, no. 51 (1937): 257–71.

Goldberg, Jonathan. *Desiring Women Writing: English Renaissance Examples.* Stanford, Calif.: Stanford University Press, 1997.

Goodrich, Jaime. "The Dedicatory Preface to Mary Roper Clarke Basset's Translation of Eusebius' *Ecclesiastical History.*" *English Literary Renaissance* 40, no. 3 (2010): 301–28.

———. "'Ensigne-Bearers of Saint Clare': Elizabeth Evelinge's Translations and the Restoration of English Franciscanism." In White, *English Women,* 83–100.

———. "Mary Tudor, Lord Morley, and St. Thomas Aquinas: The Politics of Pious Translation at the Henrician Court." *ANQ* 24, no. 1–2 (2011): 11–20.

Gouanvic, Jean-Marc. "A Bourdieusian Theory of Translation, or the Coincidence of Practical Instances: Field, 'Habitus,' Capital, and 'Illusio.'" *Translator* 11, no. 2 (2005): 147–66.

Habermas, Jürgen. *The Structural Transformation of the Public Sphere: An Inquiry into a Category of Bourgeois Society.* Translated by Thomas Burger. Cambridge, Mass.: MIT, 1989.

Hamlin, Hannibal. *Psalm Culture and Early Modern English Literature.* Cambridge: Cambridge University Press, 2004.

Hannay, Margaret P. *Philip's Phoenix: Mary Sidney, Countess of Pembroke.* Oxford: Oxford University Press, 1990.

———. "'Princes You as Men Must Dy': Genevan Advice to Monarchs in the *Psalmes* of Mary Sidney." *English Literary Renaissance* 19, no. 1 (1989): 22–41.

———. "Re-Revealing the Psalms: The Countess of Pembroke and Her Early Modern Readers." *Sidney Journal* 23, no. 1–2 (2005): 19–35.

———, ed. *Silent but for the Word: Tudor Women as Patrons, Translators, and Writers of Religious Works.* Kent, Ohio: Kent State University Press, 1985.

Hosington, Brenda M. "Lady Margaret Beaufort's Translations as Mirrors of Practical Piety." In White, *English Women,* 185–203.

———. "Translation in the Service of Politics and Religion: A Family Tradition for Thomas More, Margaret Roper, and Mary Clarke Basset." In *Between Scylla and Charybdis: Learned Letter Writers, Politics, and Religion,* edited by Jeanine de Landstheer and Hank Nellen, 93–108. Leiden: Brill, 2010.

Hovland, Carl I., Irving L. Janis, and Harold H. Kelley. *Communication and Persuasion: Psychological Studies of Opinion Change.* New Haven, Conn.: Yale University Press, 1953.

Inghilleri, Moira. "The Sociology of Bourdieu and the Construction of the 'Object' in Translation and Interpreting Studies." *Translator* 11, no. 2 (2005): 125–45.

Kelly, Louis. "Translation and Religious Belief." In Braden, Cummings, and Gillespie, *Oxford History of Literary Translation,* 24–31.

Kinnamon, Noel. "The Sidney Psalms: The Penshurst and Tixall Manuscripts." *English Manuscript Studies, 1100–1700* 2 (1990):139–61.

Krontiris, Tina. *Oppositional Voices: Women as Writers and Translators of Literature in the English Renaissance.* New York: Routledge, 1992.

Lamb, Mary Ellen. "The Cooke Sisters: Attitudes Toward Learned Women in the Renaissance." In Hannay, *Silent but for the Word,* 107–25.

———. "Margaret Roper, the Humanist Political Project, and the Problem of Agency." In *Opening the Borders: Inclusivity in Early Modern Studies; Essays in Honor of James V. Mirollo,* edited by Peter C. Herman, 83–108. Newark: University of Delaware Press, 1999.

Lefevere, André. *Translation, Rewriting, and the Manipulation of Literary Fame.* New York: Routledge, 1992.

Matthiessen, F. O. *Translation: An Elizabethan Art.* Cambridge, Mass.: Harvard University Press, 1931.

McCutcheon, Elizabeth. "The Education of Thomas More's Daughters: Concepts and Praxis." In *East Meets West: Homage to Edgar C. Knowlton, Jr.,* edited by Roger L. Hadlich and J. D. Ellsworth, 193–207. Honolulu: University of Hawaii Press, 1988.

Morini, Massimiliano. *Tudor Translation in Theory and Practice.* Aldershot, UK: Ashgate, 2006.

North, Marcy L. *The Anonymous Renaissance: Cultures of Discretion in Tudor-Stuart England.* Chicago: University of Chicago Press, 2003.

Pollnitz, Aysha. "Religion and Translation at the Court of Henry VIII: Princess Mary, Katherine Parr and the *Paraphrases* of Erasmus." In *Mary Tudor: Old and New Perspectives,* edited by Susan Doran and Thomas S. Freeman, 123–37. Houndmills, UK: Palgrave Macmillan, 2011.

Prescott, Anne Lake. "The Pearl of the Valois and Elizabeth I: Marguerite de Navarre's *Miroir* and Tudor England." In Hannay, *Silent but for the Word,* 41–76.

Quilligan, Maureen. *Incest and Agency in Elizabeth's England.* Philadelphia: University of Pennsylvania Press, 2005.

Rhodes, Neil. "Status Anxiety and English Renaissance Translation." In *Renaissance Paratexts,* edited by Helen Smith and Louise Wilson, 107–20. Cambridge: Cambridge University Press, 2011.

Schleiner, Louise. *Tudor and Stuart Women Writers.* Bloomington: Indiana University Press, 1994.

Simeoni, Daniel. "The Pivotal Status of the Translator's Habitus." *Target* 10, no. 1 (1998): 1–40.

Simon, Sherry. *Gender in Translation: Cultural Identity and the Politics of Transmission.* London: Routledge, 1996.

Spivak, Gayatri Chakravorty. "Scattered Speculations on the Subaltern and the Popular." *Postcolonial Studies* 8, no. 4 (2005): 475–86.

Summit, Jennifer. *Lost Property: The Woman Writer and English Literary History, 1380–1589.* Chicago: University of Chicago Press, 2000.

Trill, Suzanne. "Sixteenth-Century Women's Writing: Mary Sidney's *Psalmes* and the 'Femininity' of Translation." In *Writing and the English Renaissance,* edited by William Zunder and Suzanne Trill, 140–58. New York: Longman, 1996.

Uman, Deborah. *Women as Translators in Early Modern England.* Newark: University of Delaware Press, 2012.

Uman, Deborah, and Bistué Belén. "Translation as Collaborative Authorship: Margaret Tyler's *The Mirrour of Princely Deedes and Knighthood.*" *Comparative Literature Studies* 44, no. 3 (2007): 298–323.

Venuti, Lawrence. *The Translator's Invisibility: A History of Translation.* New York: Routledge, 1995.

Verbrugge, Rita M. "Margaret More Roper's Personal Expression in the *Devout Treatise upon the Pater Noster.*" In Hannay, *Silent but for the Word,* 30–42.

Wall, Wendy. *The Imprint of Gender: Authorship and Publication in the English Renaissance.* Ithaca, N.Y.: Cornell University Press, 1993.

White, Micheline, ed. *English Women, Religion, and Textual Production, 1500–1625.* Farnham, UK: Ashgate, 2011.

———. "Renaissance Englishwomen and Religious Translations: The Case of Anne Lock's *Of the Markes of the Children of God* (1590)." *English Literary Renaissance* 29, no. 3 (1999): 375–400.

Wright, Gillian. "Translating at Leisure: Gentlemen and Gentlewomen." In Braden, Cummings, and Gillespie, *Oxford History of Literary Translation,* 58–73.

INDEX

An "n" following a page number indicates an endnote; "f" indicates a figure.